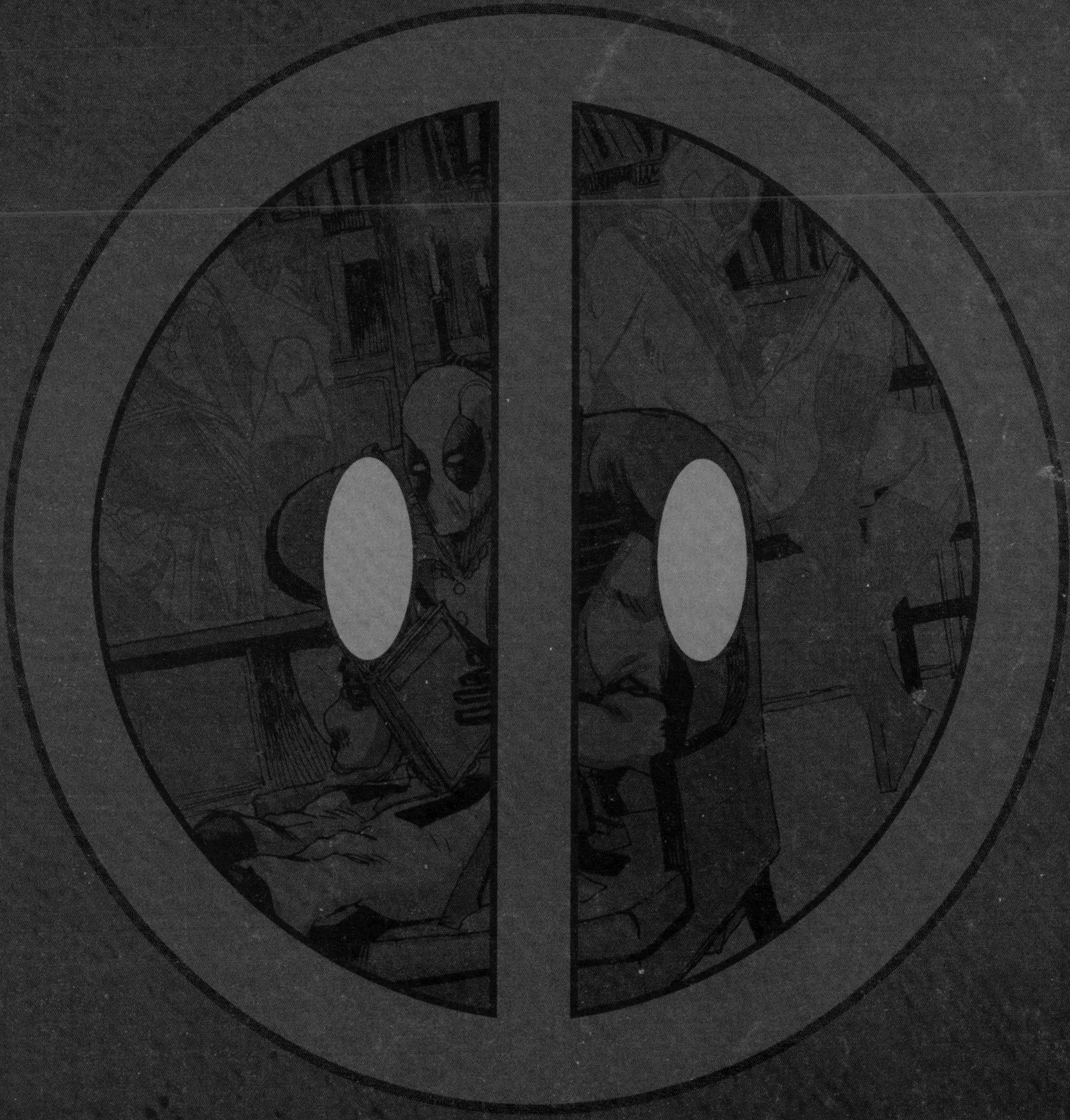

DEADPOOL created by
ROB LIEFELD & FABIAN NICIEZA

collection editor   JENNIFER GRÜNWALD
assistant editor   CAITLIN O'CONNELL
associate managing editor   KATERI WOODY
editor, special projects   MARK D. BEAZLEY
vp production & special projects   JEFF YOUNGQUIST
svp print, sales & marketing   DAVID GABRIEL
book designer   ADAM DEL RE

editor in chief   AXEL ALONSO
chief creative officer   JOE QUESADA
president   DAN BUCKLEY
executive producer   ALAN FINE

DEADPOOL: WORLD'S GREATEST VOL. 7 — DEADPOOL DOES SHAKESPEARE. Contains material originally published in magazine form as DEADPOOL #21 and #26-27. First printing 2017. ISBN# 978-1-302-90542-2. Published by MARVEL WORLDWIDE, INC., a subsidiary of MARVEL ENTERTAINMENT, LLC. OFFICE OF PUBLICATION: 135 West 50th Street, New York, NY 10020. Copyright © 2017 MARVEL. No similarity between any of the names, characters, persons, and/or institutions in this magazine with those of any living or dead person or institution is intended, and any such similarity which may exist is purely coincidental. Printed in Canada. DAN BUCKLEY, President, Marvel Entertainment; JOE QUESADA, Chief Creative Officer; TOM BREVOORT, SVP of Publishing; DAVID BOGART, SVP of Business Affairs & Operations, Publishing & Partnership; C.B. CEBULSKI, VP of Brand Management & Development, Asia; DAVID GABRIEL, SVP of Sales & Marketing, Publishing; JEFF YOUNGQUIST, VP of Production & Special Projects; DAN CARR, Executive Director of Publishing Technology; ALEX MORALES, Director of Publishing Operations; SUSAN CRESPI, Production Manager; STAN LEE, Chairman Emeritus. For information regarding advertising in Marvel Comics or on Marvel.com, please contact Vit DeBellis, Integrated Sales Manager, at vdebellis@marvel.com. For Marvel subscription inquiries, please call 888-511-5480. Manufactured between 3/31/2017 and 5/2/2017 by SOLISCO PRINTERS, SCOTT, QC, CANADA.

10 9 8 7 6 5 4 3 2 1

THE WORLD'S GREATEST COMIC MAGAZINE!

DEADPOOL

DEADPOOL DOES SHAKESPEARE

ISSUE #26

GERRY DUGGAN
writer

SCOTT HEPBURN WITH **PAOLO VILLANELLI**
artists

JAVA TARTAGLIA & IRMA KNIIVILA
colorists

DAVID LOPEZ
cover art

ISSUE #27

GERRY DUGGAN
writer

SEAN IZAAKSE & SALVA ESPIN
artists

VERONICA GANDINI
colorist

DAVID LOPEZ
cover art

"MUCH ADO ABOUT DEADPOOL"

IAN DOESCHER
writer

BRUNO OLIVEIRA
artist

NICK FILARDI
colorist

VC's JOE SABINO
letterer

HEATHER ANTOS
assistant editor

JORDAN D. WHITE
editor

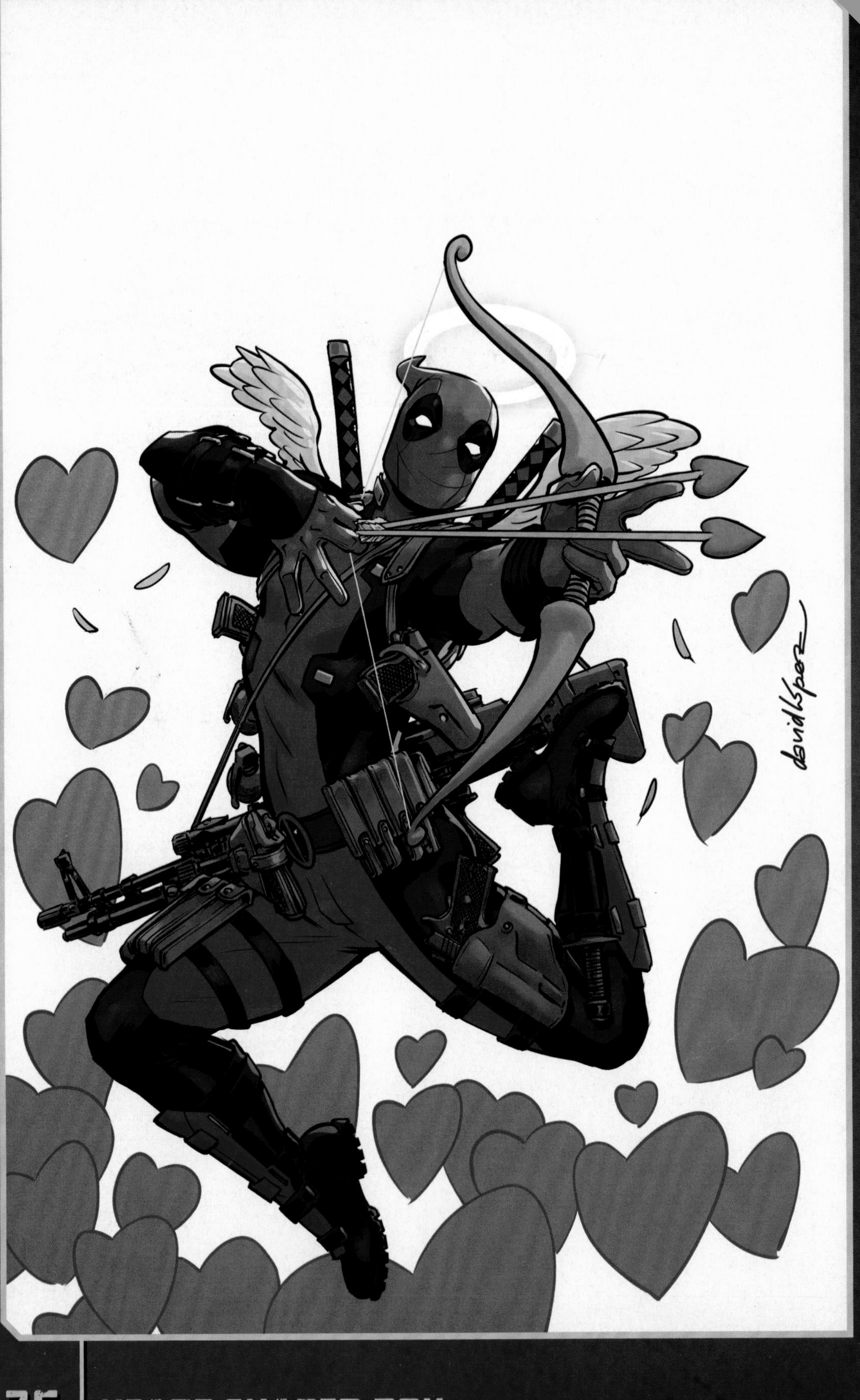

Avenger...Assassin...Superstar...Smelly person...Possibly the world's most skilled mercenary, definitely the world's most annoying, Wade Wilson was chosen for a top-secret government program that gave him a healing factor allowing him to heal from any wound. Somehow, despite making his money as a gun for hire, Wade has become one of the most beloved "heroes" in the world. Call him the Merc with the Mouth...call him the Regeneratin' Degenerate...call him...

DEADPOOL

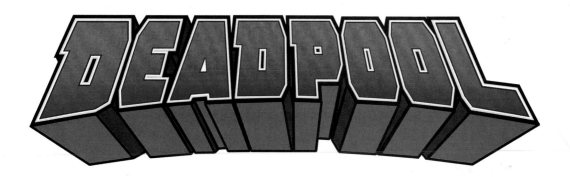

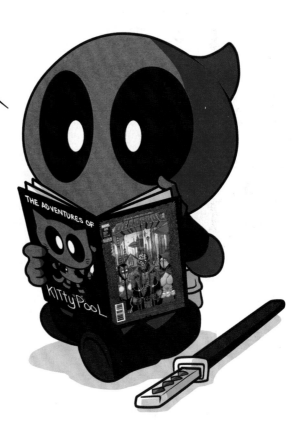

HEY THERE, FOLKS-- **DEADPOOL** HERE!
HOPE YOU'RE ALL DOING GOOD THIS ROMANTIC HOLIDAY!
LET'S SEE...WHAT DO YOU NEED TO KNOW?
WELL, FIRST OFF, THINGS AIN'T GREAT WITH MY WIFE, ***SHIKLAH***, DEMON QUEEN OF THE MONSTER METROPOLIS UNDER MANHATTAN. WE'VE BEEN FIGHTING. BUT AT LEAST WE'RE STILL MARRIED!
SECOND, ***MADCAP*** IS STILL OUT THERE SOMEWHERE, COMPLETELY SADISTIC AND INSANE, AND SWEARING TO GET TERRIBLE REVENGE ON ME.
ANYWAY... IF YOU DON'T HAVE A VALENTINE THIS YEAR...YOU CAN TOTALLY CLAIM ME. I'LL TAKE ALL COMERS.
THE ADVENTURES OF
KITtyPooL

LI'L DEADPOOL ART BY
IRENE Y. LEE

HEART-SHAPED BOX

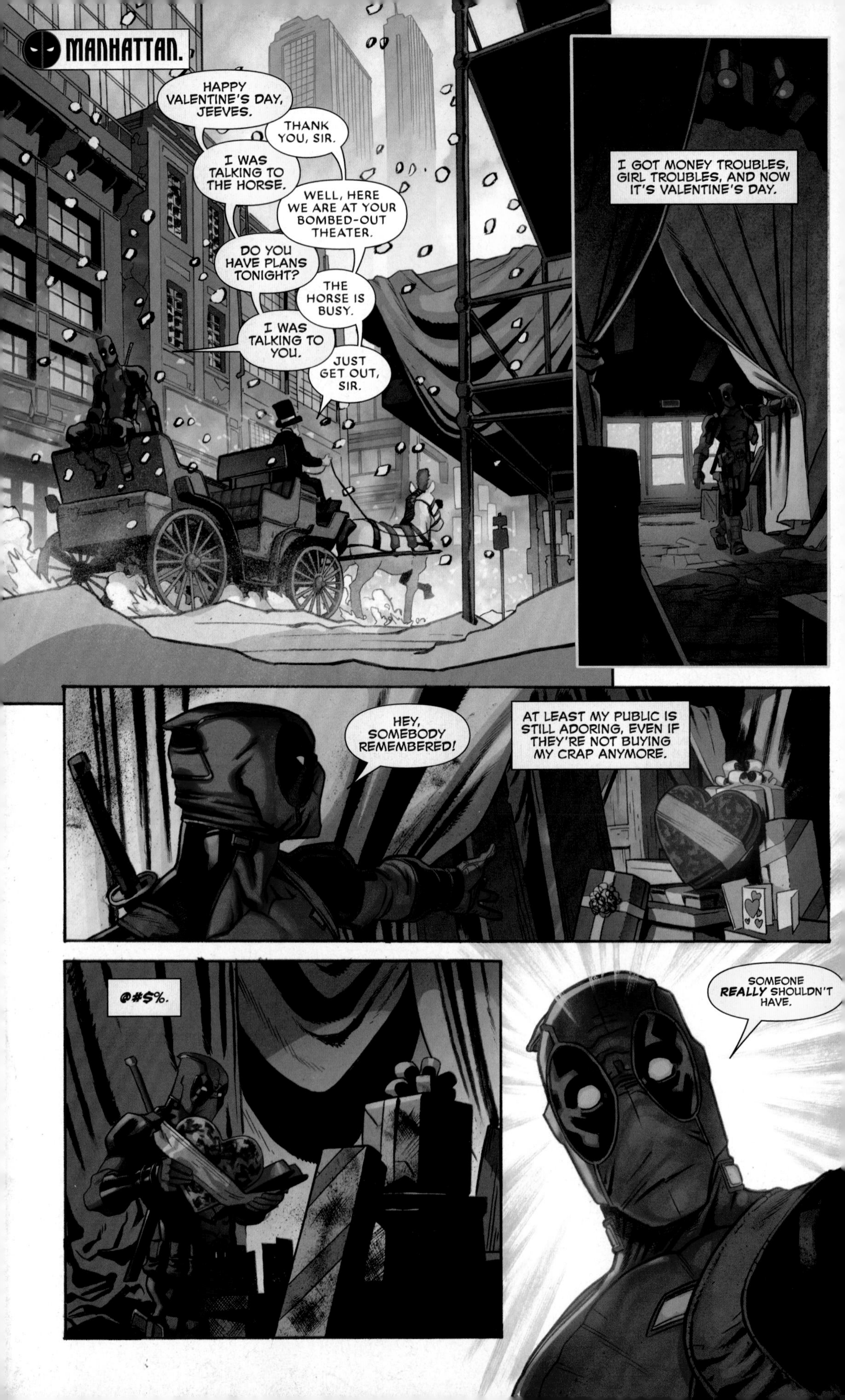
MANHATTAN.
HAPPY VALENTINE'S DAY, JEEVES.
THANK YOU, SIR.
I WAS TALKING TO THE HORSE.
WELL, HERE WE ARE AT YOUR BOMBED-OUT THEATER.
DO YOU HAVE PLANS TONIGHT?
THE HORSE IS BUSY.
I WAS TALKING TO YOU.
JUST GET OUT, SIR.
I GOT MONEY TROUBLES, GIRL TROUBLES, AND NOW IT'S VALENTINE'S DAY.
HEY, SOMEBODY REMEMBERED!
AT LEAST MY PUBLIC IS STILL ADORING, EVEN IF THEY'RE NOT BUYING MY CRAP ANYMORE.
@#$%.
SOMEONE REALLY SHOULDN'T HAVE.

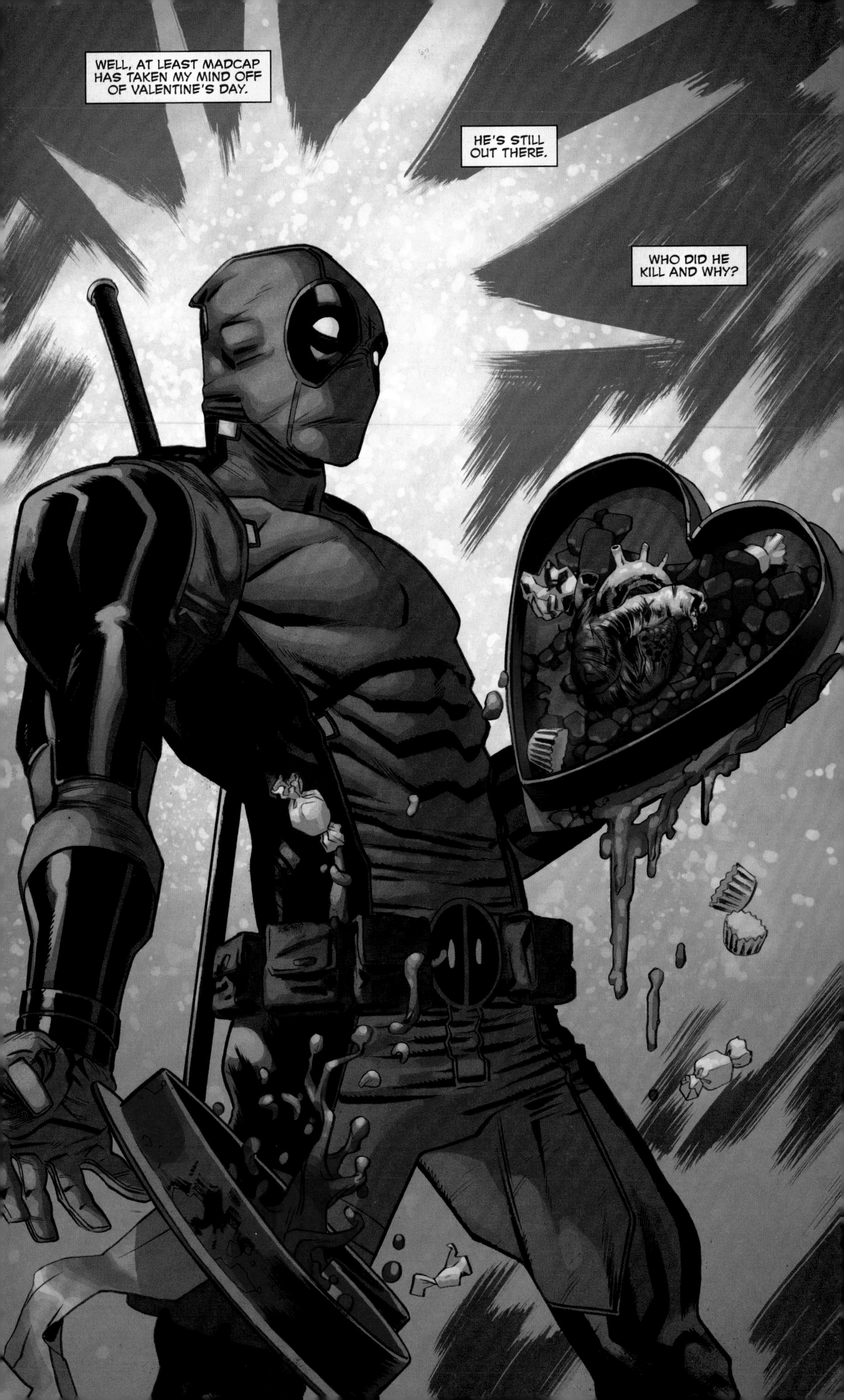
WELL, AT LEAST MADCAP HAS TAKEN MY MIND OFF OF VALENTINE'S DAY.
HE'S STILL OUT THERE.
WHO DID HE KILL AND WHY?

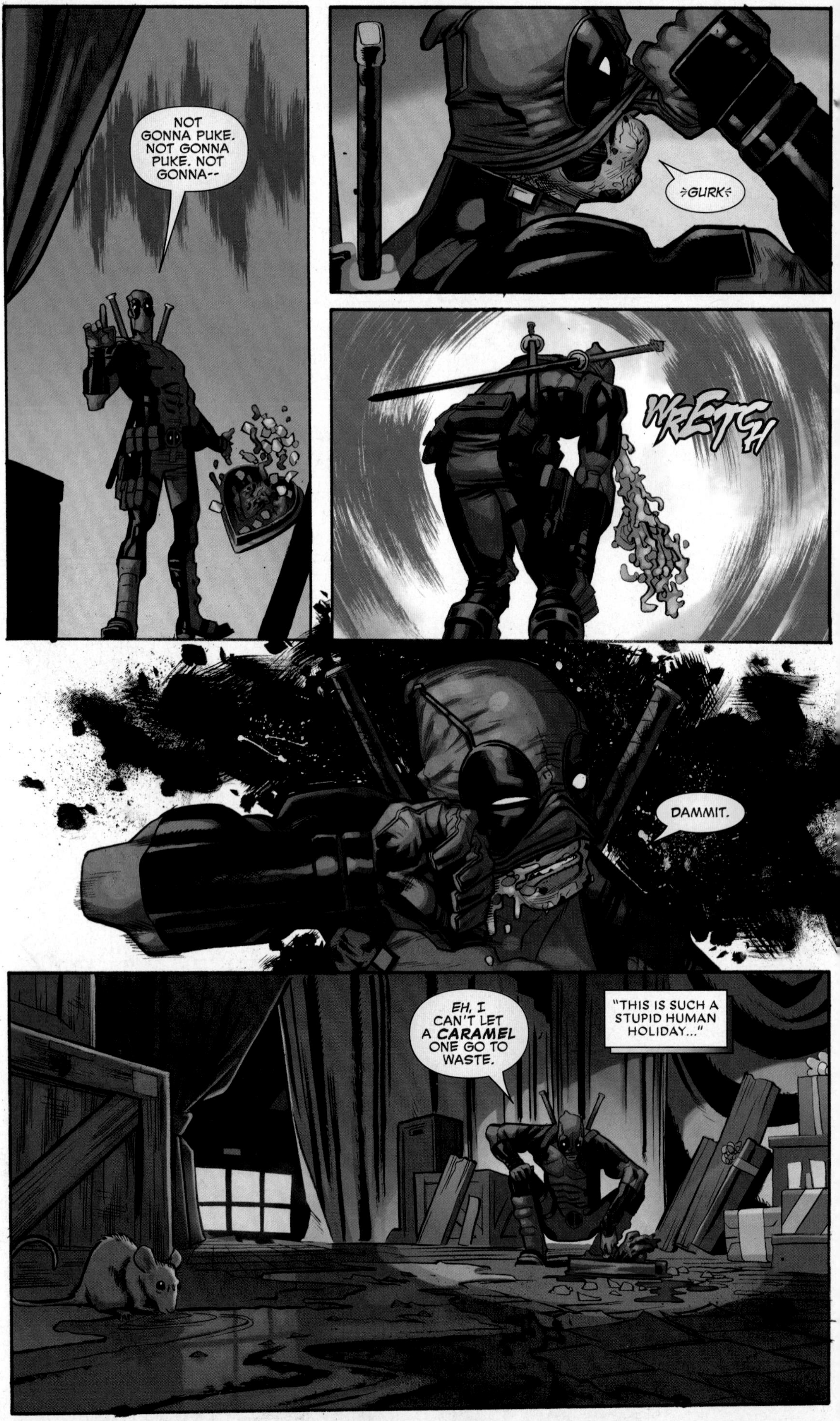
NOT GONNA PUKE. NOT GONNA PUKE. NOT GONNA--
GURK
WRETCH
DAMMIT.
EH, I CAN'T LET A CARAMEL ONE GO TO WASTE.
"THIS IS SUCH A STUPID HUMAN HOLIDAY..."

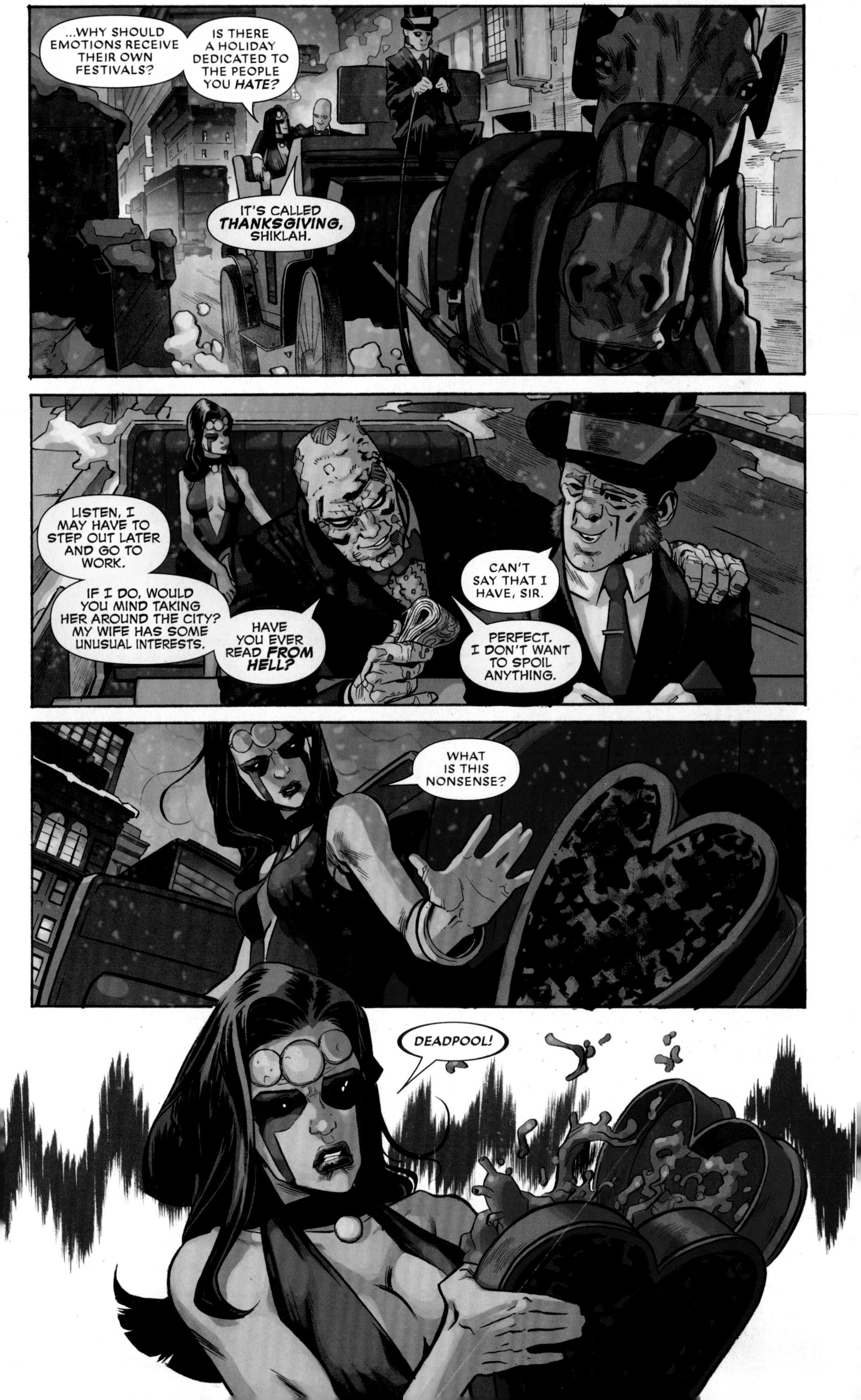
...WHY SHOULD EMOTIONS RECEIVE THEIR OWN FESTIVALS?
IS THERE A HOLIDAY DEDICATED TO THE PEOPLE YOU HATE?
IT'S CALLED THANKSGIVING, SHIKLAH.
LISTEN, I MAY HAVE TO STEP OUT LATER AND GO TO WORK.
IF I DO, WOULD YOU MIND TAKING HER AROUND THE CITY? MY WIFE HAS SOME UNUSUAL INTERESTS.
HAVE YOU EVER READ FROM HELL?
CAN'T SAY THAT I HAVE, SIR.
PERFECT. I DON'T WANT TO SPOIL ANYTHING.
WHAT IS THIS NONSENSE?
DEADPOOL!

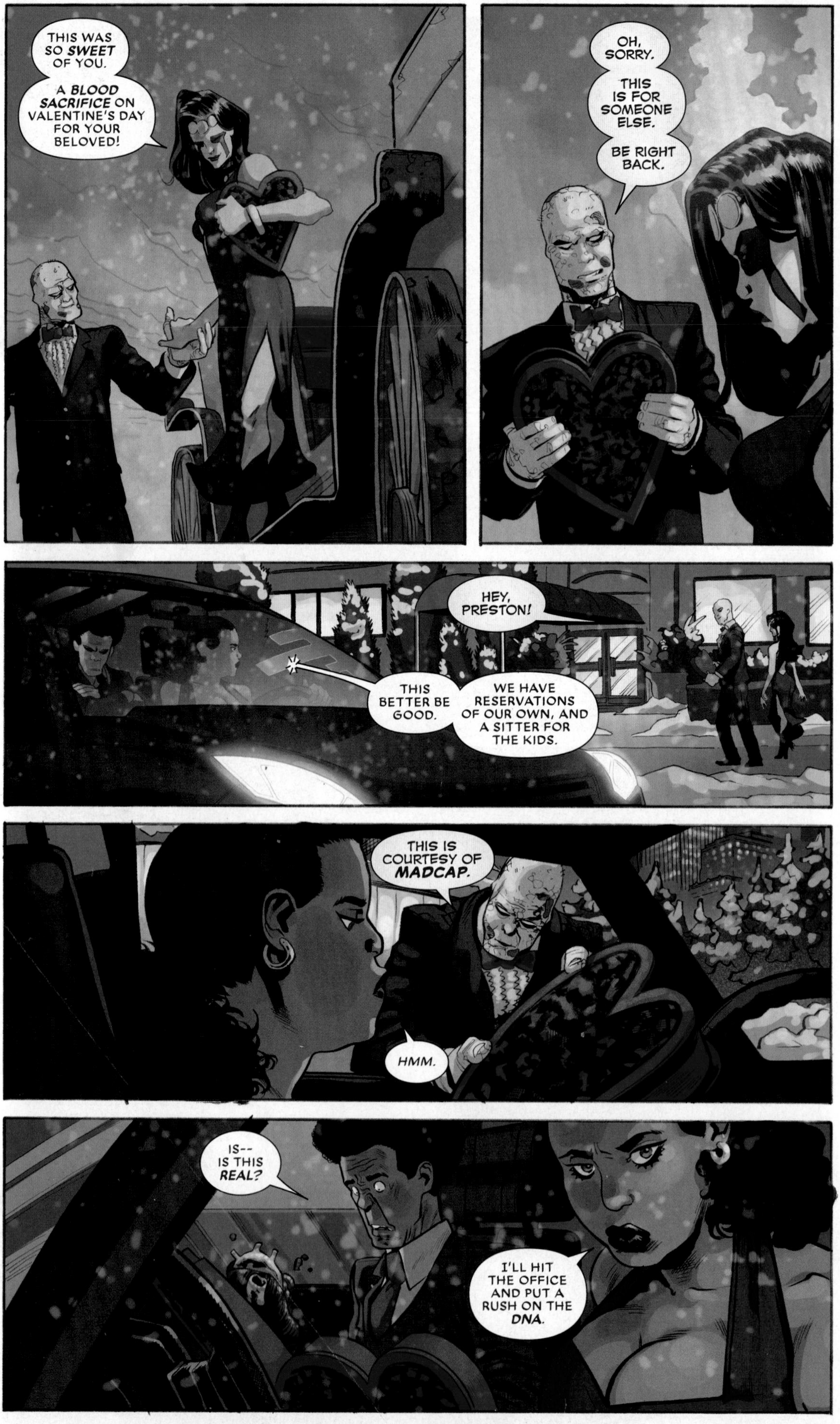
THIS WAS SO *SWEET* OF YOU.
A ***BLOOD SACRIFICE*** ON VALENTINE'S DAY FOR YOUR BELOVED!
OH, SORRY.
THIS IS FOR SOMEONE ELSE.
BE RIGHT BACK.
HEY, PRESTON!
THIS BETTER BE GOOD.
WE HAVE RESERVATIONS OF OUR OWN, AND A SITTER FOR THE KIDS.
THIS IS COURTESY OF ***MADCAP.***
HMM.
IS-- IS THIS ***REAL?***
I'LL HIT THE OFFICE AND PUT A RUSH ON THE ***DNA.***

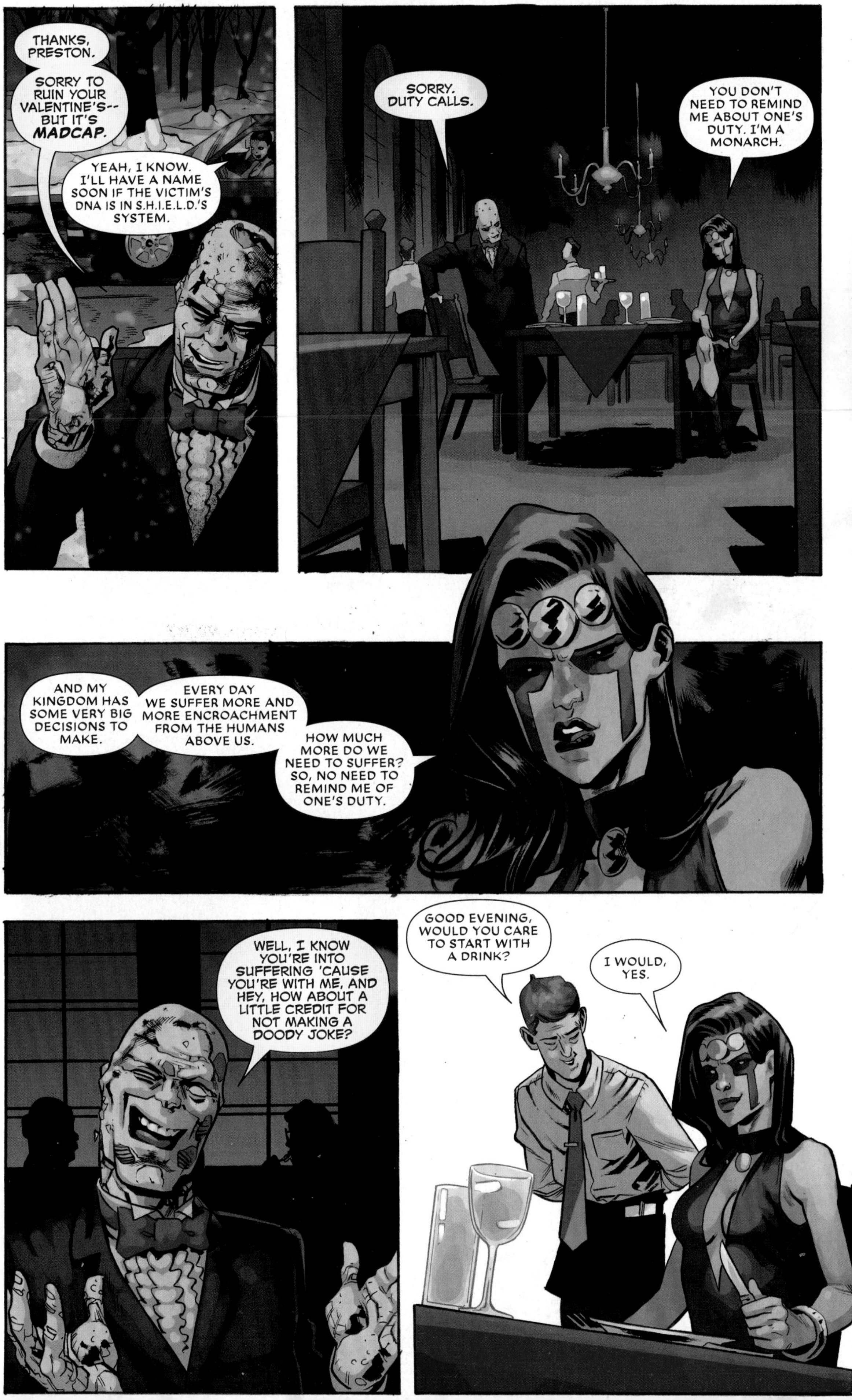
THANKS, PRESTON.
SORRY TO RUIN YOUR VALENTINE'S-- BUT IT'S MADCAP.
YEAH, I KNOW. I'LL HAVE A NAME SOON IF THE VICTIM'S DNA IS IN S.H.I.E.L.D.'S SYSTEM.
SORRY. DUTY CALLS.
YOU DON'T NEED TO REMIND ME ABOUT ONE'S DUTY. I'M A MONARCH.
AND MY KINGDOM HAS SOME VERY BIG DECISIONS TO MAKE.
EVERY DAY WE SUFFER MORE AND MORE ENCROACHMENT FROM THE HUMANS ABOVE US.
HOW MUCH MORE DO WE NEED TO SUFFER? SO, NO NEED TO REMIND ME OF ONE'S DUTY.
WELL, I KNOW YOU'RE INTO SUFFERING 'CAUSE YOU'RE WITH ME, AND HEY, HOW ABOUT A LITTLE CREDIT FOR NOT MAKING A DOODY JOKE?
GOOD EVENING, WOULD YOU CARE TO START WITH A DRINK?
I WOULD, YES.

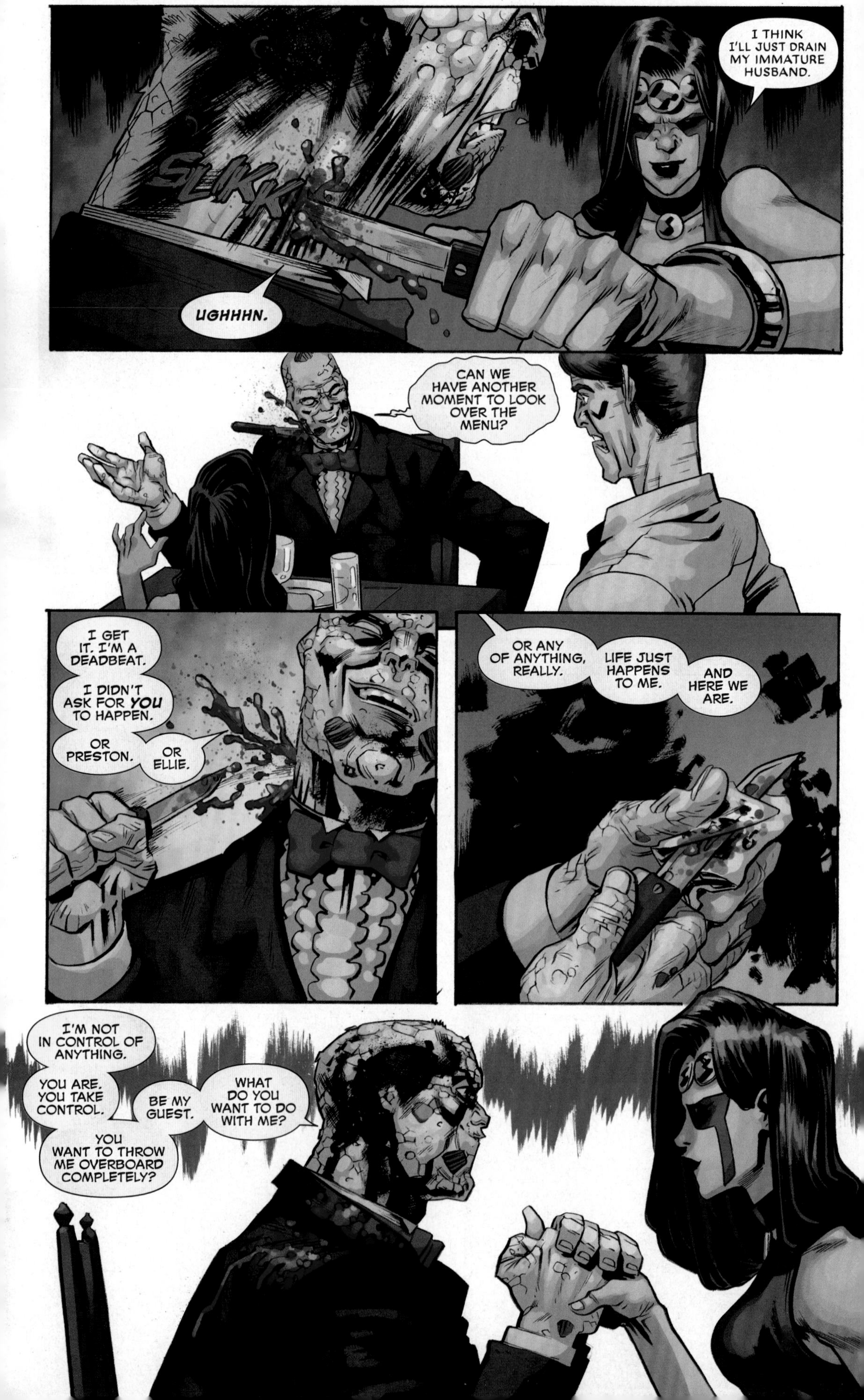
I THINK I'LL JUST DRAIN MY IMMATURE HUSBAND.
SLIKK
UGHHHN.
CAN WE HAVE ANOTHER MOMENT TO LOOK OVER THE MENU?
I GET IT. I'M A DEADBEAT.
I DIDN'T ASK FOR *YOU* TO HAPPEN.
OR PRESTON.
OR ELLIE.
OR ANY OF ANYTHING, REALLY.
LIFE JUST HAPPENS TO ME.
AND HERE WE ARE.
I'M NOT IN CONTROL OF ANYTHING.
YOU ARE. YOU TAKE CONTROL.
BE MY GUEST.
WHAT DO YOU WANT TO DO WITH ME?
YOU WANT TO THROW ME OVERBOARD COMPLETELY?

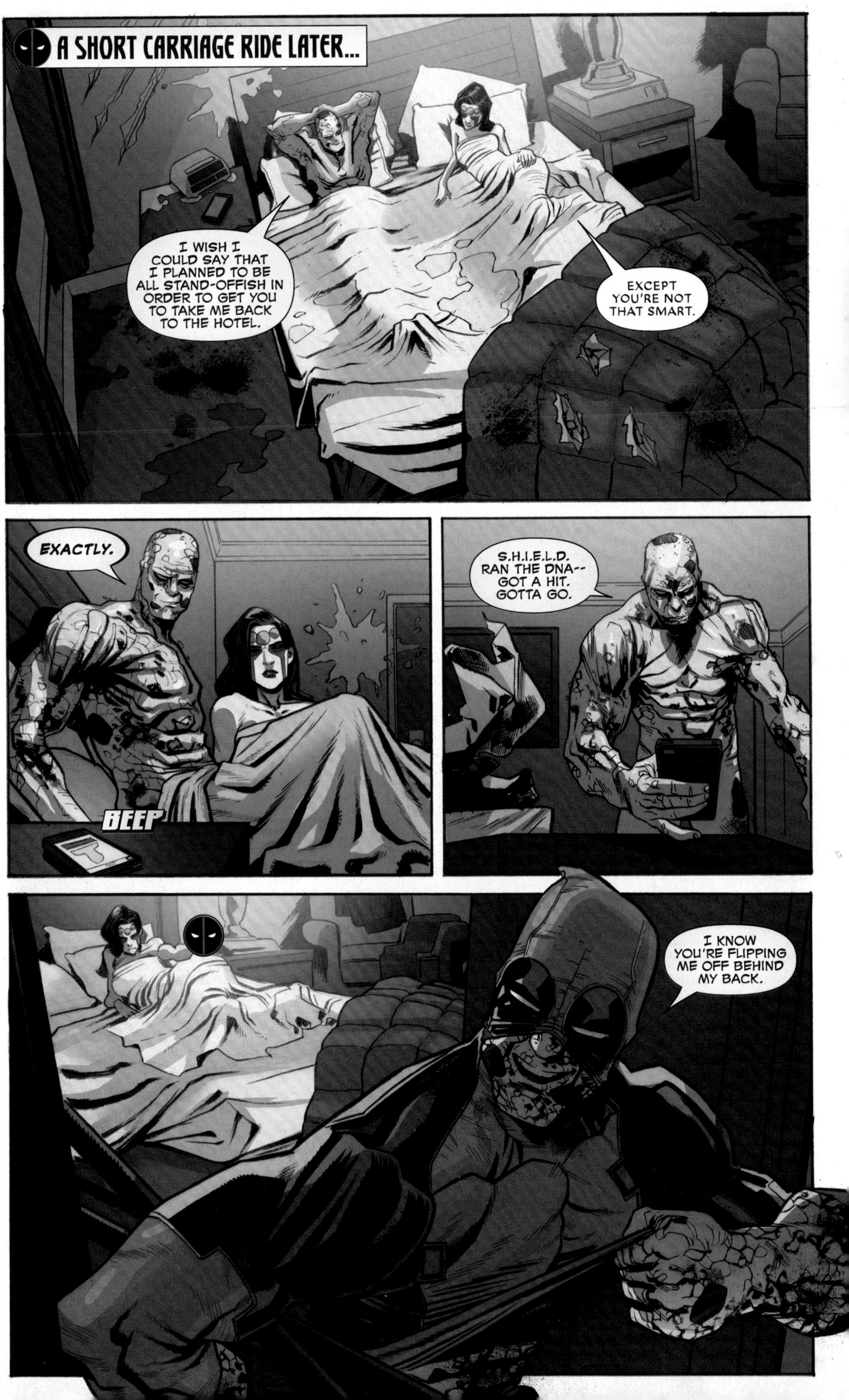
A SHORT CARRIAGE RIDE LATER...
I WISH I COULD SAY THAT I PLANNED TO BE ALL STAND-OFFISH IN ORDER TO GET YOU TO TAKE ME BACK TO THE HOTEL.
EXCEPT YOU'RE NOT THAT SMART.
EXACTLY.
BEEP
S.H.I.E.L.D. RAN THE DNA--GOT A HIT. GOTTA GO.
I KNOW YOU'RE FLIPPING ME OFF BEHIND MY BACK.

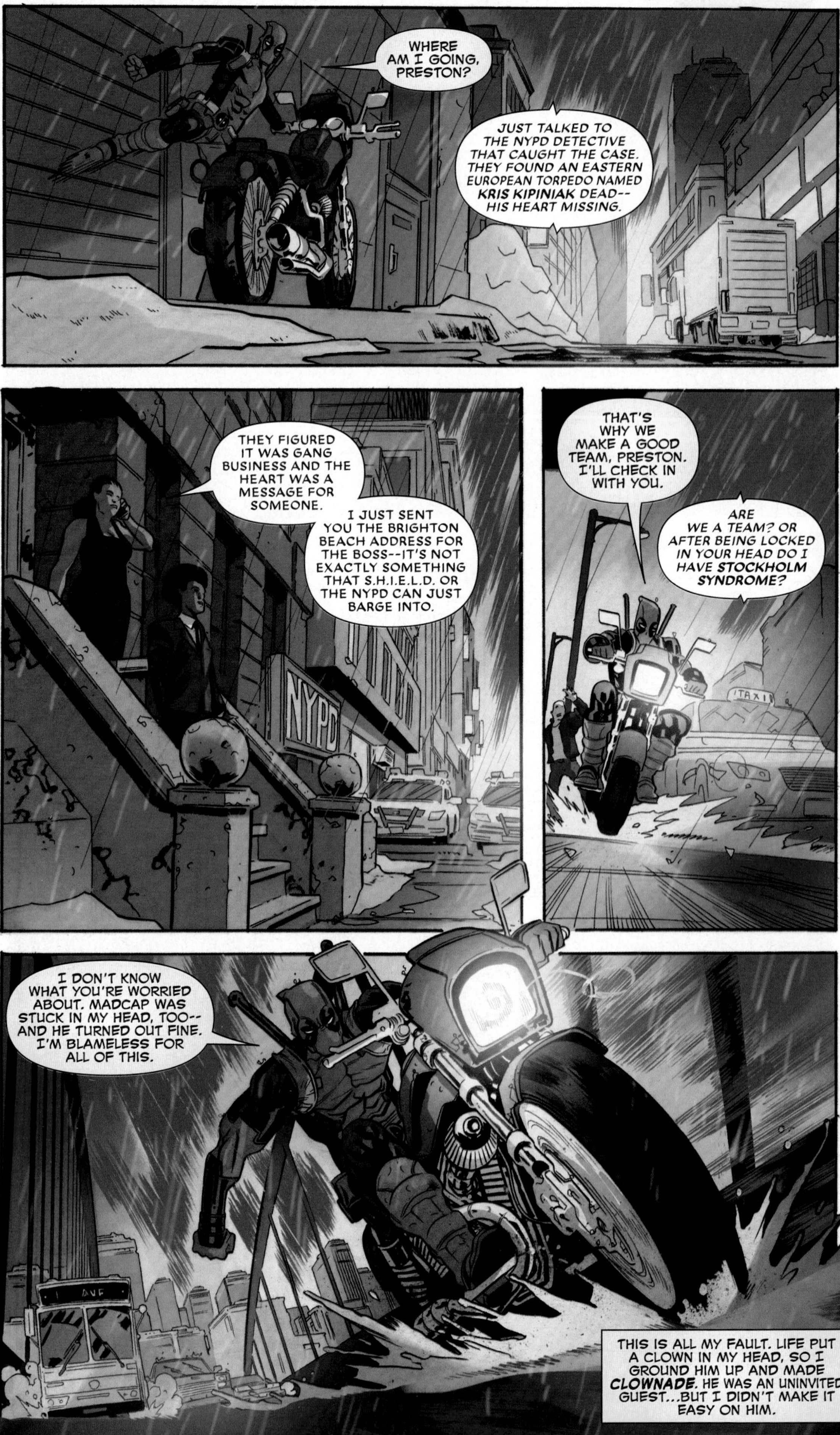

WHERE AM I GOING, PRESTON?
JUST TALKED TO THE NYPD DETECTIVE THAT CAUGHT THE CASE. THEY FOUND AN EASTERN EUROPEAN TORPEDO NAMED KRIS KIPINIAK DEAD--HIS HEART MISSING.
THEY FIGURED IT WAS GANG BUSINESS AND THE HEART WAS A MESSAGE FOR SOMEONE.
I JUST SENT YOU THE BRIGHTON BEACH ADDRESS FOR THE BOSS--IT'S NOT EXACTLY SOMETHING THAT S.H.I.E.L.D. OR THE NYPD CAN JUST BARGE INTO.
NYPD
THAT'S WHY WE MAKE A GOOD TEAM, PRESTON. I'LL CHECK IN WITH YOU.
ARE WE A TEAM? OR AFTER BEING LOCKED IN YOUR HEAD DO I HAVE STOCKHOLM SYNDROME?
TAXI
I DON'T KNOW WHAT YOU'RE WORRIED ABOUT. MADCAP WAS STUCK IN MY HEAD, TOO--AND HE TURNED OUT FINE. I'M BLAMELESS FOR ALL OF THIS.
THIS IS ALL MY FAULT. LIFE PUT A CLOWN IN MY HEAD, SO I GROUND HIM UP AND MADE CLOWNADE. HE WAS AN UNINVITED GUEST...BUT I DIDN'T MAKE IT EASY ON HIM.

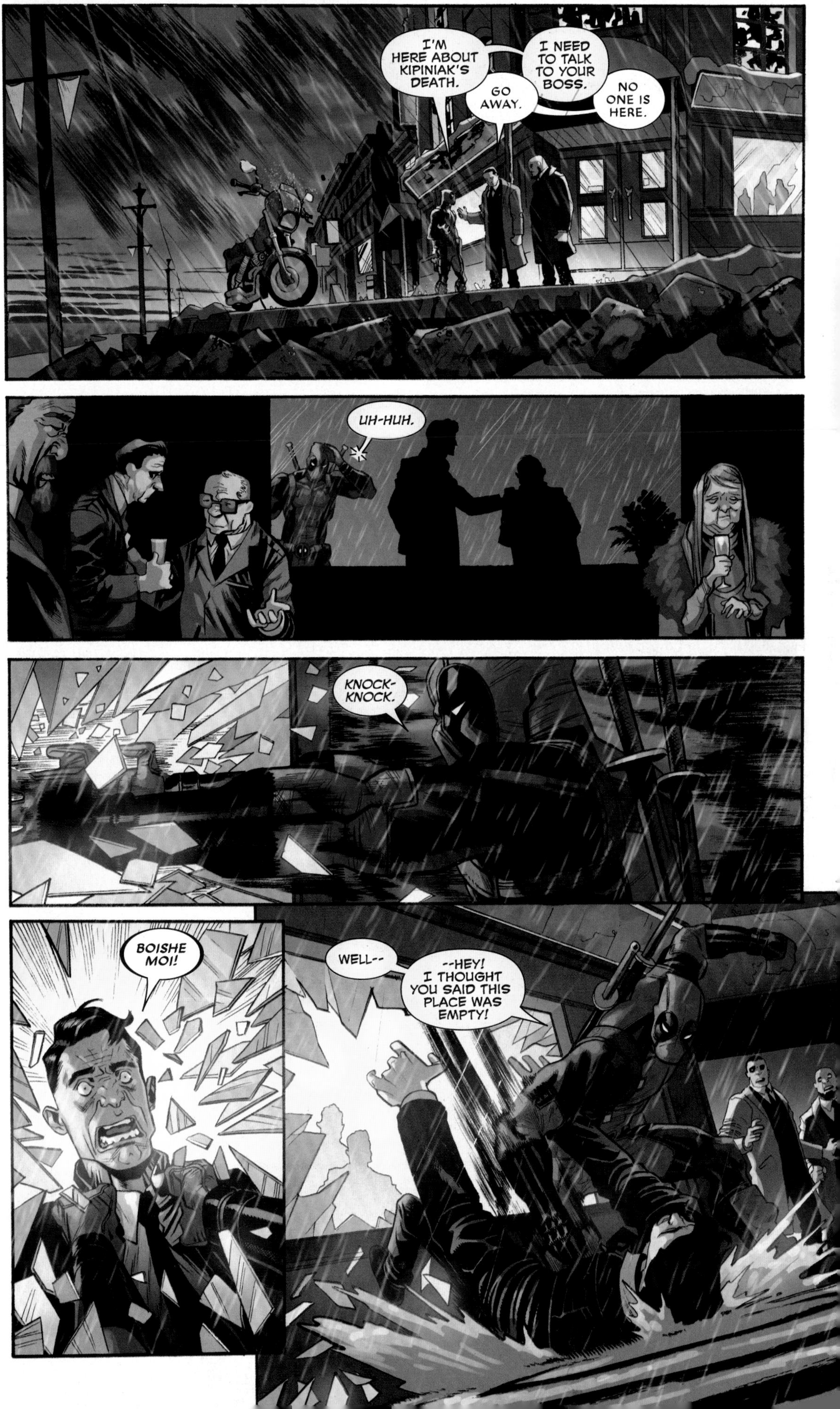

I'M HERE ABOUT KIPINIAK'S DEATH.
GO AWAY.
I NEED TO TALK TO YOUR BOSS.
NO ONE IS HERE.
UH-HUH.
KNOCK-KNOCK.
BOISHE MOI!
WELL--
--HEY! I THOUGHT YOU SAID THIS PLACE WAS EMPTY!

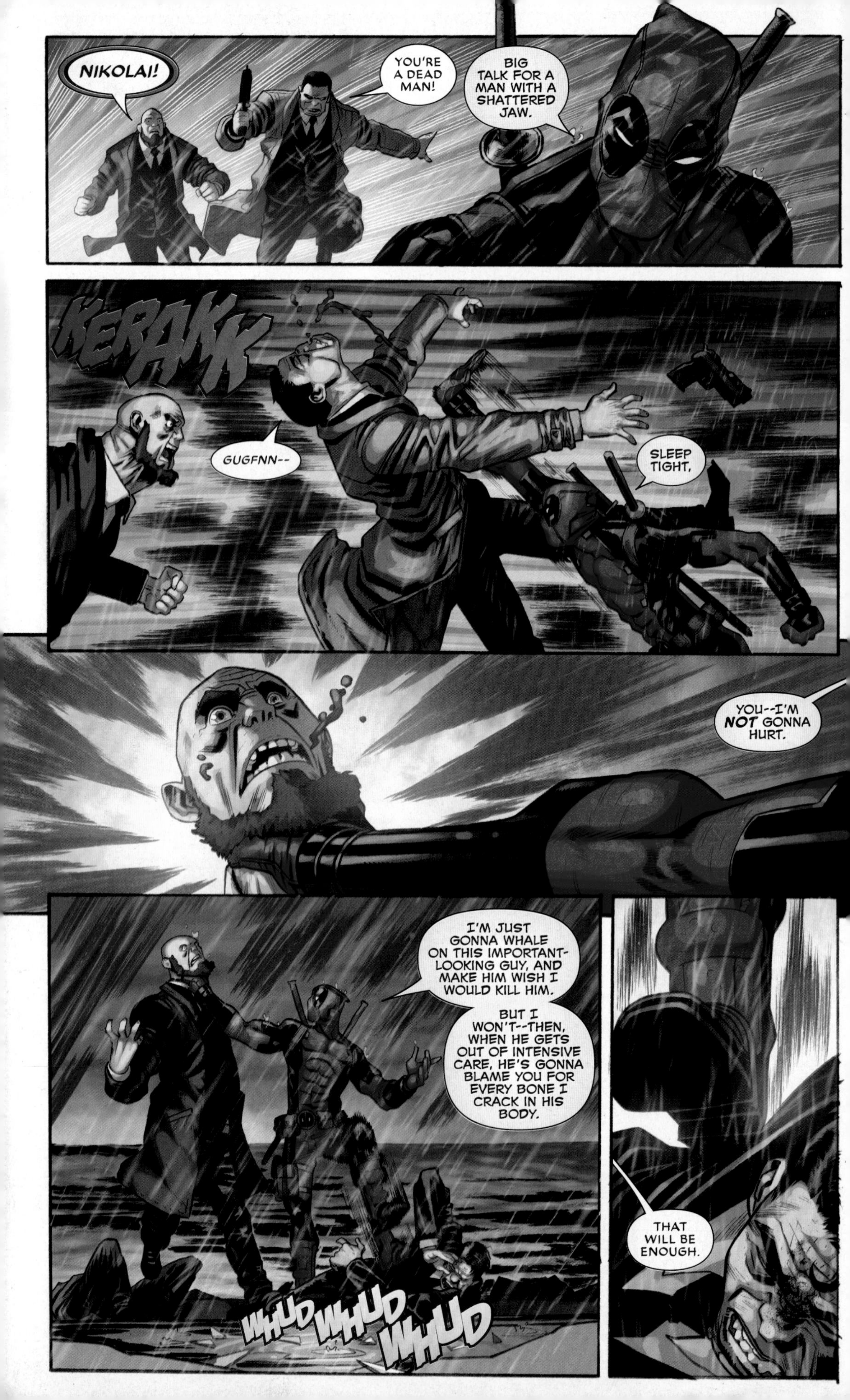
NIKOLAI!
YOU'RE A DEAD MAN!
BIG TALK FOR A MAN WITH A SHATTERED JAW.
KERAKK
GUGFNN--
SLEEP TIGHT,
YOU--I'M NOT GONNA HURT.
I'M JUST GONNA WHALE ON THIS IMPORTANT-LOOKING GUY, AND MAKE HIM WISH I WOULD KILL HIM.
BUT I WON'T--THEN, WHEN HE GETS OUT OF INTENSIVE CARE, HE'S GONNA BLAME YOU FOR EVERY BONE I CRACK IN HIS BODY.
WHUD WHUD WHUD
THAT WILL BE ENOUGH.

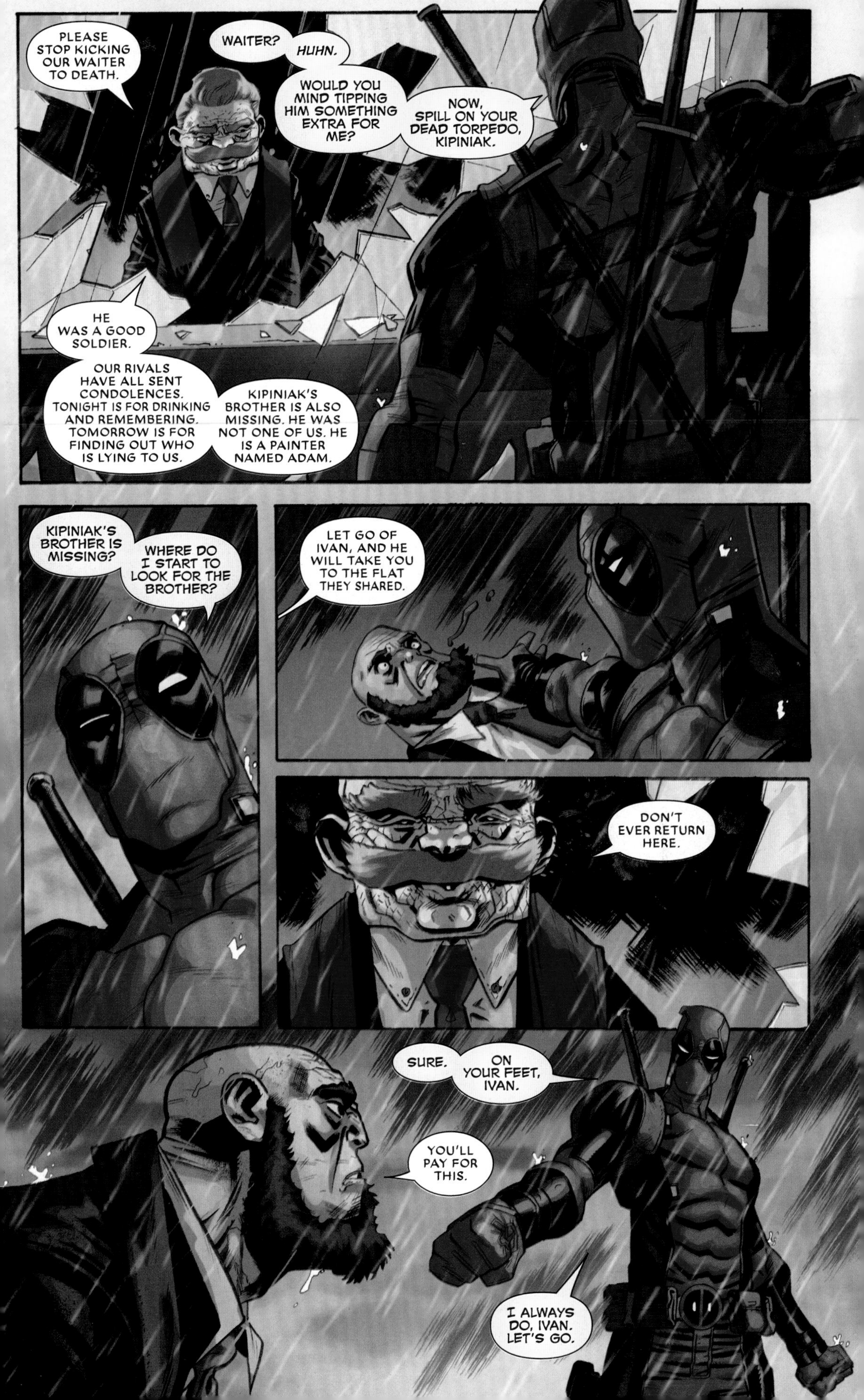
PLEASE STOP KICKING OUR WAITER TO DEATH.
WAITER? HUHN.
WOULD YOU MIND TIPPING HIM SOMETHING EXTRA FOR ME?
NOW, SPILL ON YOUR DEAD TORPEDO, KIPINIAK.
HE WAS A GOOD SOLDIER.
OUR RIVALS HAVE ALL SENT CONDOLENCES. TONIGHT IS FOR DRINKING AND REMEMBERING. TOMORROW IS FOR FINDING OUT WHO IS LYING TO US.
KIPINIAK'S BROTHER IS ALSO MISSING. HE WAS NOT ONE OF US. HE IS A PAINTER NAMED ADAM.
KIPINIAK'S BROTHER IS MISSING?
WHERE DO I START TO LOOK FOR THE BROTHER?
LET GO OF IVAN, AND HE WILL TAKE YOU TO THE FLAT THEY SHARED.
DON'T EVER RETURN HERE.
SURE.
ON YOUR FEET, IVAN.
YOU'LL PAY FOR THIS.
I ALWAYS DO, IVAN. LET'S GO.

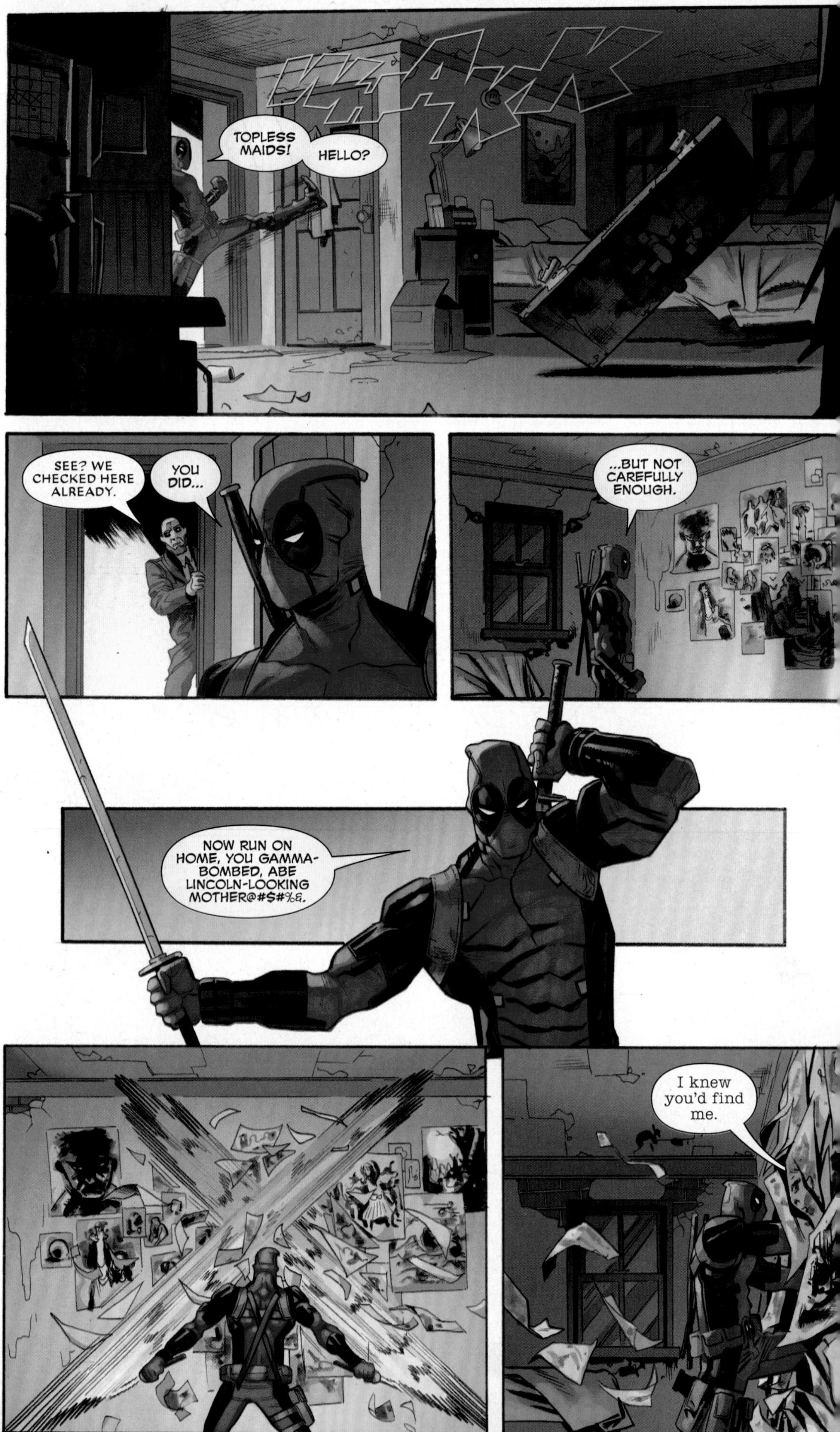
WHAK
TOPLESS MAIDS!
HELLO?
SEE? WE CHECKED HERE ALREADY.
YOU DID...
...BUT NOT CAREFULLY ENOUGH.
NOW RUN ON HOME, YOU GAMMA-BOMBED, ABE LINCOLN-LOOKING MOTHER@#$#%&.
I knew you'd find me.

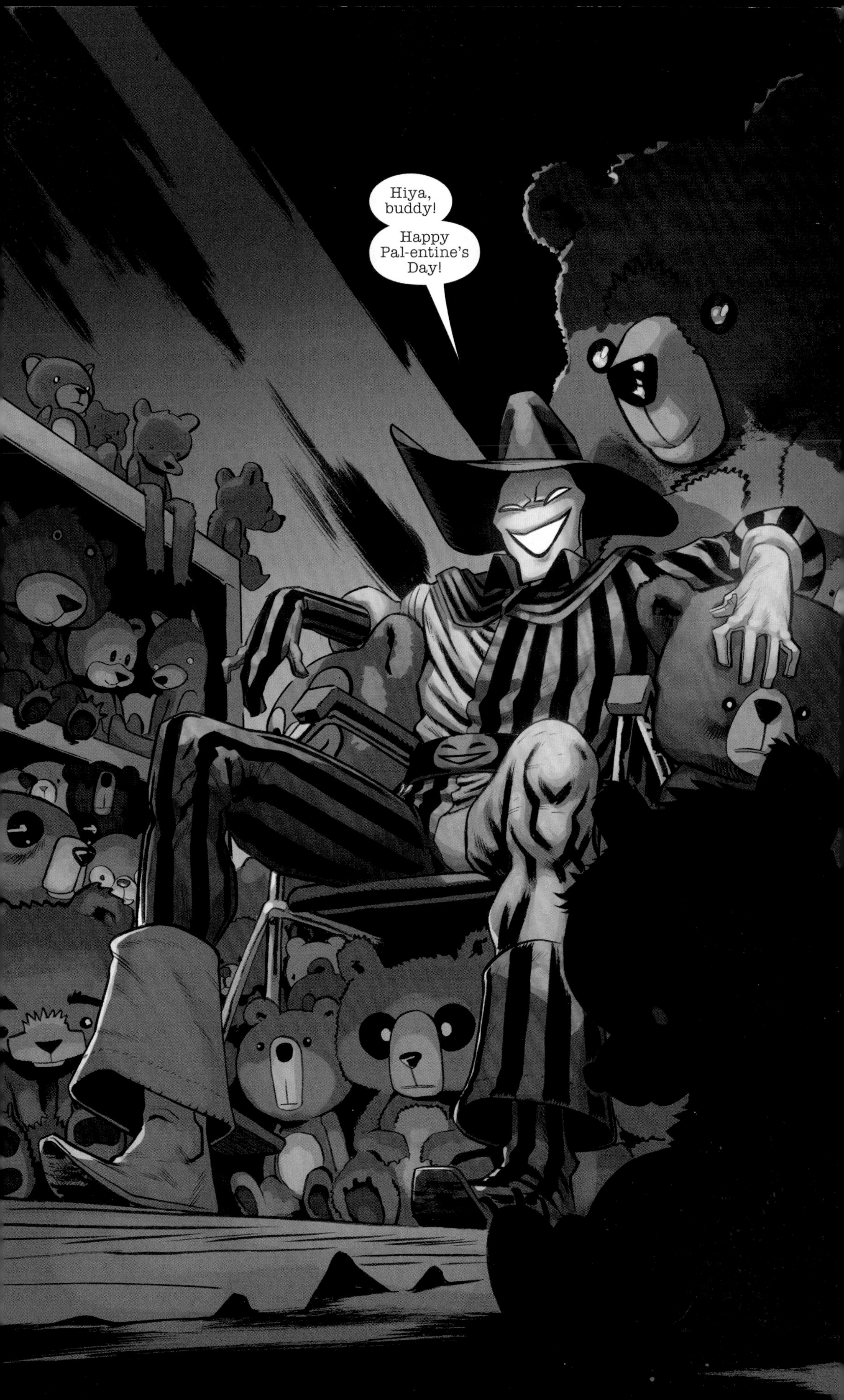
Hiya, buddy!
Happy Pal-entine's Day!

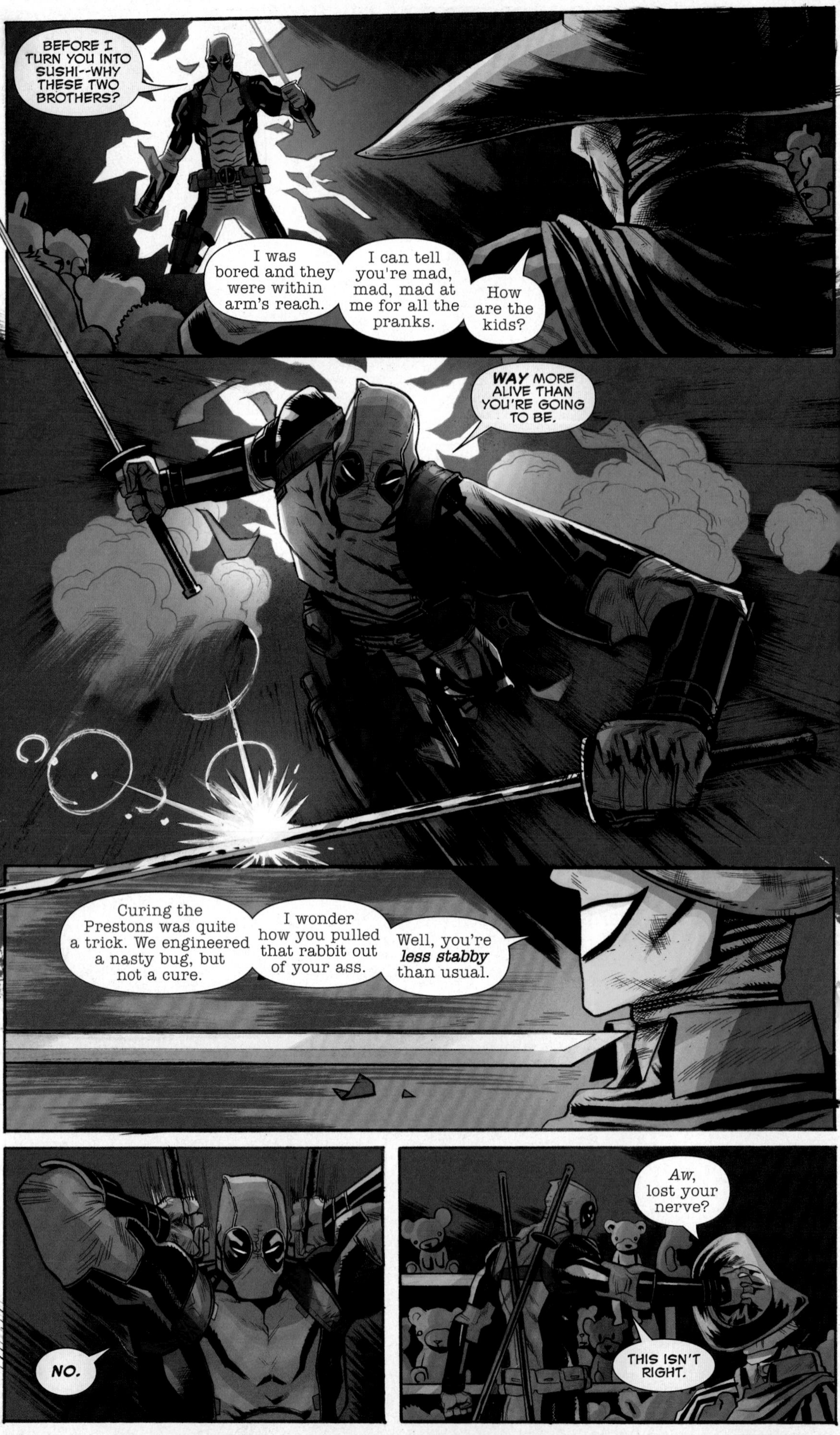
BEFORE I TURN YOU INTO SUSHI--WHY THESE TWO BROTHERS?
I was bored and they were within arm's reach.
I can tell you're mad, mad, mad at me for all the pranks.
How are the kids?
WAY MORE ALIVE THAN YOU'RE GOING TO BE.
Curing the Prestons was quite a trick. We engineered a nasty bug, but not a cure.
I wonder how you pulled that rabbit out of your ass.
Well, you're less stabby than usual.
NO.
Aw, lost your nerve?
THIS ISN'T RIGHT.

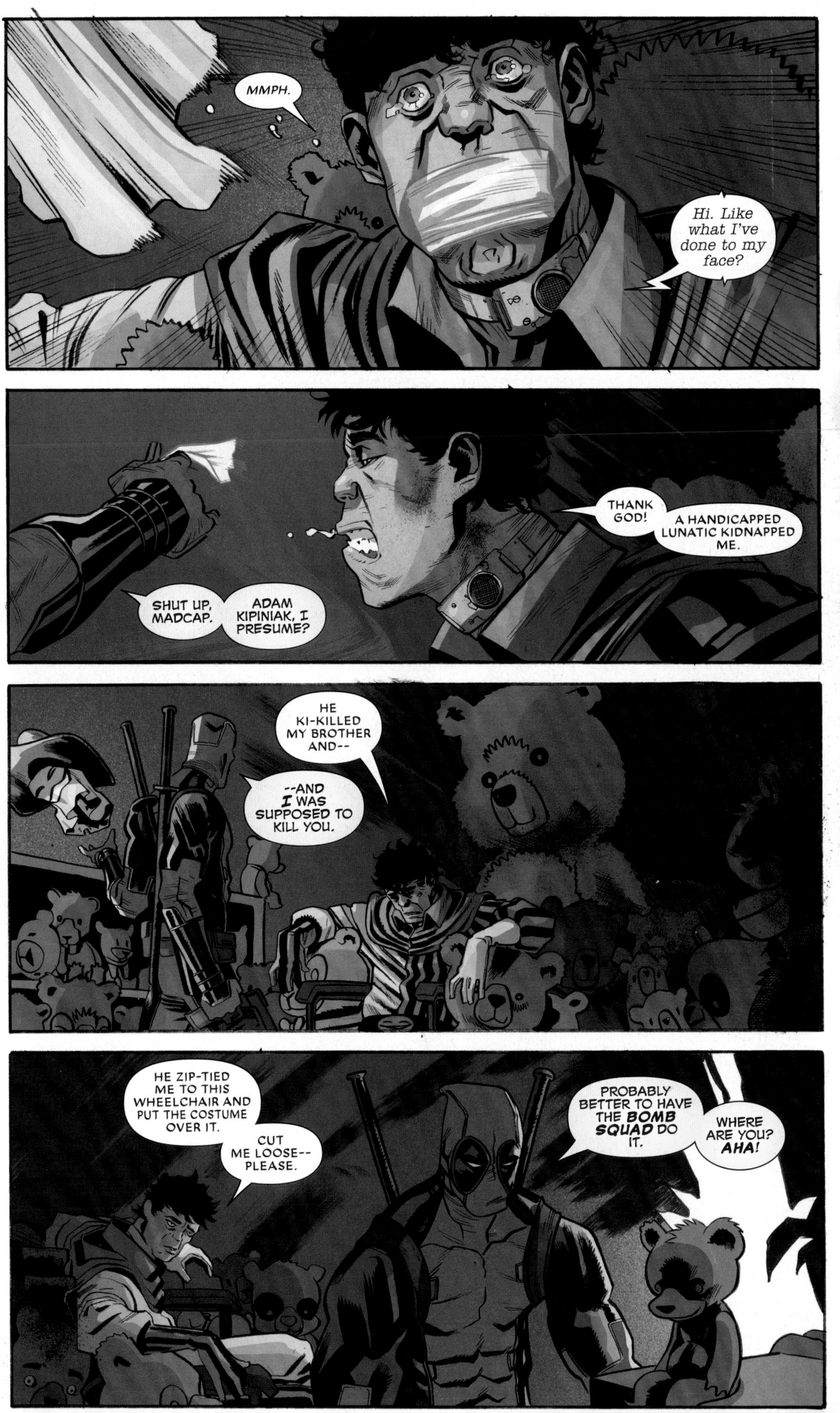
MMPH.
Hi. Like what I've done to my face?
THANK GOD!
A HANDICAPPED LUNATIC KIDNAPPED ME.
SHUT UP, MADCAP.
ADAM KIPINIAK, I PRESUME?
HE KI-KILLED MY BROTHER AND--
--AND I WAS SUPPOSED TO KILL YOU.
HE ZIP-TIED ME TO THIS WHEELCHAIR AND PUT THE COSTUME OVER IT.
CUT ME LOOSE-- PLEASE.
PROBABLY BETTER TO HAVE THE BOMB SQUAD DO IT.
WHERE ARE YOU? AHA!

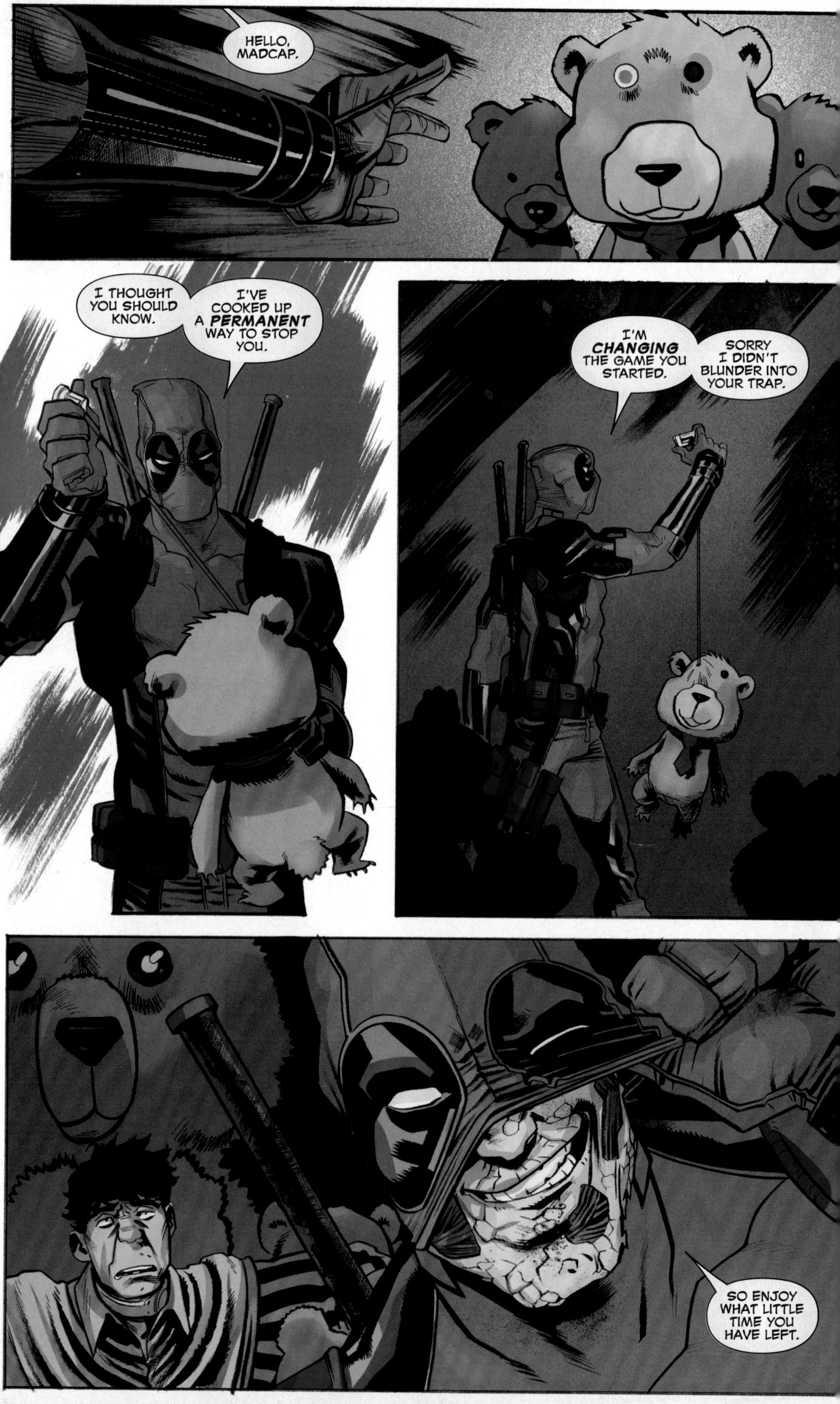
HELLO, MADCAP.
I THOUGHT YOU SHOULD KNOW.
I'VE COOKED UP A **PERMANENT** WAY TO STOP YOU.
I'M **CHANGING** THE GAME YOU STARTED.
SORRY I DIDN'T BLUNDER INTO YOUR TRAP.
SO ENJOY WHAT LITTLE TIME YOU HAVE LEFT.

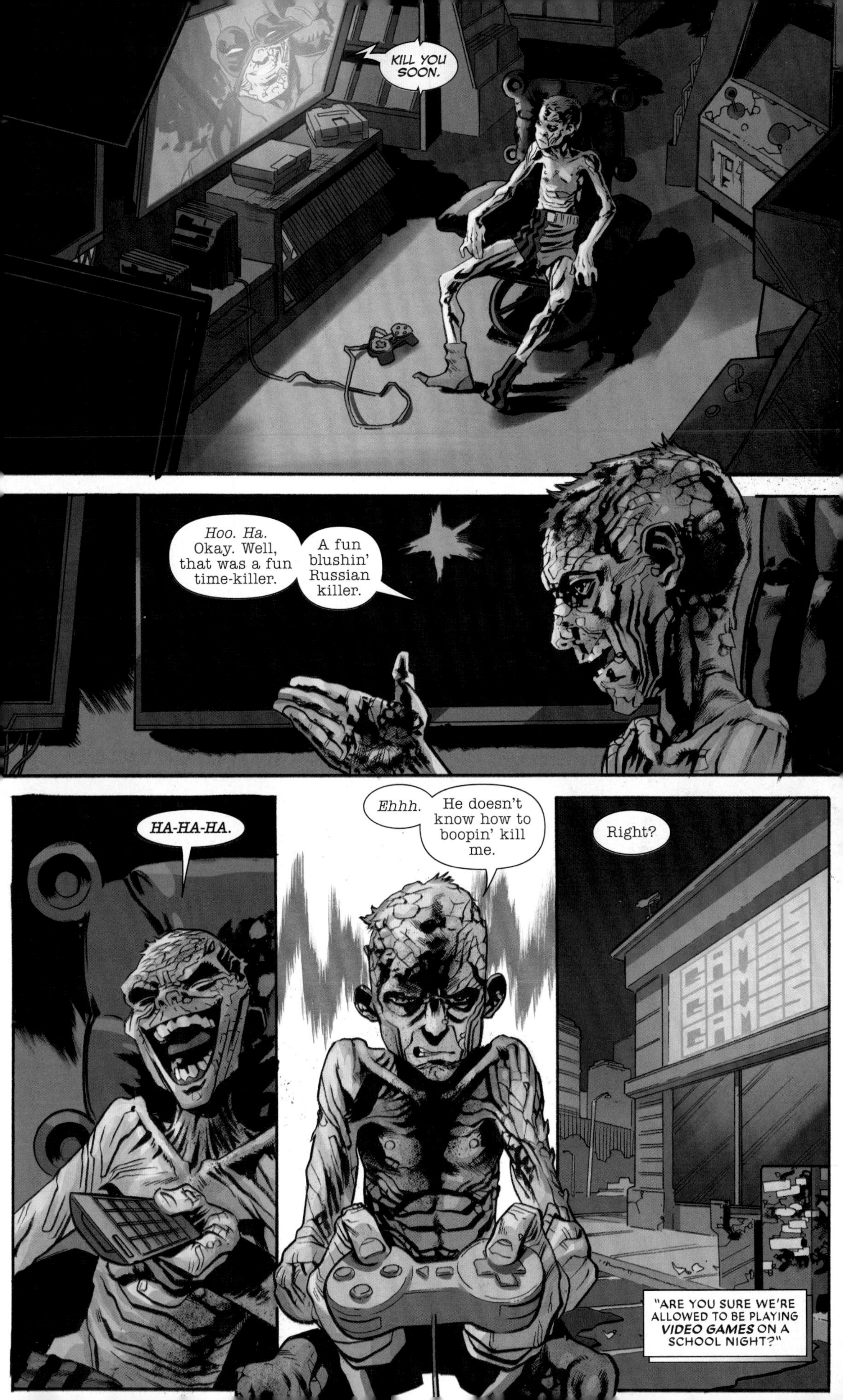

KILL YOU SOON.
Hoo. Ha. Okay. Well, that was a fun time-killer.
A fun blushin' Russian killer.
HA-HA-HA.
Ehhh.
He doesn't know how to boopin' kill me.
Right?
GAMES GAMES GAMES
"ARE YOU SURE WE'RE ALLOWED TO BE PLAYING VIDEO GAMES ON A SCHOOL NIGHT?"

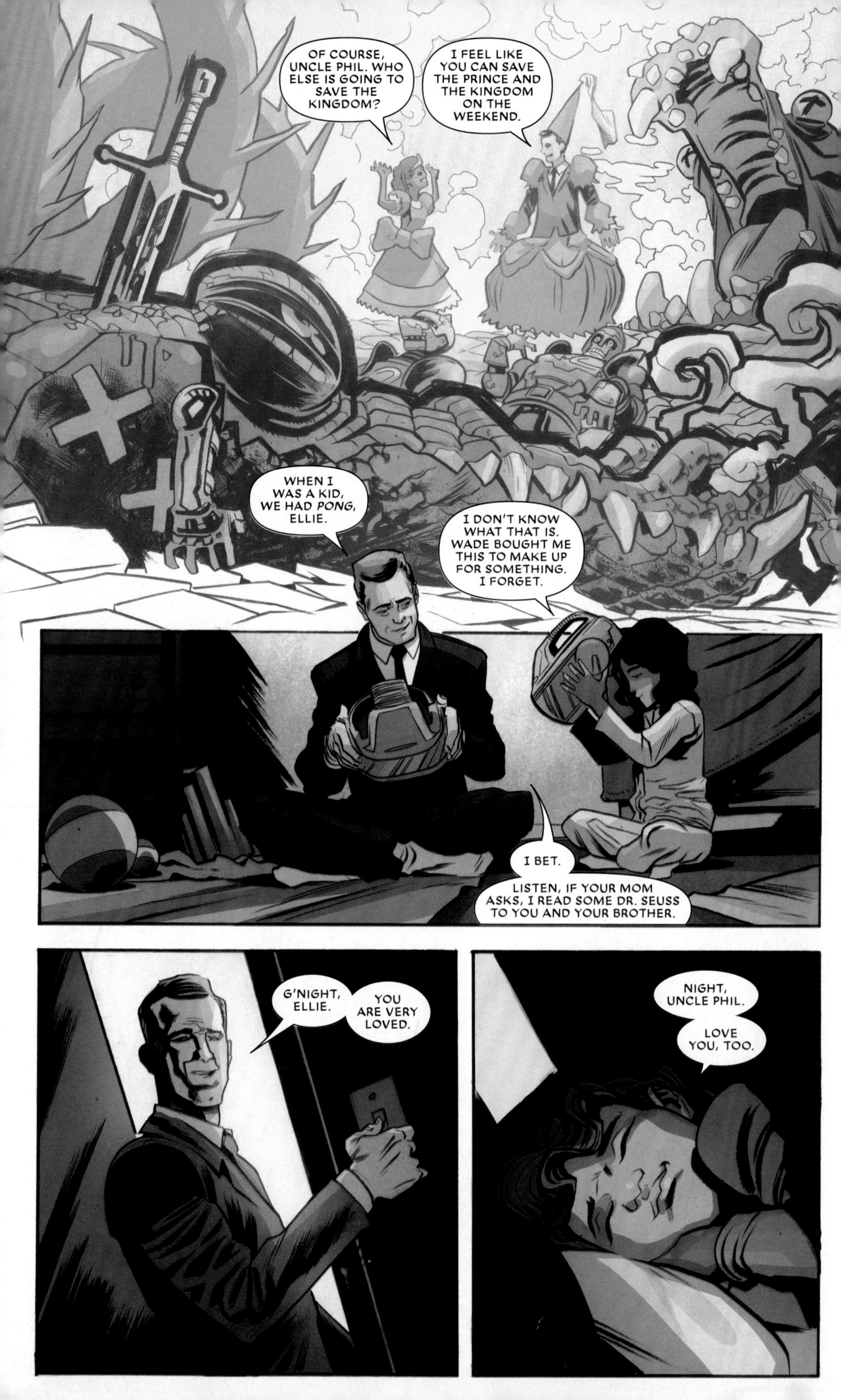

OF COURSE, UNCLE PHIL. WHO ELSE IS GOING TO SAVE THE KINGDOM?
I FEEL LIKE YOU CAN SAVE THE PRINCE AND THE KINGDOM ON THE WEEKEND.
WHEN I WAS A KID, WE HAD *PONG*, ELLIE.
I DON'T KNOW WHAT THAT IS. WADE BOUGHT ME THIS TO MAKE UP FOR SOMETHING. I FORGET.
I BET.
LISTEN, IF YOUR MOM ASKS, I READ SOME DR. SEUSS TO YOU AND YOUR BROTHER.
G'NIGHT, ELLIE.
YOU ARE VERY LOVED.
NIGHT, UNCLE PHIL.
LOVE YOU, TOO.

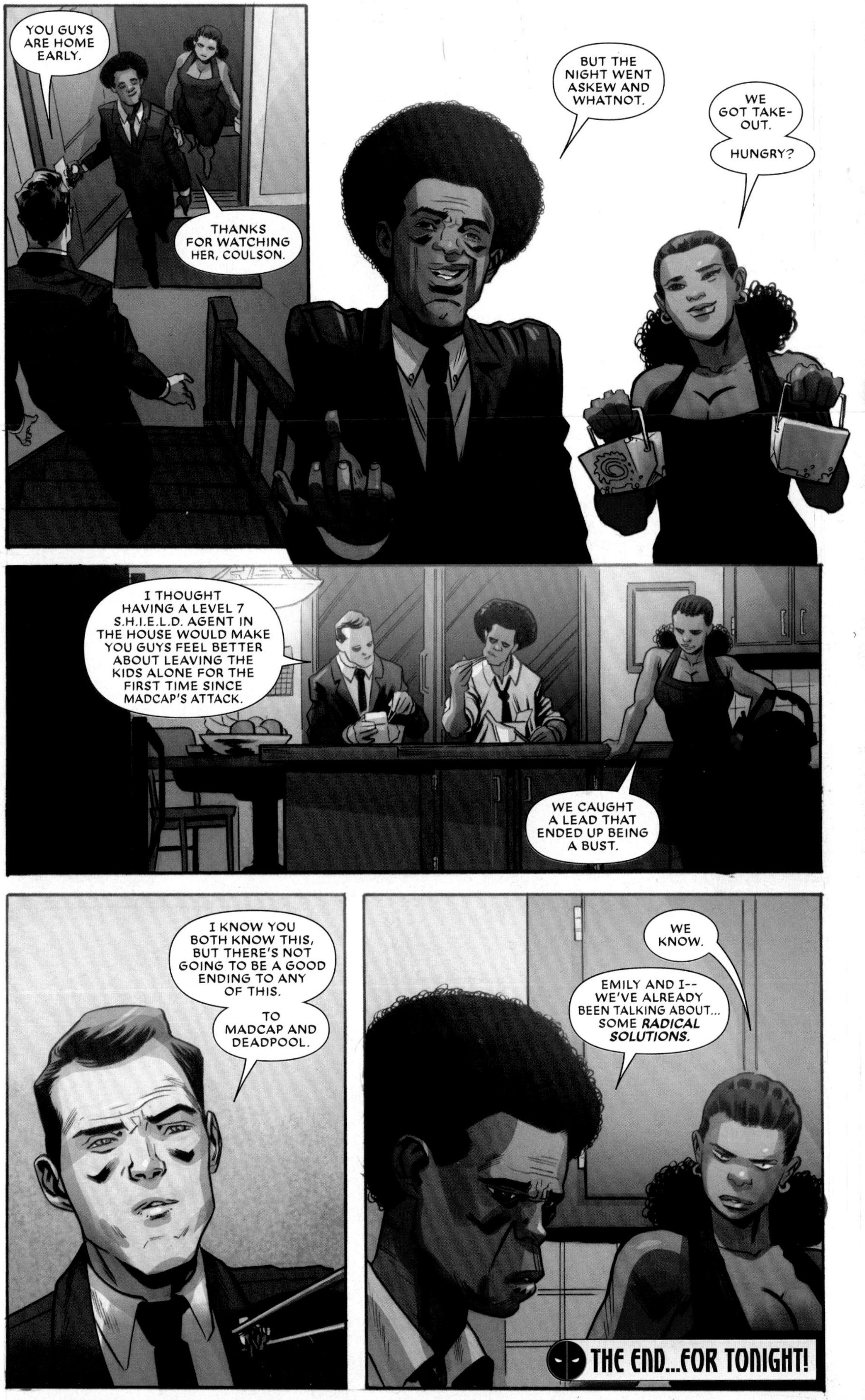
YOU GUYS ARE HOME EARLY.
THANKS FOR WATCHING HER, COULSON.
BUT THE NIGHT WENT ASKEW AND WHATNOT.
WE GOT TAKE-OUT.
HUNGRY?
I THOUGHT HAVING A LEVEL 7 S.H.I.E.L.D. AGENT IN THE HOUSE WOULD MAKE YOU GUYS FEEL BETTER ABOUT LEAVING THE KIDS ALONE FOR THE FIRST TIME SINCE MADCAP'S ATTACK.
WE CAUGHT A LEAD THAT ENDED UP BEING A BUST.
I KNOW YOU BOTH KNOW THIS, BUT THERE'S NOT GOING TO BE A GOOD ENDING TO ANY OF THIS.
TO MADCAP AND DEADPOOL.
WE KNOW.
EMILY AND I-- WE'VE ALREADY BEEN TALKING ABOUT... SOME *RADICAL SOLUTIONS.*
THE END...FOR TONIGHT!

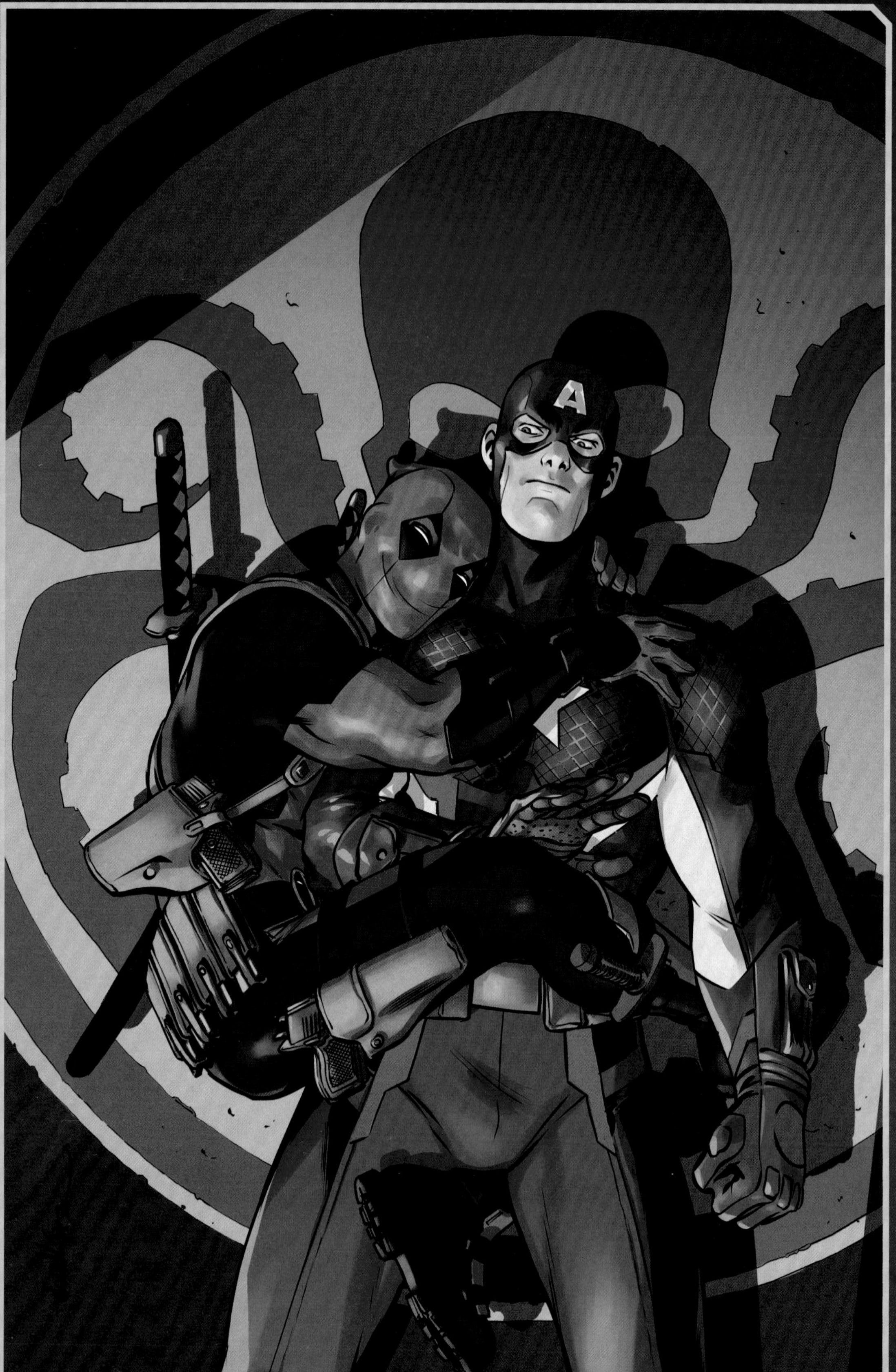

27 | AND NOW FOR SOMETHING COMPLETELY DIFFERENT

Avenger...Assassin...Superstar...Smelly person...Possibly the world's most skilled mercenary, definitely the world's most annoying, Wade Wilson was chosen for a top-secret government program that gave him a healing factor allowing him to heal from any wound. Somehow, despite making his money as a gun for hire, Wade has become one of the most beloved "heroes" in the world. Call him the Merc with the Mouth...call him the Regeneratin' Degenerate...call him...

DEADPOOL

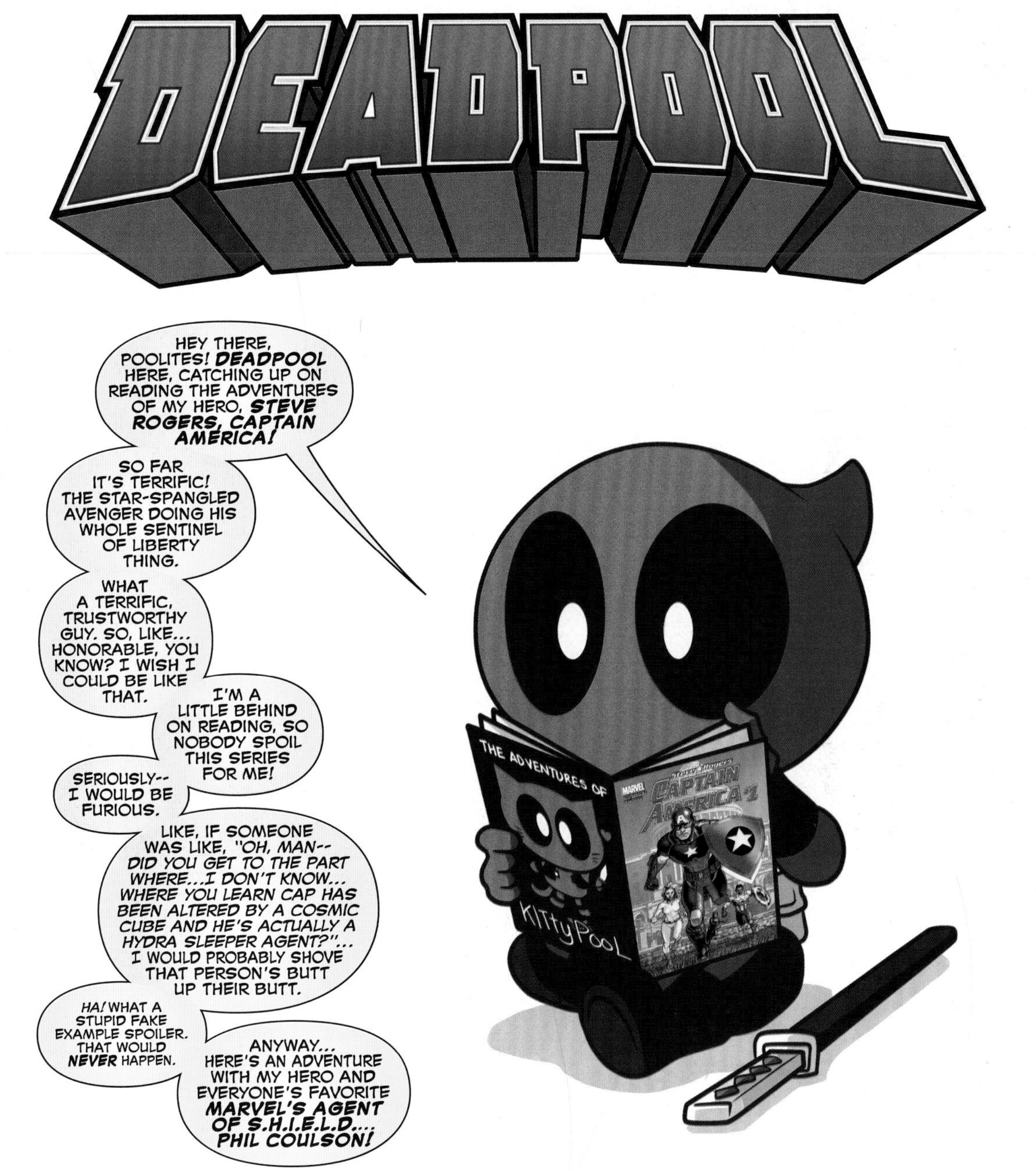
HEY THERE, POOLITES! DEADPOOL HERE, CATCHING UP ON READING THE ADVENTURES OF MY HERO, STEVE ROGERS, CAPTAIN AMERICA!
SO FAR IT'S TERRIFIC! THE STAR-SPANGLED AVENGER DOING HIS WHOLE SENTINEL OF LIBERTY THING.
WHAT A TERRIFIC, TRUSTWORTHY GUY. SO, LIKE... HONORABLE, YOU KNOW? I WISH I COULD BE LIKE THAT.
I'M A LITTLE BEHIND ON READING, SO NOBODY SPOIL THIS SERIES FOR ME!
SERIOUSLY-- I WOULD BE FURIOUS.
LIKE, IF SOMEONE WAS LIKE, "OH, MAN-- DID YOU GET TO THE PART WHERE...I DON'T KNOW... WHERE YOU LEARN CAP HAS BEEN ALTERED BY A COSMIC CUBE AND HE'S ACTUALLY A HYDRA SLEEPER AGENT?"... I WOULD PROBABLY SHOVE THAT PERSON'S BUTT UP THEIR BUTT.
HA! WHAT A STUPID FAKE EXAMPLE SPOILER. THAT WOULD NEVER HAPPEN.
ANYWAY... HERE'S AN ADVENTURE WITH MY HERO AND EVERYONE'S FAVORITE MARVEL'S AGENT OF S.H.I.E.L.D.... PHIL COULSON!
THE ADVENTURES OF
KITtyPooL
MARVEL
CAPTAIN AMERICA
#1

LI'L DEADPOOL ART BY
IRENE Y. LEE

AND NOW FOR SOMETHING COMPLETELY DIFFERENT

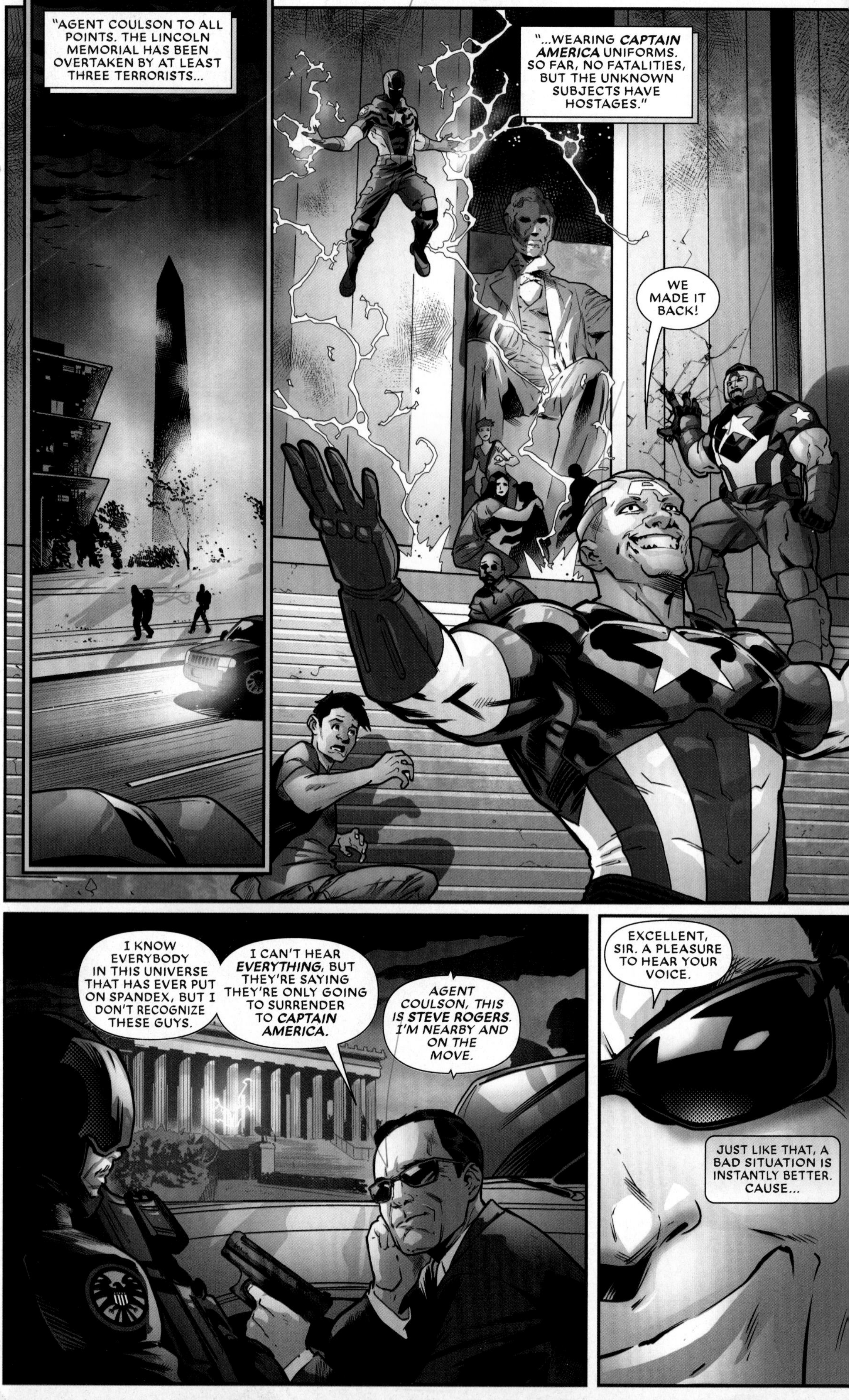
"AGENT COULSON TO ALL POINTS. THE LINCOLN MEMORIAL HAS BEEN OVERTAKEN BY AT LEAST THREE TERRORISTS...
"...WEARING CAPTAIN AMERICA UNIFORMS. SO FAR, NO FATALITIES, BUT THE UNKNOWN SUBJECTS HAVE HOSTAGES."
WE MADE IT BACK!
I KNOW EVERYBODY IN THIS UNIVERSE THAT HAS EVER PUT ON SPANDEX, BUT I DON'T RECOGNIZE THESE GUYS.
I CAN'T HEAR EVERYTHING, BUT THEY'RE SAYING THEY'RE ONLY GOING TO SURRENDER TO CAPTAIN AMERICA.
AGENT COULSON, THIS IS STEVE ROGERS. I'M NEARBY AND ON THE MOVE.
EXCELLENT, SIR. A PLEASURE TO HEAR YOUR VOICE.
JUST LIKE THAT, A BAD SITUATION IS INSTANTLY BETTER. CAUSE...

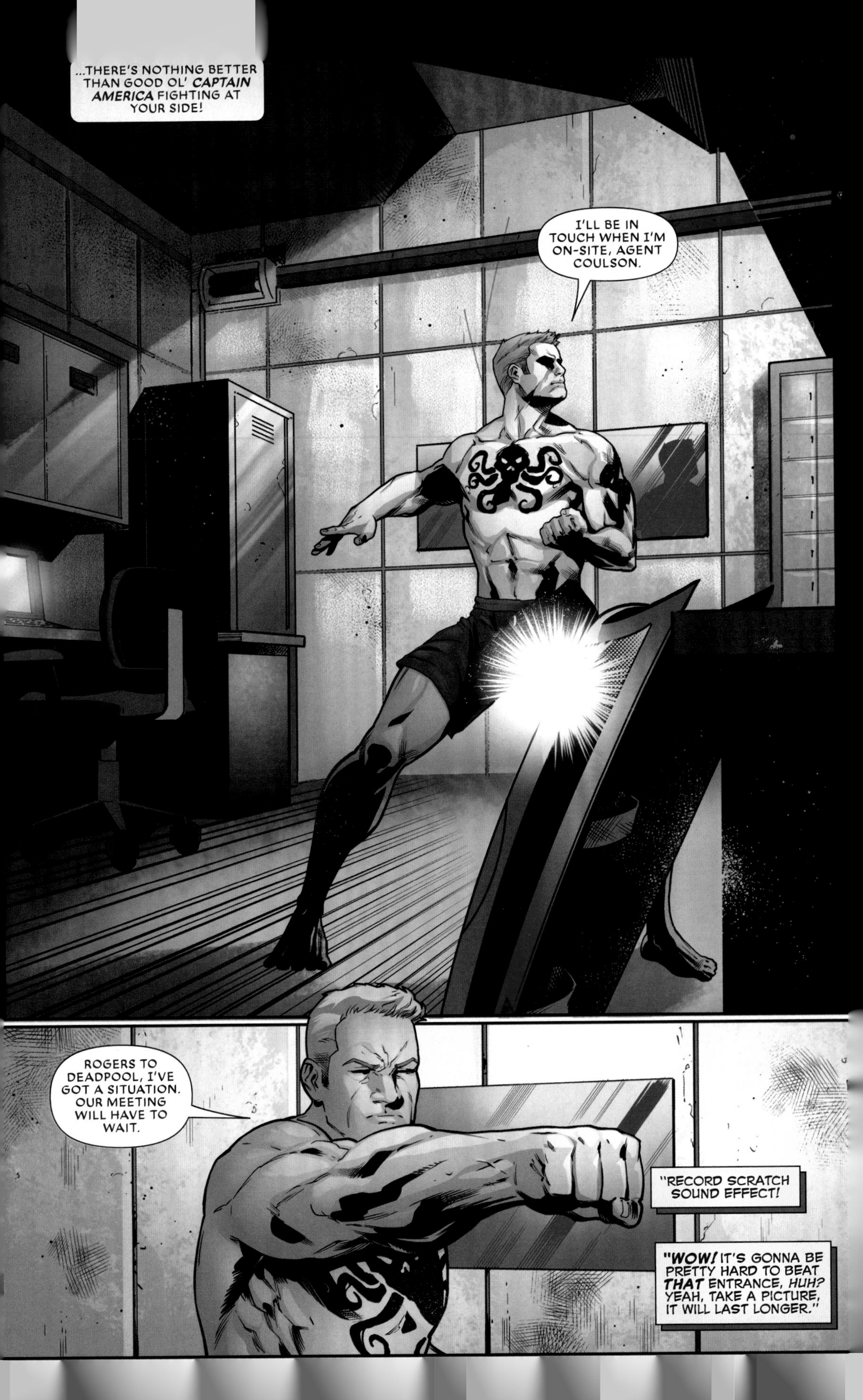
...THERE'S NOTHING BETTER THAN GOOD OL' CAPTAIN AMERICA FIGHTING AT YOUR SIDE!
I'LL BE IN TOUCH WHEN I'M ON-SITE, AGENT COULSON.
ROGERS TO DEADPOOL, I'VE GOT A SITUATION. OUR MEETING WILL HAVE TO WAIT.
"RECORD SCRATCH SOUND EFFECT!
"WOW! IT'S GONNA BE PRETTY HARD TO BEAT THAT ENTRANCE, HUH? YEAH, TAKE A PICTURE, IT WILL LAST LONGER."

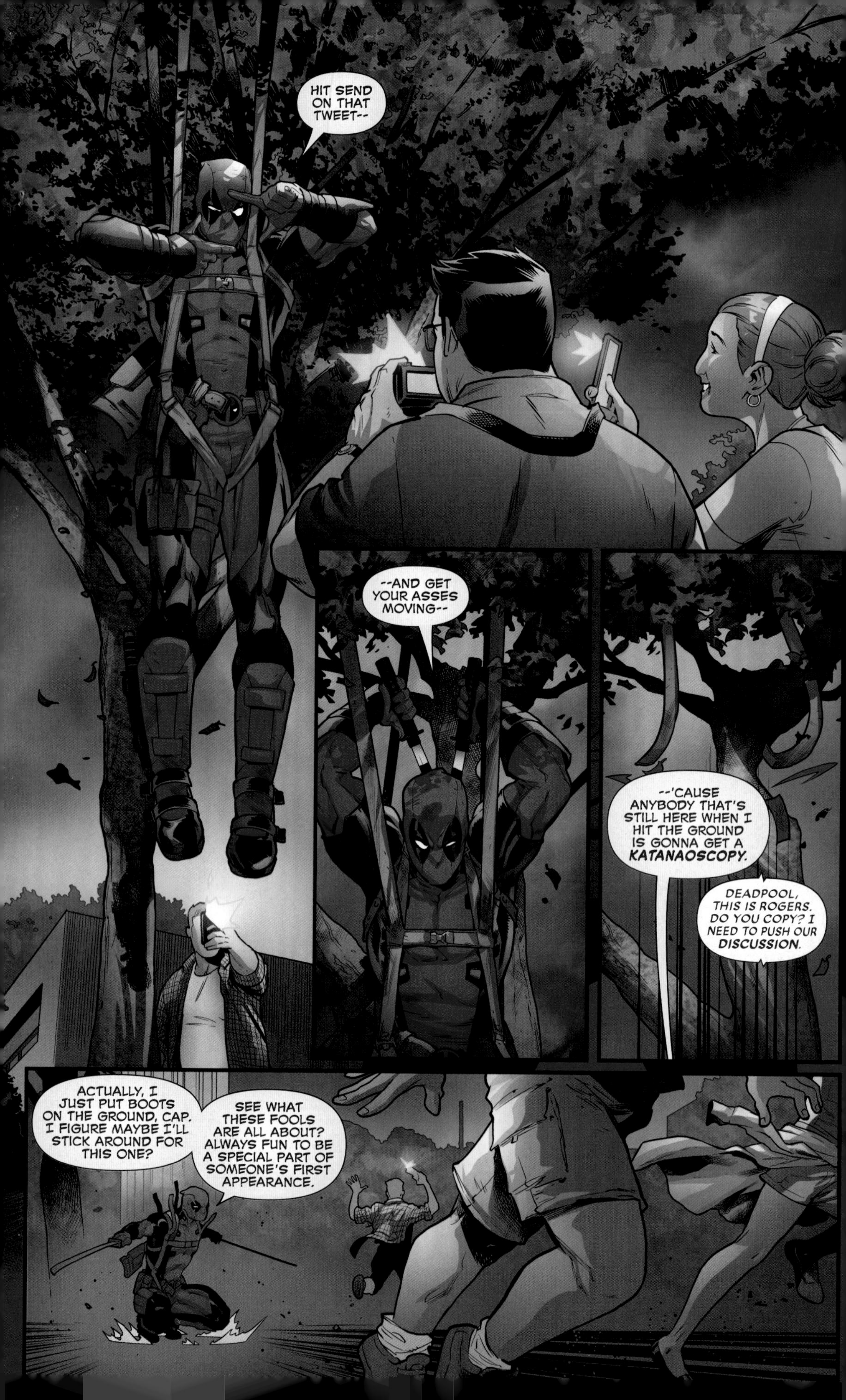
HIT SEND ON THAT TWEET--
--AND GET YOUR ASSES MOVING--
--'CAUSE ANYBODY THAT'S STILL HERE WHEN I HIT THE GROUND IS GONNA GET A **KATANAOSCOPY**.
DEADPOOL, THIS IS ROGERS. DO YOU COPY? I NEED TO PUSH OUR **DISCUSSION**.
ACTUALLY, I JUST PUT BOOTS ON THE GROUND, CAP. I FIGURE MAYBE I'LL STICK AROUND FOR THIS ONE?
SEE WHAT THESE FOOLS ARE ALL ABOUT? ALWAYS FUN TO BE A SPECIAL PART OF SOMEONE'S FIRST APPEARANCE.

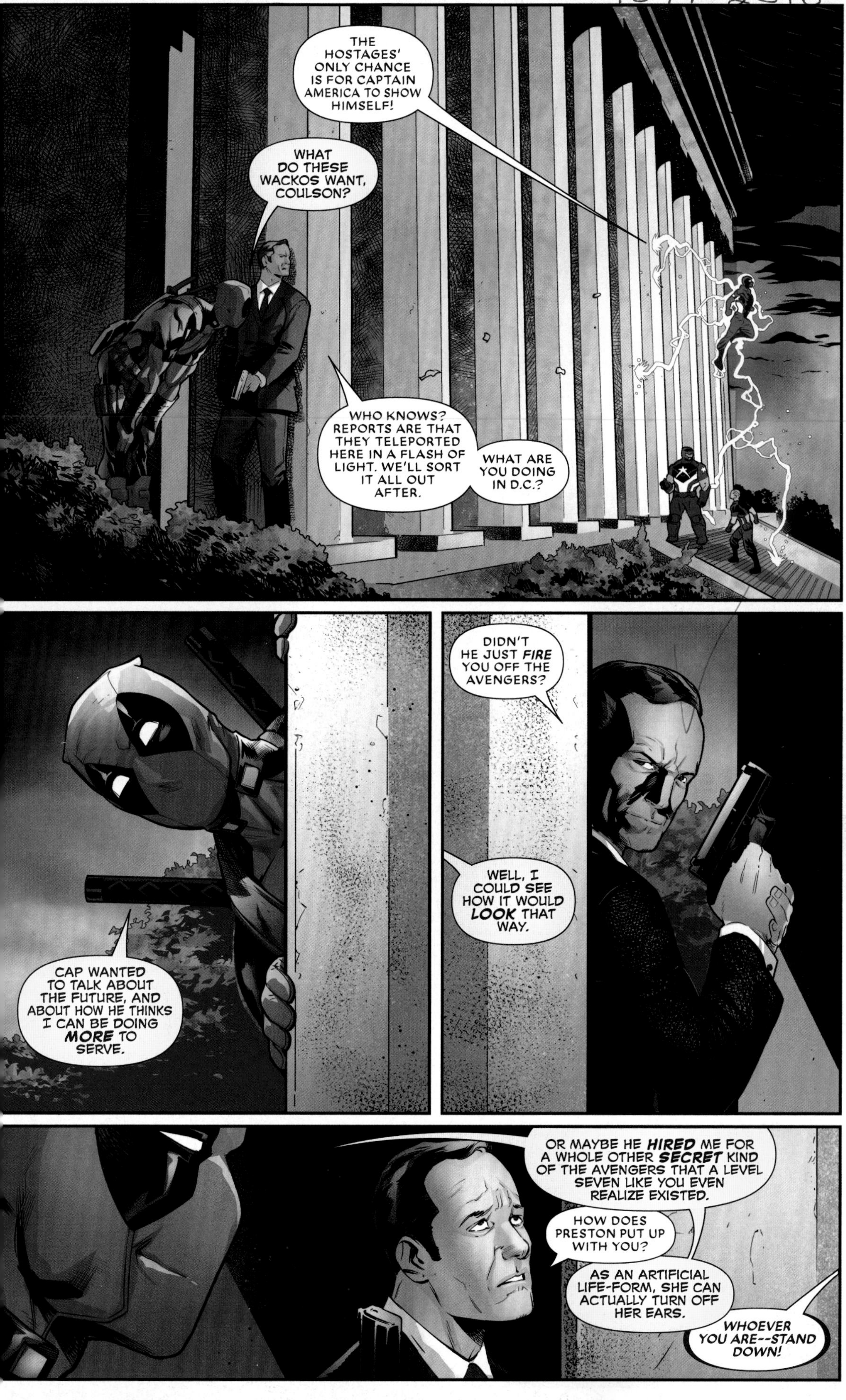

THE HOSTAGES' ONLY CHANCE IS FOR CAPTAIN AMERICA TO SHOW HIMSELF!
WHAT DO THESE WACKOS WANT, COULSON?
WHO KNOWS? REPORTS ARE THAT THEY TELEPORTED HERE IN A FLASH OF LIGHT. WE'LL SORT IT ALL OUT AFTER.
WHAT ARE YOU DOING IN D.C.?
CAP WANTED TO TALK ABOUT THE FUTURE, AND ABOUT HOW HE THINKS I CAN BE DOING MORE TO SERVE.
DIDN'T HE JUST FIRE YOU OFF THE AVENGERS?
WELL, I COULD SEE HOW IT WOULD LOOK THAT WAY.
OR MAYBE HE HIRED ME FOR A WHOLE OTHER SECRET KIND OF THE AVENGERS THAT A LEVEL SEVEN LIKE YOU EVEN REALIZE EXISTED.
HOW DOES PRESTON PUT UP WITH YOU?
AS AN ARTIFICIAL LIFE-FORM, SHE CAN ACTUALLY TURN OFF HER EARS.
WHOEVER YOU ARE--STAND DOWN!

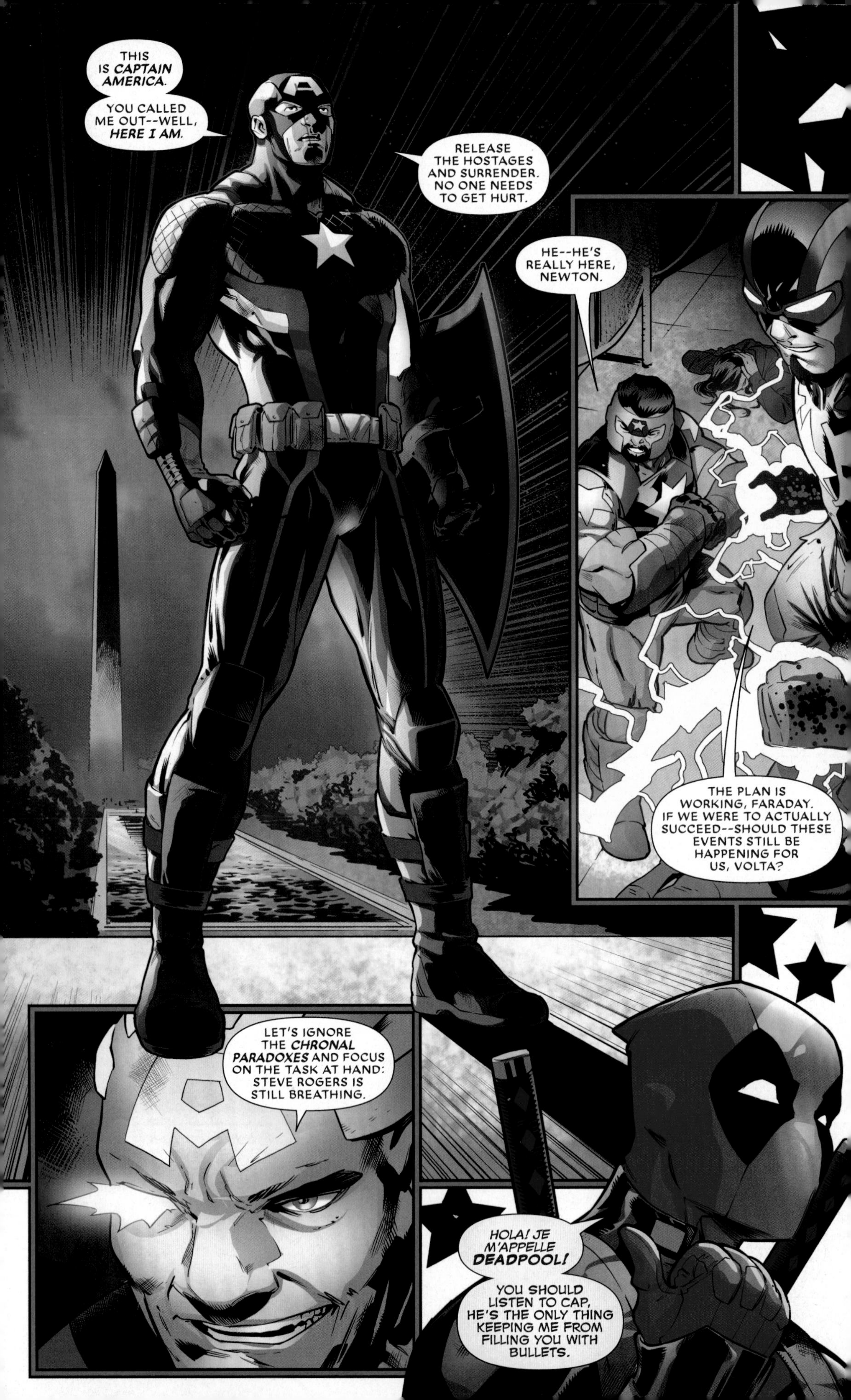
THIS IS CAPTAIN AMERICA.
YOU CALLED ME OUT--WELL, HERE I AM.
RELEASE THE HOSTAGES AND SURRENDER. NO ONE NEEDS TO GET HURT.
HE--HE'S REALLY HERE, NEWTON.
THE PLAN IS WORKING, FARADAY. IF WE WERE TO ACTUALLY SUCCEED--SHOULD THESE EVENTS STILL BE HAPPENING FOR US, VOLTA?
LET'S IGNORE THE CHRONAL PARADOXES AND FOCUS ON THE TASK AT HAND: STEVE ROGERS IS STILL BREATHING.
HOLA! JE M'APPELLE DEADPOOL!
YOU SHOULD LISTEN TO CAP, HE'S THE ONLY THING KEEPING ME FROM FILLING YOU WITH BULLETS.

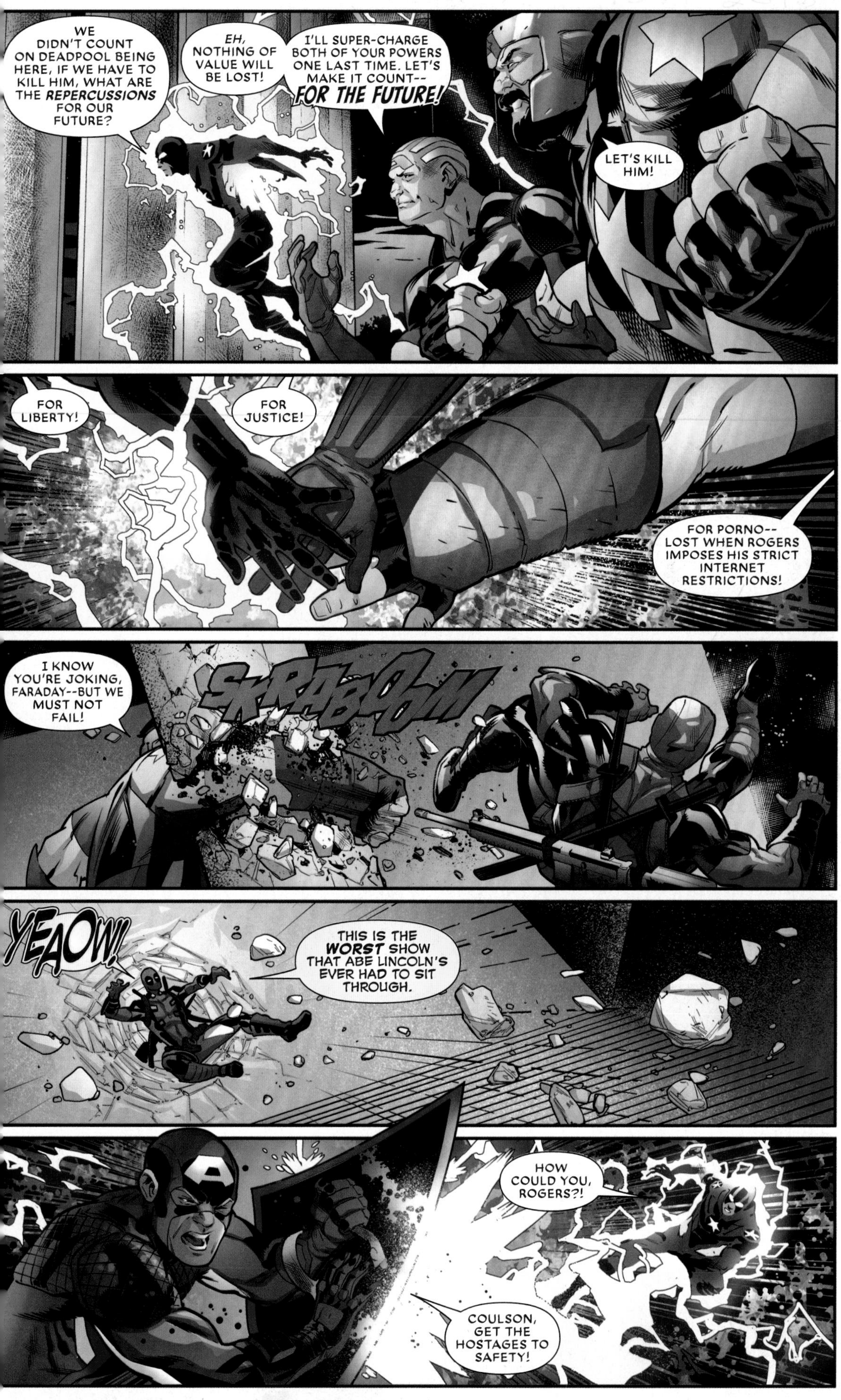
WE DIDN'T COUNT ON DEADPOOL BEING HERE, IF WE HAVE TO KILL HIM, WHAT ARE THE *REPERCUSSIONS* FOR OUR FUTURE?
EH, NOTHING OF VALUE WILL BE LOST!
I'LL SUPER-CHARGE BOTH OF YOUR POWERS ONE LAST TIME. LET'S MAKE IT COUNT-- *FOR THE FUTURE!*
LET'S KILL HIM!
FOR LIBERTY!
FOR JUSTICE!
FOR PORNO-- LOST WHEN ROGERS IMPOSES HIS STRICT INTERNET RESTRICTIONS!
I KNOW YOU'RE JOKING, FARADAY--BUT WE MUST NOT FAIL!
SKRABOOM
YEAOW!!
THIS IS THE *WORST* SHOW THAT ABE LINCOLN'S EVER HAD TO SIT THROUGH.
HOW COULD YOU, ROGERS?!
COULSON, GET THE HOSTAGES TO SAFETY!

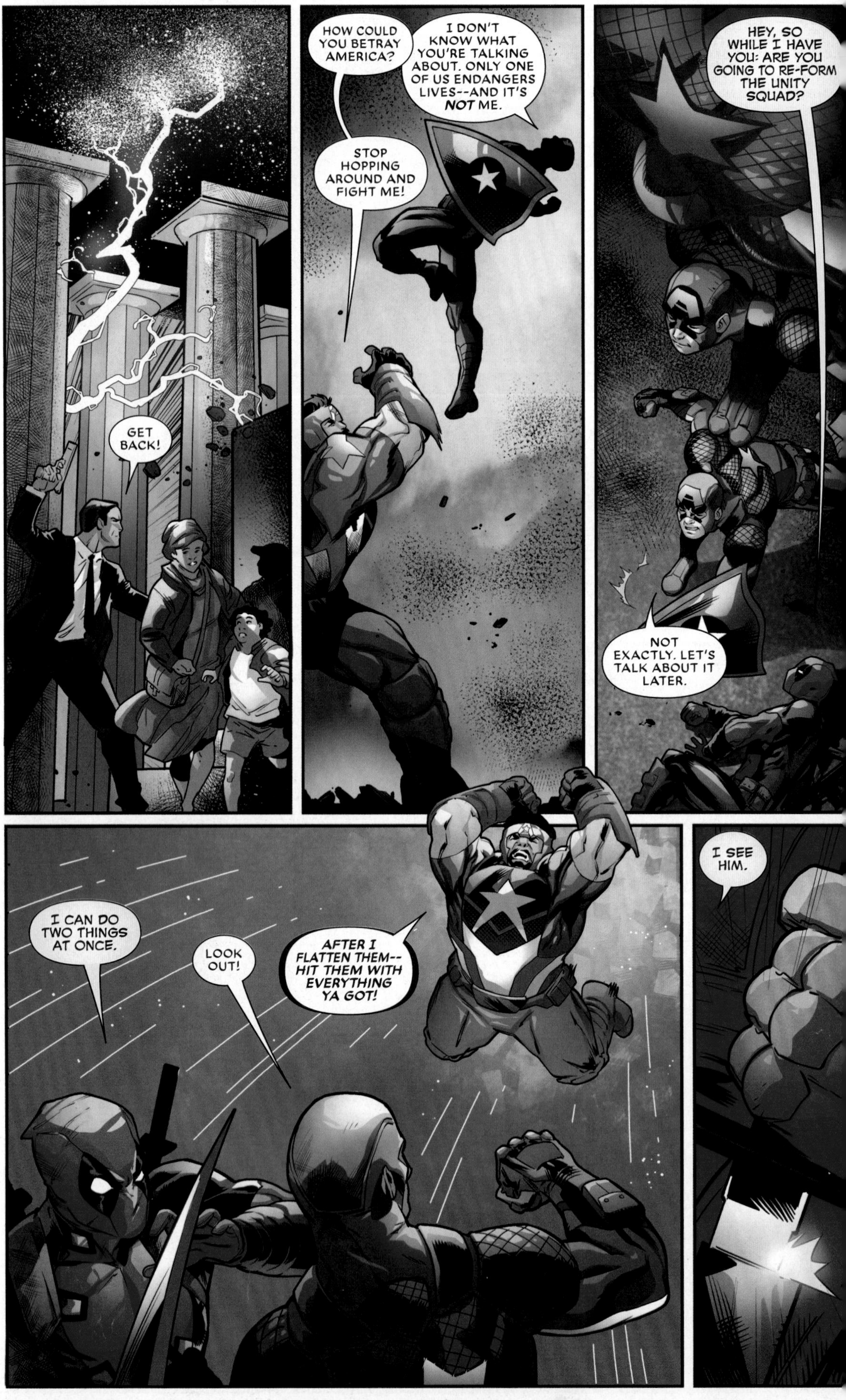
GET BACK!
HOW COULD YOU BETRAY AMERICA?
I DON'T KNOW WHAT YOU'RE TALKING ABOUT. ONLY ONE OF US ENDANGERS LIVES--AND IT'S *NOT* ME.
STOP HOPPING AROUND AND FIGHT ME!
HEY, SO WHILE I HAVE YOU: ARE YOU GOING TO RE-FORM THE UNITY SQUAD?
NOT EXACTLY. LET'S TALK ABOUT IT LATER.
I CAN DO TWO THINGS AT ONCE.
LOOK OUT!
AFTER I FLATTEN THEM--HIT THEM WITH EVERYTHING YA GOT!
I SEE HIM.

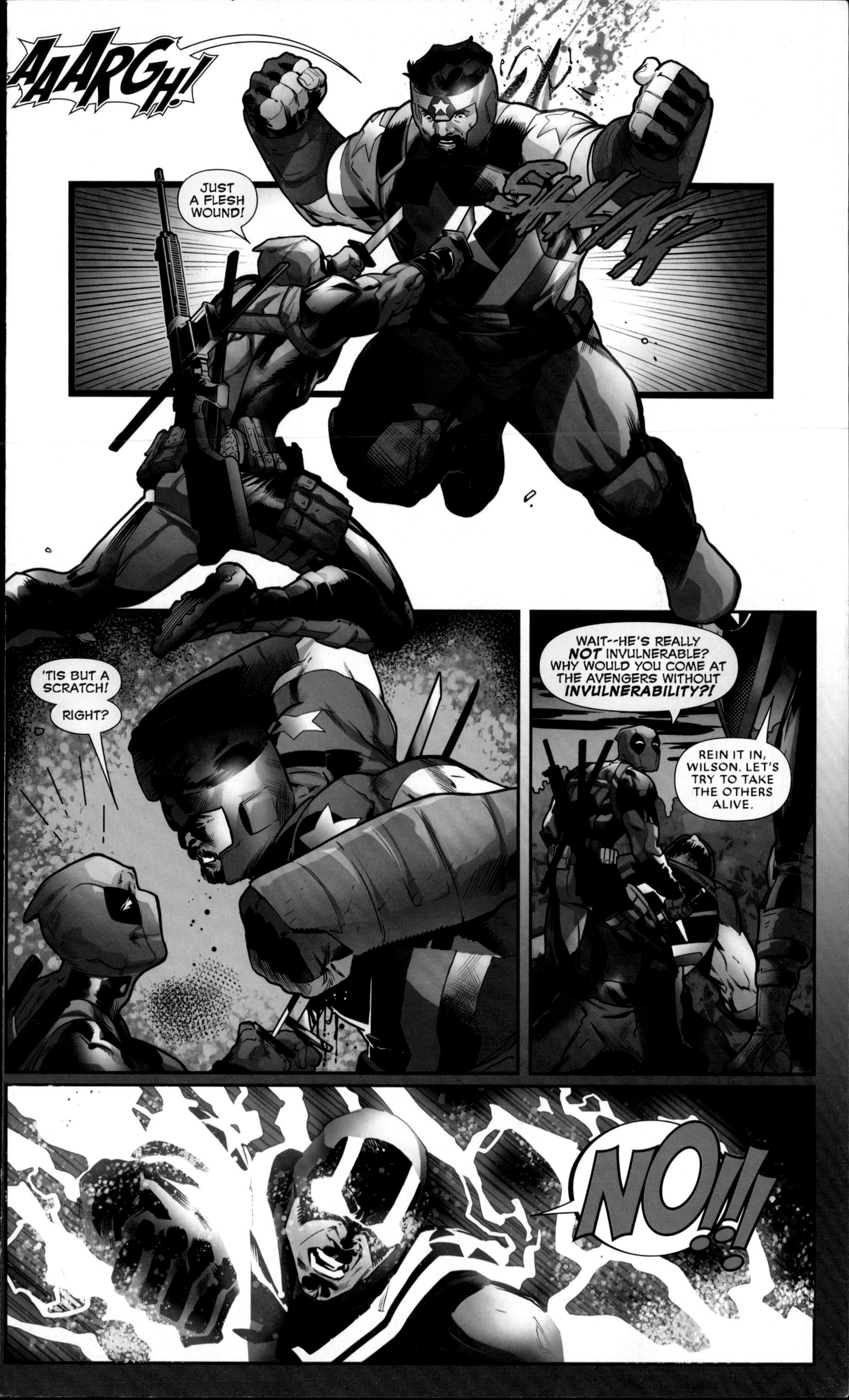
AAARGH!
JUST A FLESH WOUND!
SHHHK
'TIS BUT A SCRATCH!
RIGHT?
WAIT--HE'S REALLY **NOT** INVULNERABLE? WHY WOULD YOU COME AT THE AVENGERS WITHOUT ***INVULNERABILITY?!***
REIN IT IN, WILSON. LET'S TRY TO TAKE THE OTHERS ALIVE.
NO!!

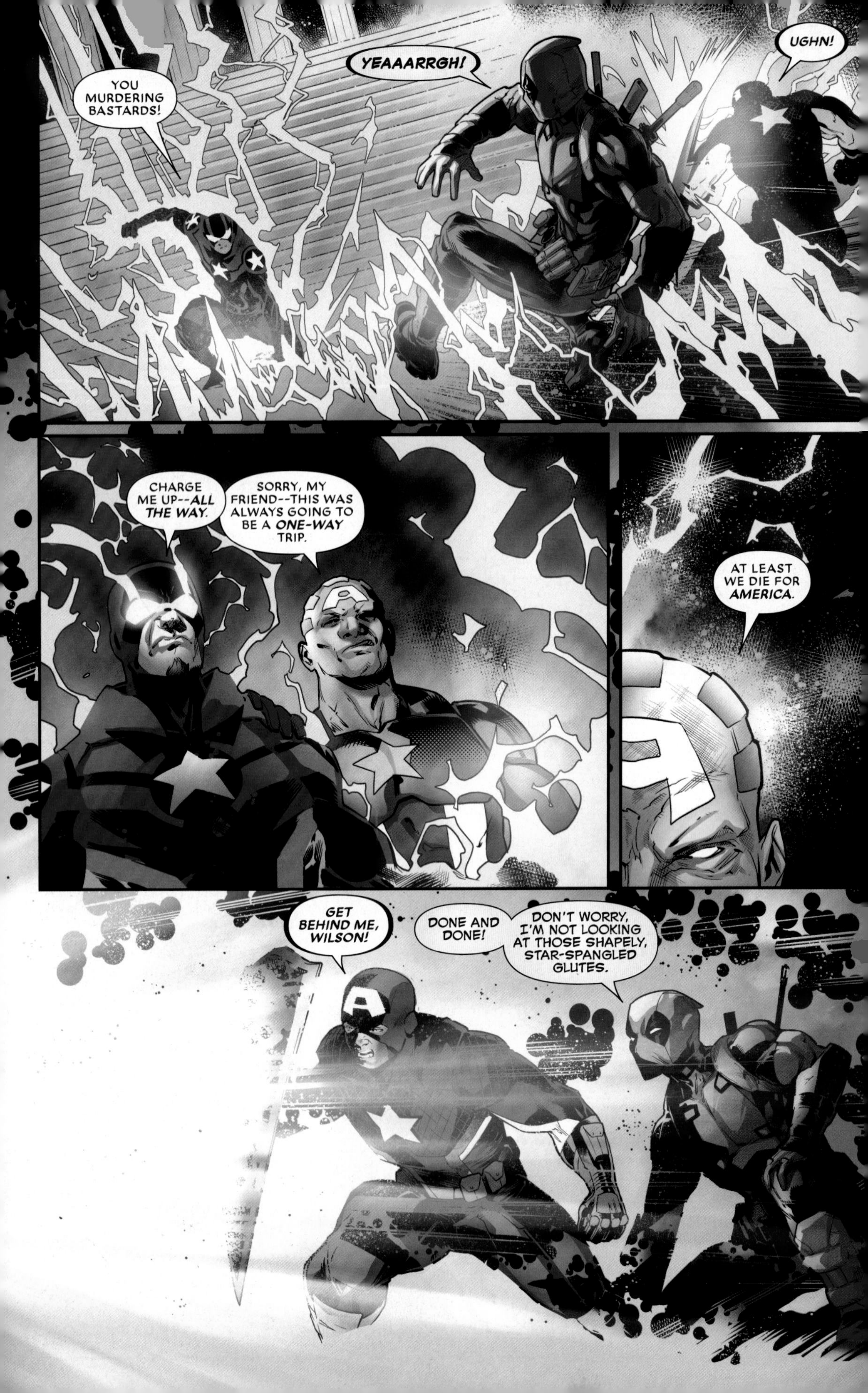
YOU MURDERING BASTARDS!
YEAAARRGH!
UGHN!
CHARGE ME UP--ALL THE WAY.
SORRY, MY FRIEND--THIS WAS ALWAYS GOING TO BE A ONE-WAY TRIP.
AT LEAST WE DIE FOR AMERICA.
GET BEHIND ME, WILSON!
DONE AND DONE!
DON'T WORRY, I'M NOT LOOKING AT THOSE SHAPELY, STAR-SPANGLED GLUTES.

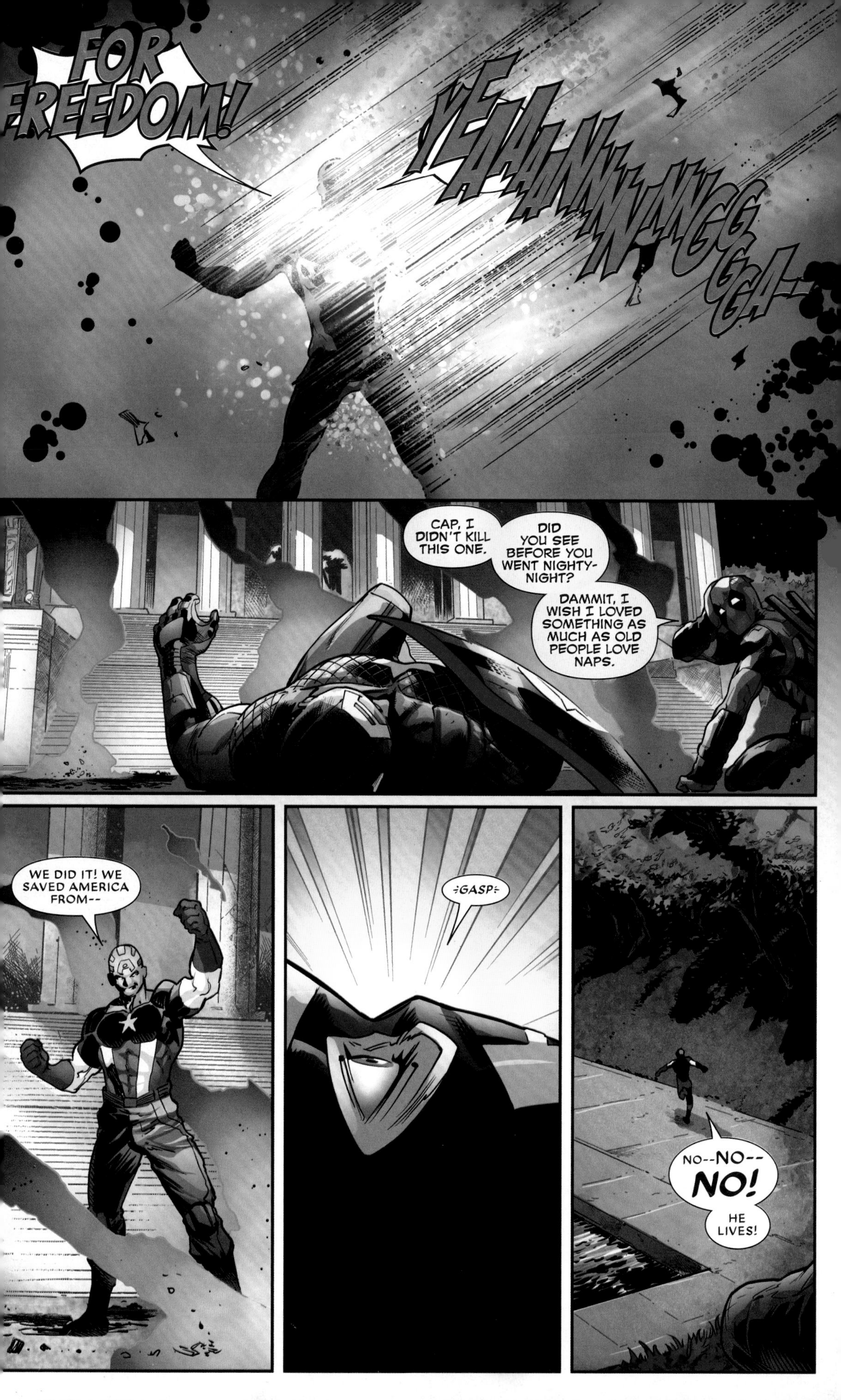
FOR FREEDOM!
YEAAANNNNNGGGA--
CAP, I DIDN'T KILL THIS ONE.
DID YOU SEE BEFORE YOU WENT NIGHTY-NIGHT?
DAMMIT, I WISH I LOVED SOMETHING AS MUCH AS OLD PEOPLE LOVE NAPS.
WE DID IT! WE SAVED AMERICA FROM--
GASP
NO--NO--NO!
HE LIVES!

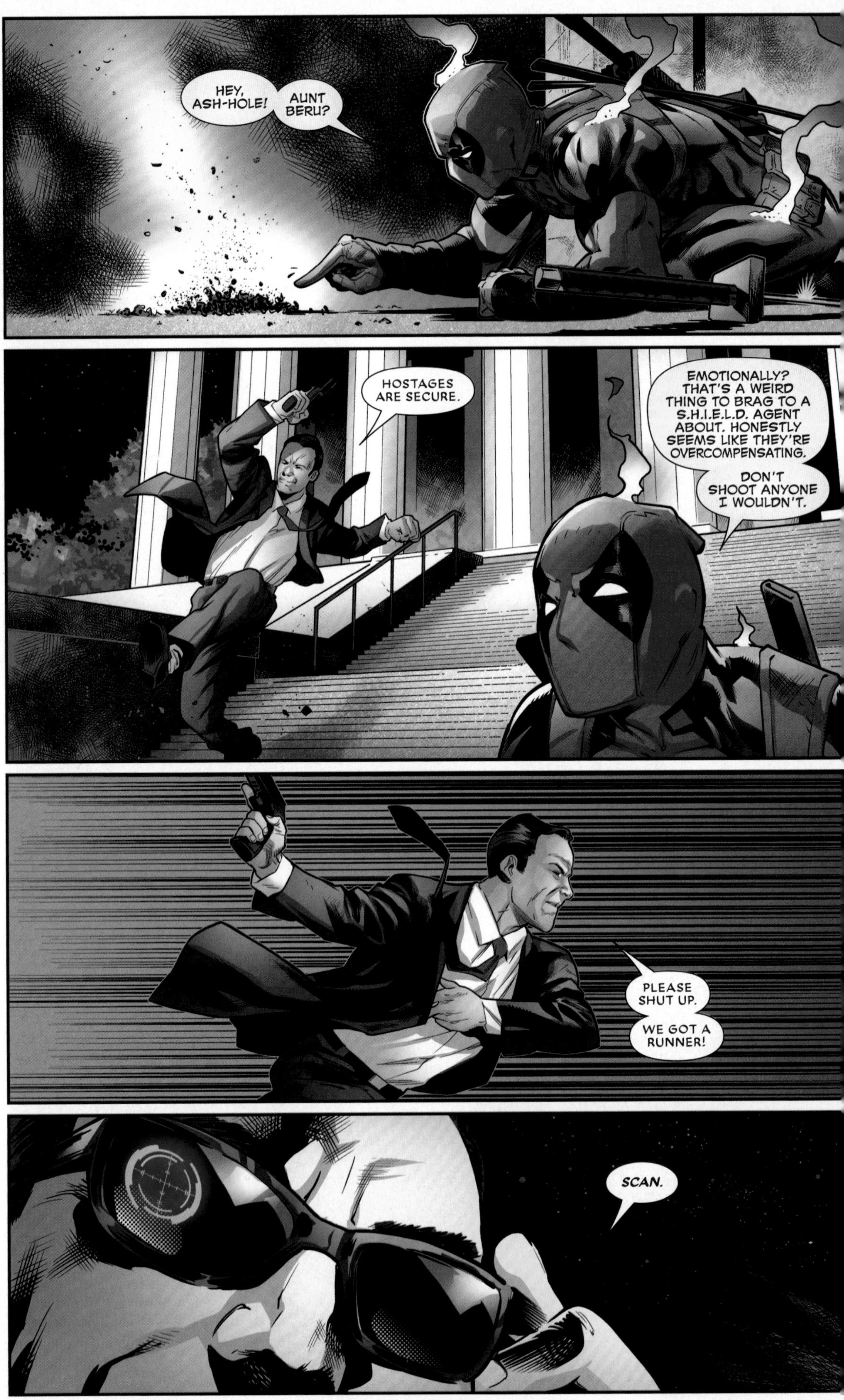

HEY, ASH-HOLE!
AUNT BERU?
HOSTAGES ARE SECURE.
EMOTIONALLY? THAT'S A WEIRD THING TO BRAG TO A S.H.I.E.L.D. AGENT ABOUT. HONESTLY SEEMS LIKE THEY'RE OVERCOMPENSATING.
DON'T SHOOT ANYONE I WOULDN'T.
PLEASE SHUT UP.
WE GOT A RUNNER!
SCAN.

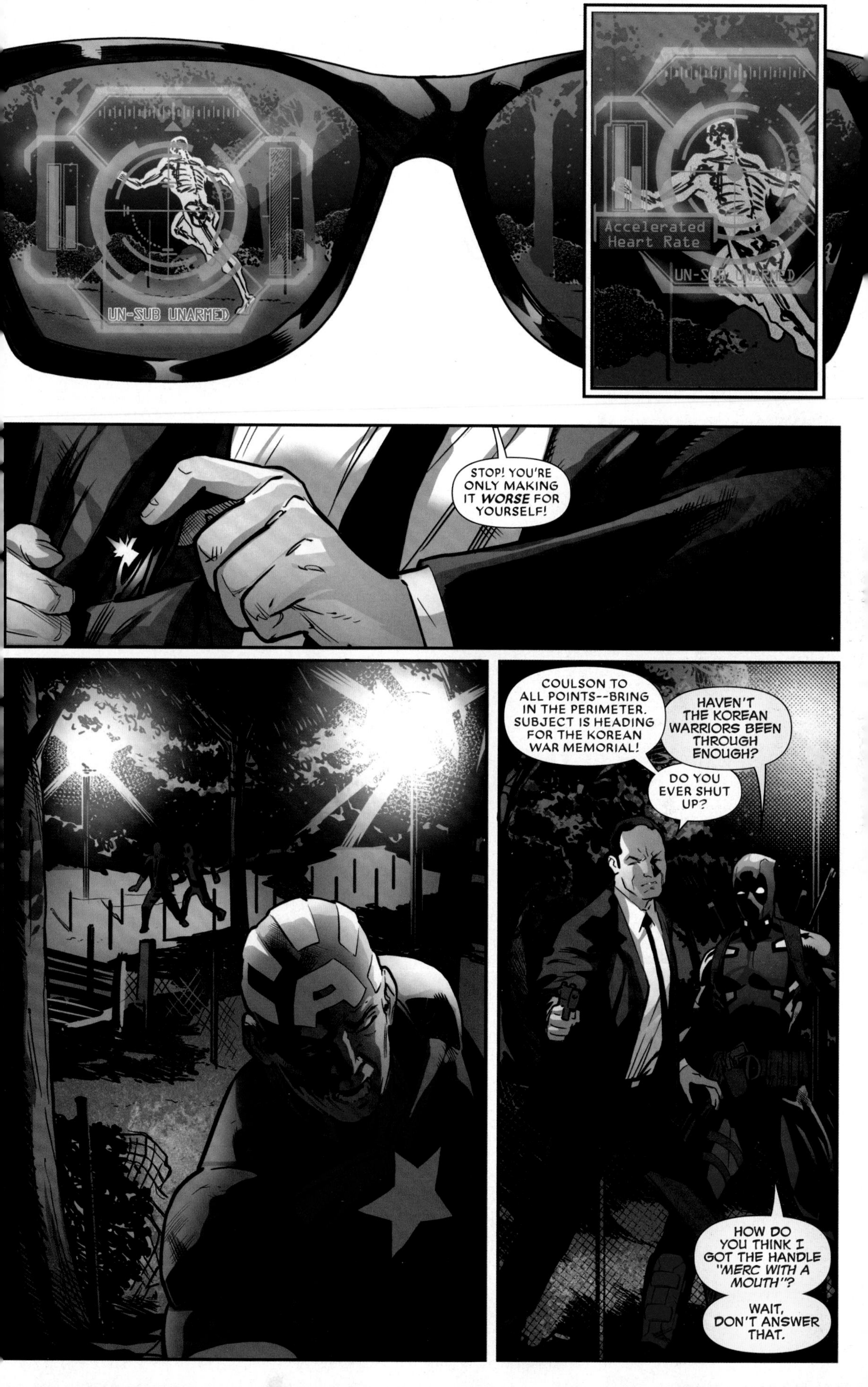
UN-SUB UNARMED
Accelerated Heart Rate
UN-SUB UNARMED
STOP! YOU'RE ONLY MAKING IT WORSE FOR YOURSELF!
COULSON TO ALL POINTS--BRING IN THE PERIMETER. SUBJECT IS HEADING FOR THE KOREAN WAR MEMORIAL!
HAVEN'T THE KOREAN WARRIORS BEEN THROUGH ENOUGH?
DO YOU EVER SHUT UP?
HOW DO YOU THINK I GOT THE HANDLE "MERC WITH A MOUTH"?
WAIT, DON'T ANSWER THAT.

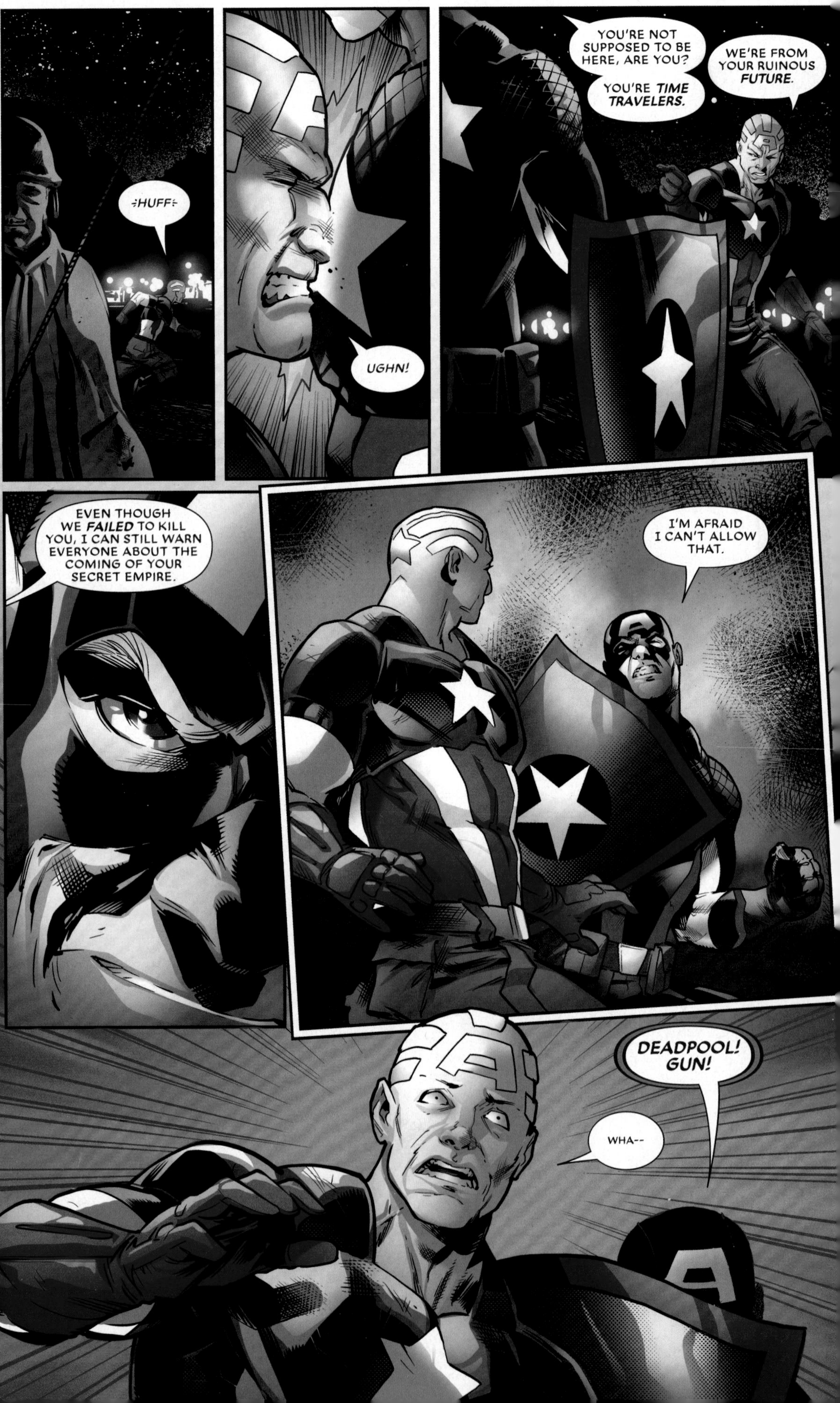

HUFF
UGHN!
YOU'RE NOT SUPPOSED TO BE HERE, ARE YOU?
YOU'RE *TIME TRAVELERS.*
WE'RE FROM YOUR RUINOUS *FUTURE.*
EVEN THOUGH WE *FAILED* TO KILL YOU, I CAN STILL WARN EVERYONE ABOUT THE COMING OF YOUR SECRET EMPIRE.
I'M AFRAID I CAN'T ALLOW THAT.
DEADPOOL! GUN!
WHA--

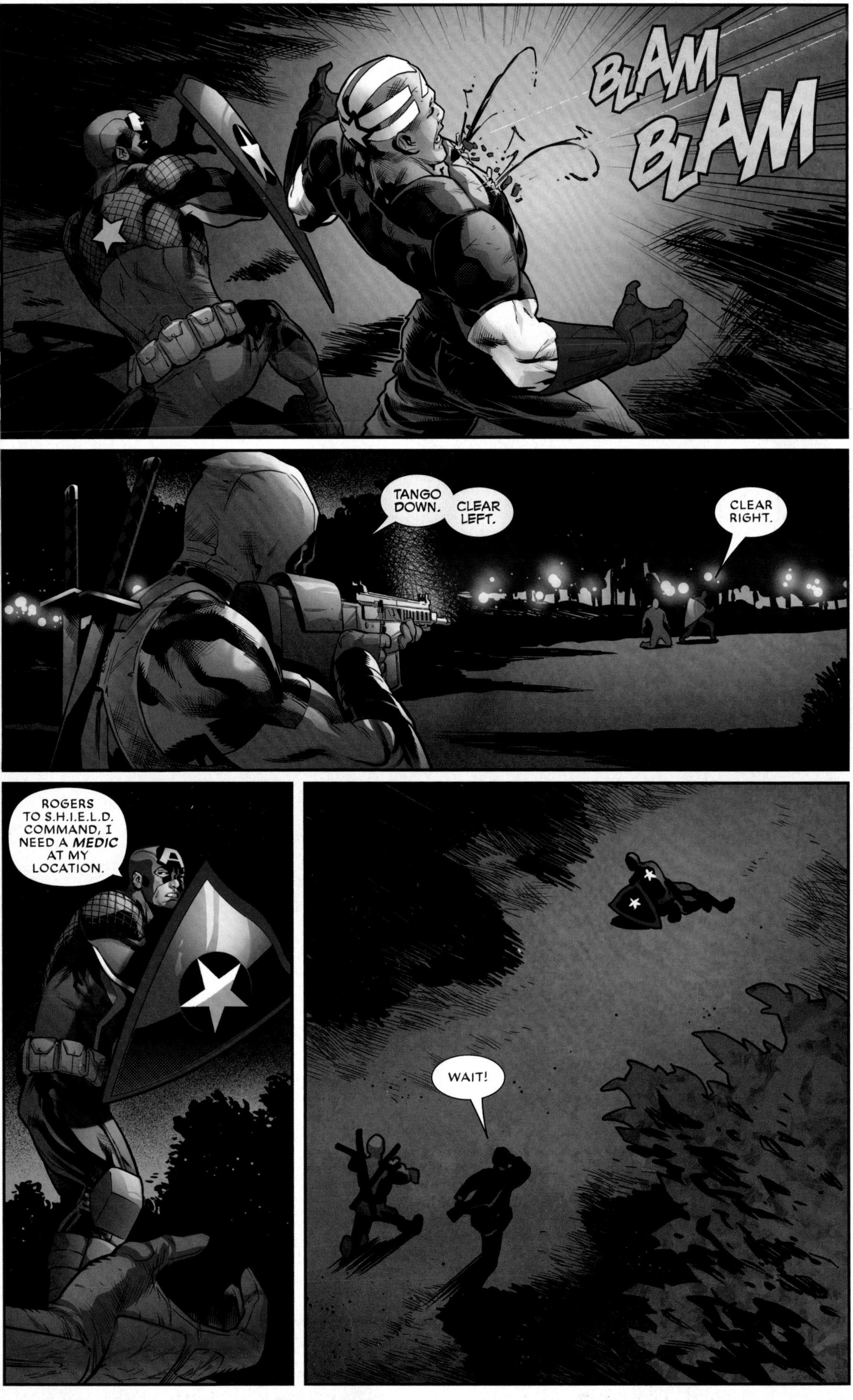
BLAM
BLAM
TANGO DOWN.
CLEAR LEFT.
CLEAR RIGHT.
ROGERS TO S.H.I.E.L.D. COMMAND, I NEED A *MEDIC* AT MY LOCATION.
WAIT!

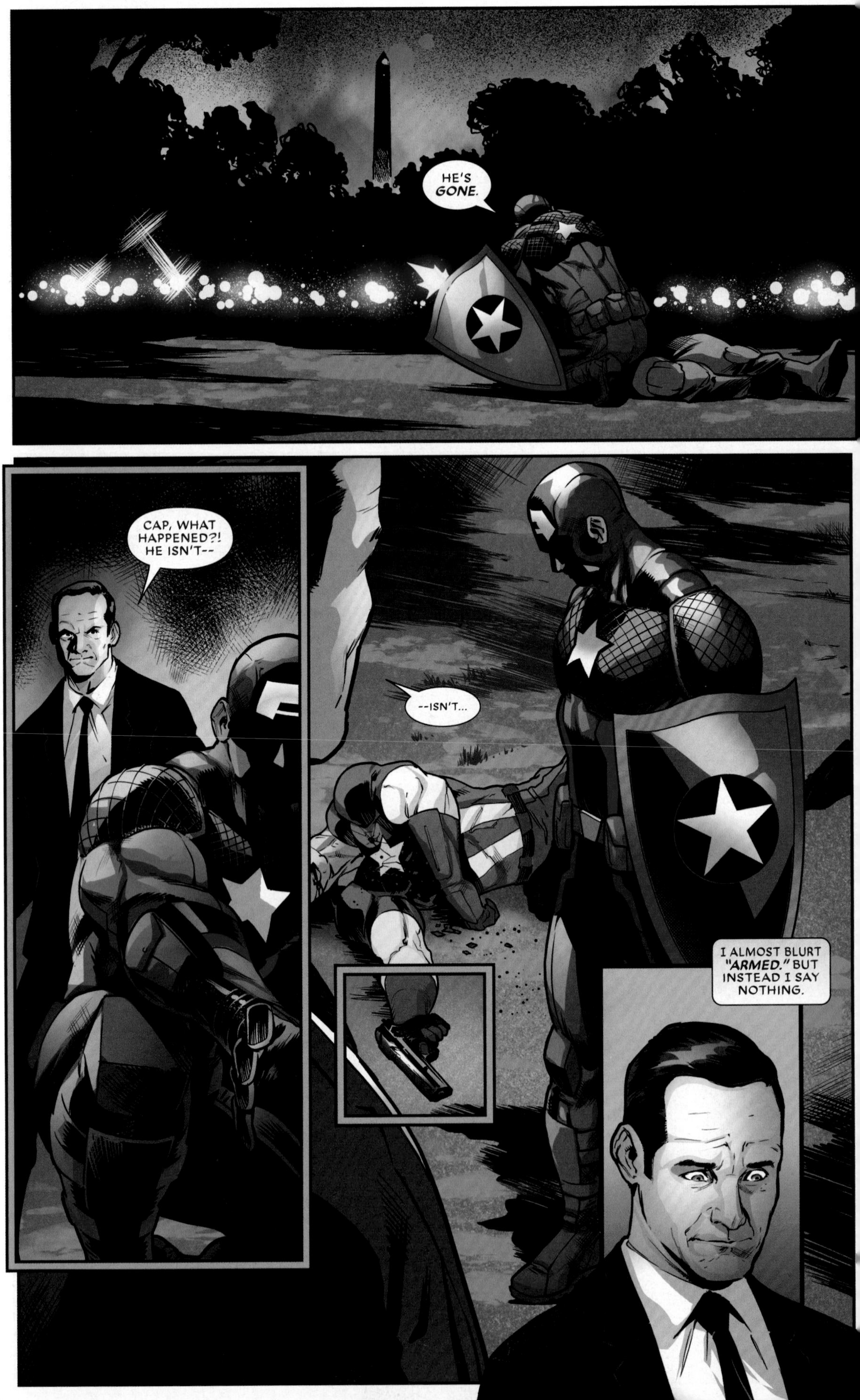
HE'S GONE.
CAP, WHAT HAPPENED?! HE ISN'T--
--ISN'T...
I ALMOST BLURT "ARMED." BUT INSTEAD I SAY NOTHING.

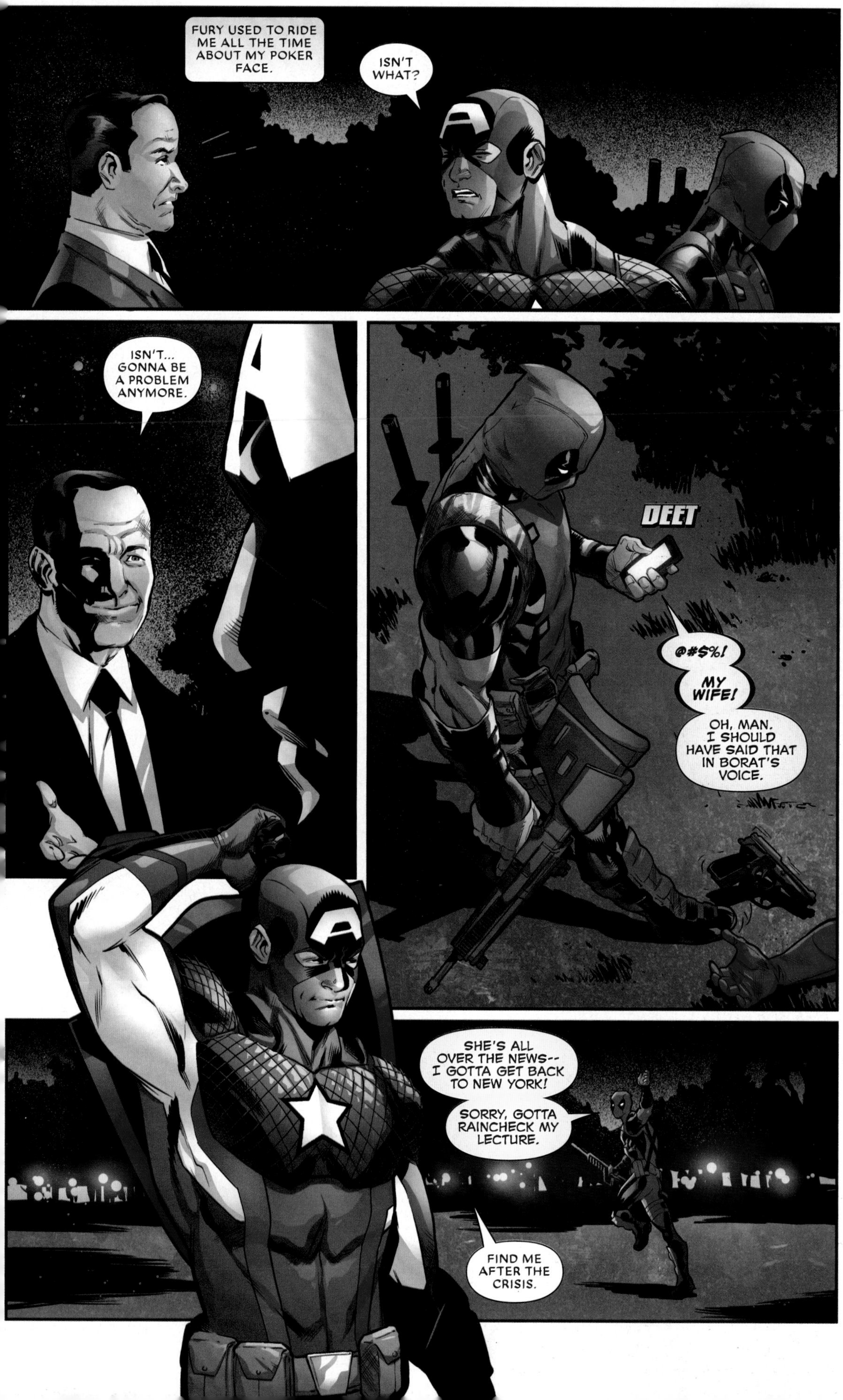
FURY USED TO RIDE ME ALL THE TIME ABOUT MY POKER FACE.
ISN'T WHAT?
ISN'T... GONNA BE A PROBLEM ANYMORE.
DEET
@#$%!
MY WIFE!
OH, MAN. I SHOULD HAVE SAID THAT IN BORAT'S VOICE.
SHE'S ALL OVER THE NEWS-- I GOTTA GET BACK TO NEW YORK!
SORRY, GOTTA RAINCHECK MY LECTURE.
FIND ME AFTER THE CRISIS.

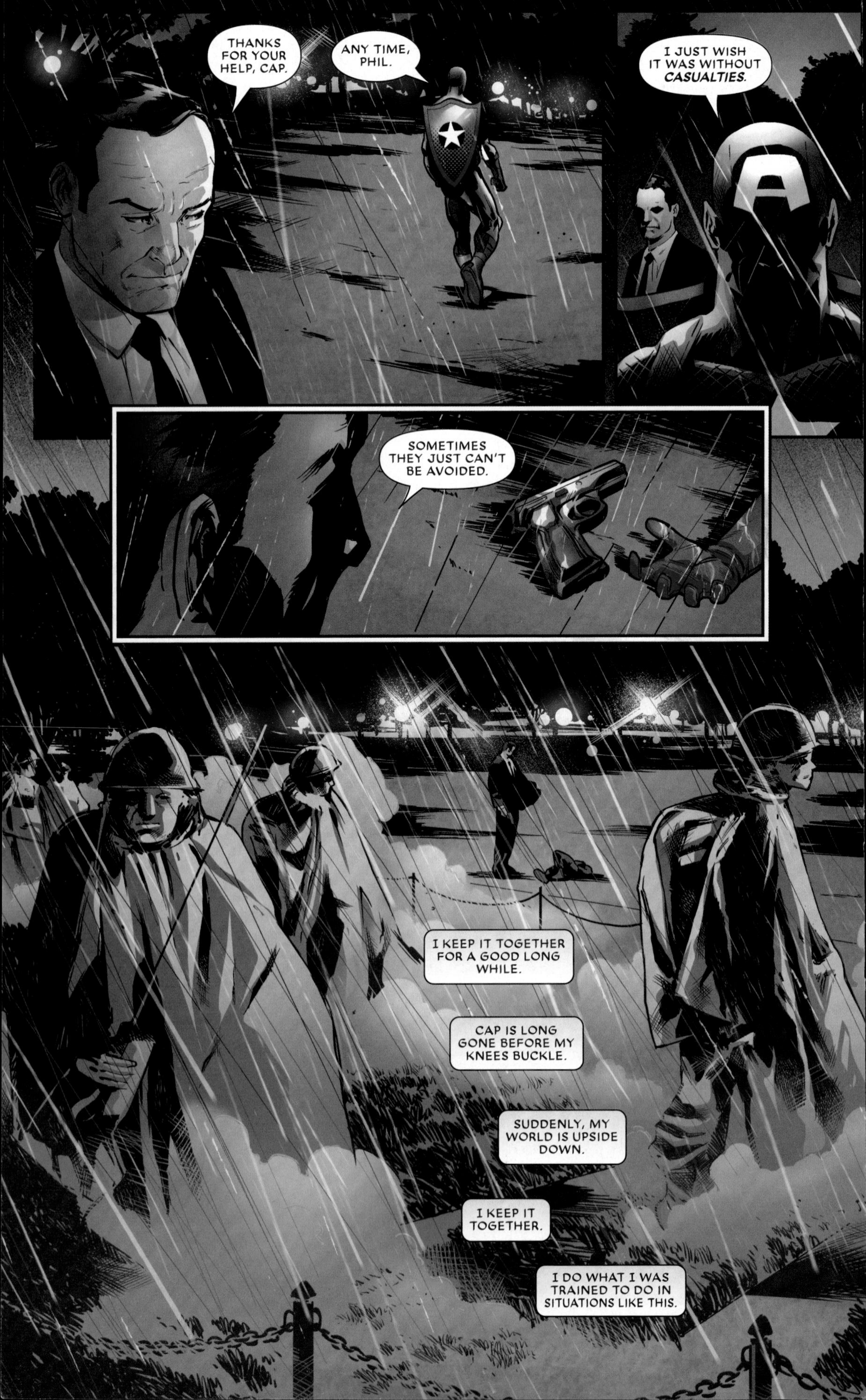
THANKS FOR YOUR HELP, CAP.
ANY TIME, PHIL.
I JUST WISH IT WAS WITHOUT *CASUALTIES*.
SOMETIMES THEY JUST CAN'T BE AVOIDED.
I KEEP IT TOGETHER FOR A GOOD LONG WHILE.
CAP IS LONG GONE BEFORE MY KNEES BUCKLE.
SUDDENLY, MY WORLD IS UPSIDE DOWN.
I KEEP IT TOGETHER.
I DO WHAT I WAS TRAINED TO DO IN SITUATIONS LIKE THIS.

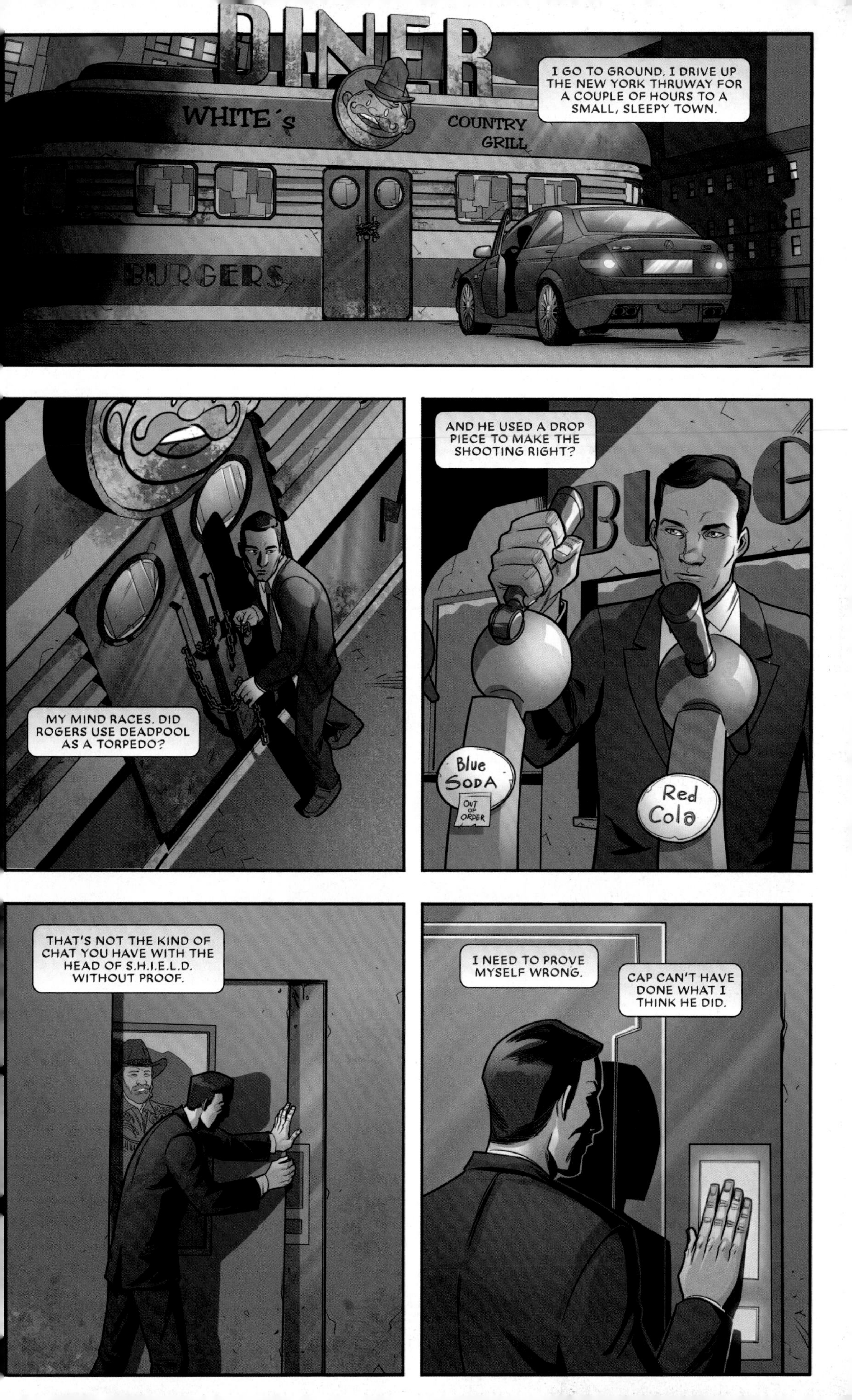
DINER
WHITE's
COUNTRY GRILL
BURGERS
I GO TO GROUND. I DRIVE UP THE NEW YORK THRUWAY FOR A COUPLE OF HOURS TO A SMALL, SLEEPY TOWN.
MY MIND RACES. DID ROGERS USE DEADPOOL AS A TORPEDO?
AND HE USED A DROP PIECE TO MAKE THE SHOOTING RIGHT?
Blue SODA
OUT OF ORDER
Red Cola
THAT'S NOT THE KIND OF CHAT YOU HAVE WITH THE HEAD OF S.H.I.E.L.D. WITHOUT PROOF.
I NEED TO PROVE MYSELF WRONG.
CAP CAN'T HAVE DONE WHAT I THINK HE DID.

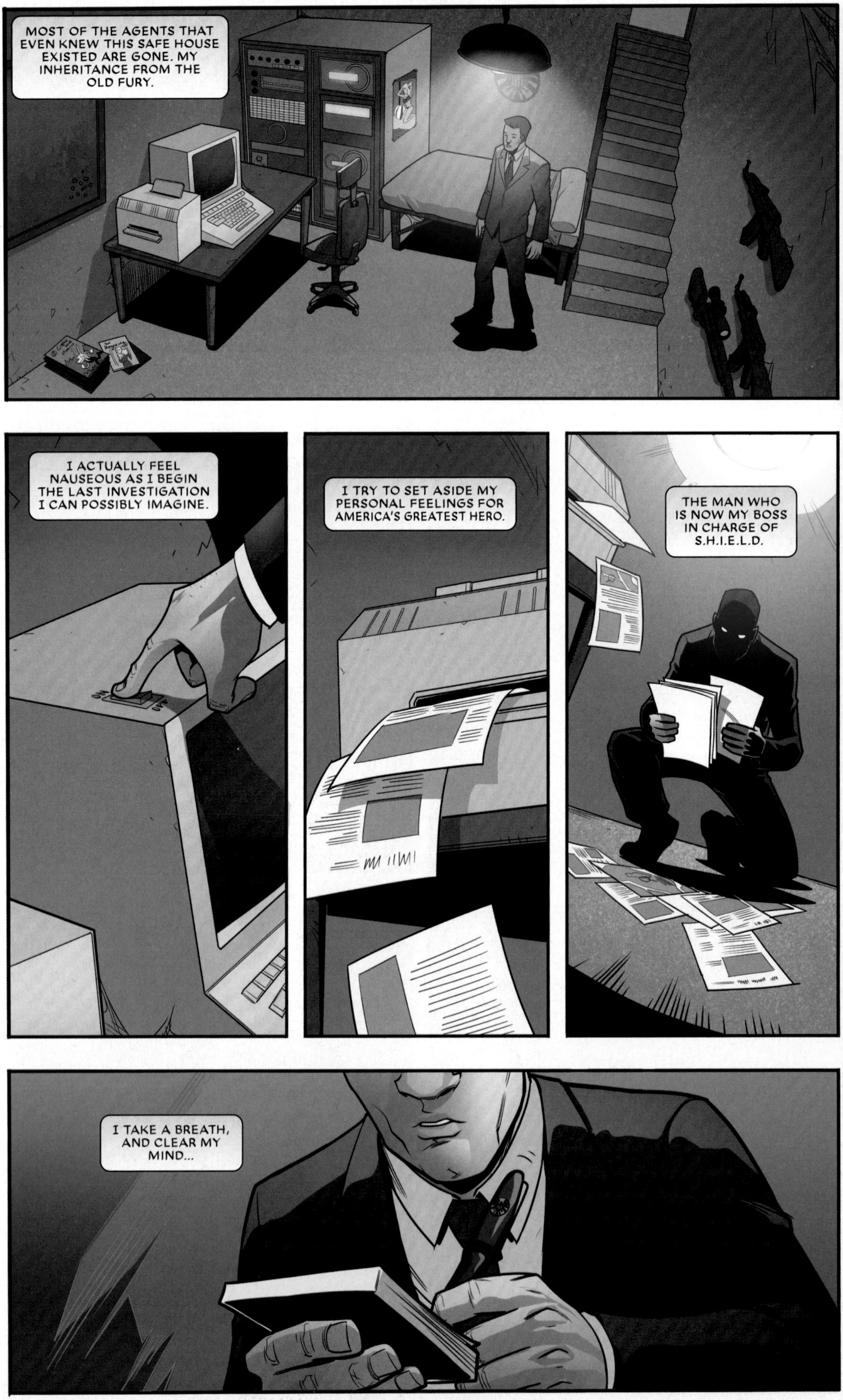
MOST OF THE AGENTS THAT EVEN KNEW THIS SAFE HOUSE EXISTED ARE GONE. MY INHERITANCE FROM THE OLD FURY.
I ACTUALLY FEEL NAUSEOUS AS I BEGIN THE LAST INVESTIGATION I CAN POSSIBLY IMAGINE.
I TRY TO SET ASIDE MY PERSONAL FEELINGS FOR AMERICA'S GREATEST HERO.
THE MAN WHO IS NOW MY BOSS IN CHARGE OF S.H.I.E.L.D.
I TAKE A BREATH, AND CLEAR MY MIND...

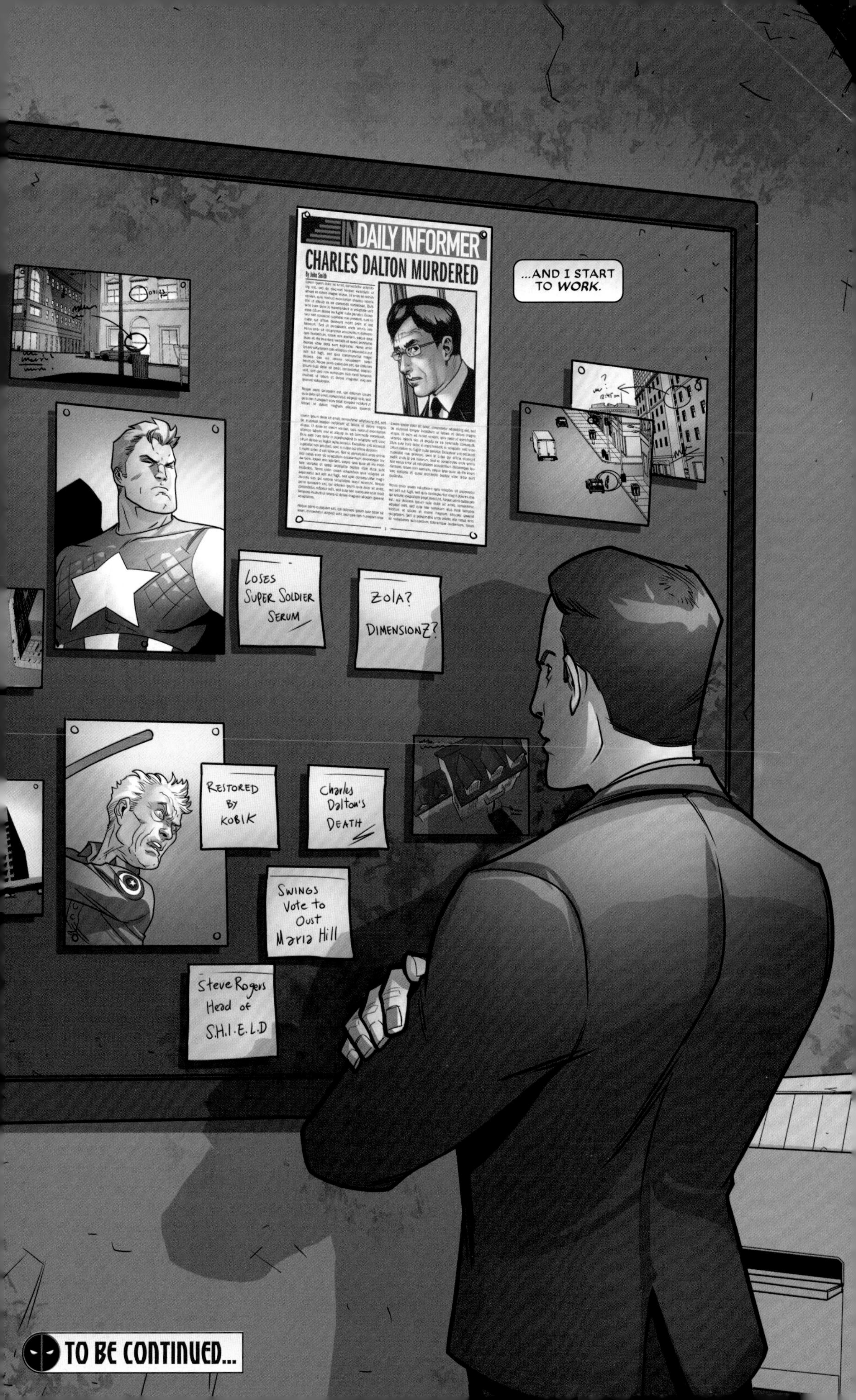
DAILY INFORMER
CHARLES DALTON MURDERED
By John Smith
...AND I START TO WORK.
LOSES SUPER SOLDIER SERUM
ZOLA? DIMENSION Z?
RESTORED BY KOBIK
Charles Dalton's DEATH
SWINGS Vote to Oust Maria Hill
Steve Rogers Head of S.H.I.E.L.D
TO BE CONTINUED...

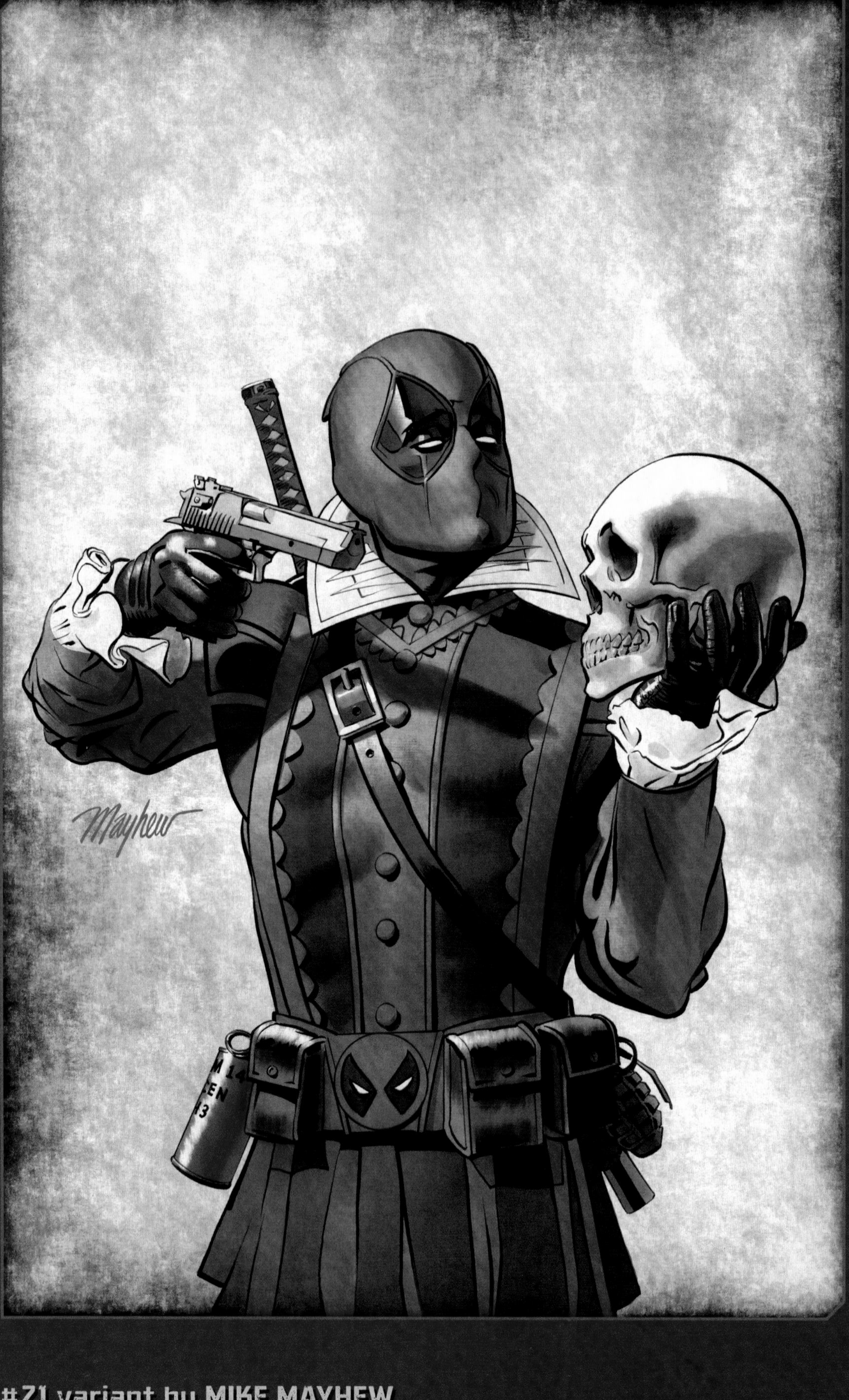
Mayhew

#21 variant by **MIKE MAYHEW**

His *MAJESTY's* most Marvelous company of Comics
This present *Wednesday*, being the 26th of October,
will present

MUCH ADO ABOUT
DEADPOOL

Written by *some hack pretending to be*

M A S T E R   W I L L I A M   S H A K E S P E A R E

Being the most lamentable T R A G E D Y of
A Ghastly G H O S T
A Dashing D A M S E L
A Sly S H R E W
A Kingly K N A V E
And the M E R C of M E N A C E

IN FIVE ACTS

The Writer by Mr. Ian Doescher
The Artist by Mr. Bruno Oliveira
The Colorist by Mr. Nick Filardi
The Letterer by Mr. Joe Sabino

Rosencrantz by Ms. Heather Antos
Gravedigger-in-Chief by Mr. Axel Alonso
Pubtender by Mr. Dan Buckley

Guildenstern by Mr. Jordan D. White
Chief Naval Officer by Mr. Joe Quesada
Executive Messenger by Mr. Alan Fine

✝ *No Persons to be admitted behind the Scenes,
nor any Money to be returned after the Pages are drawn up.*

Act l

Something's Rotten in the State of Deadpool

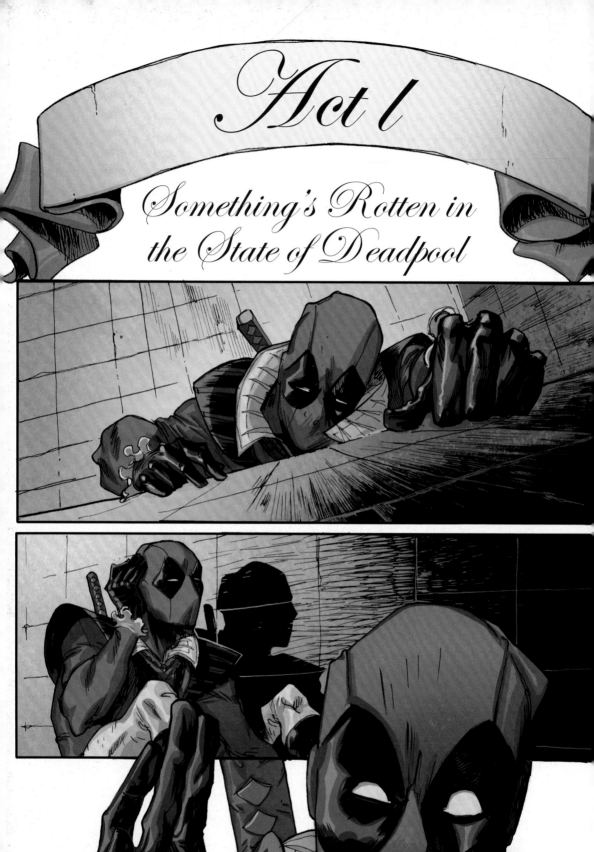

WHAT COUNTRY, FRIENDS, IS THIS? AND WHAT THE @#$&?

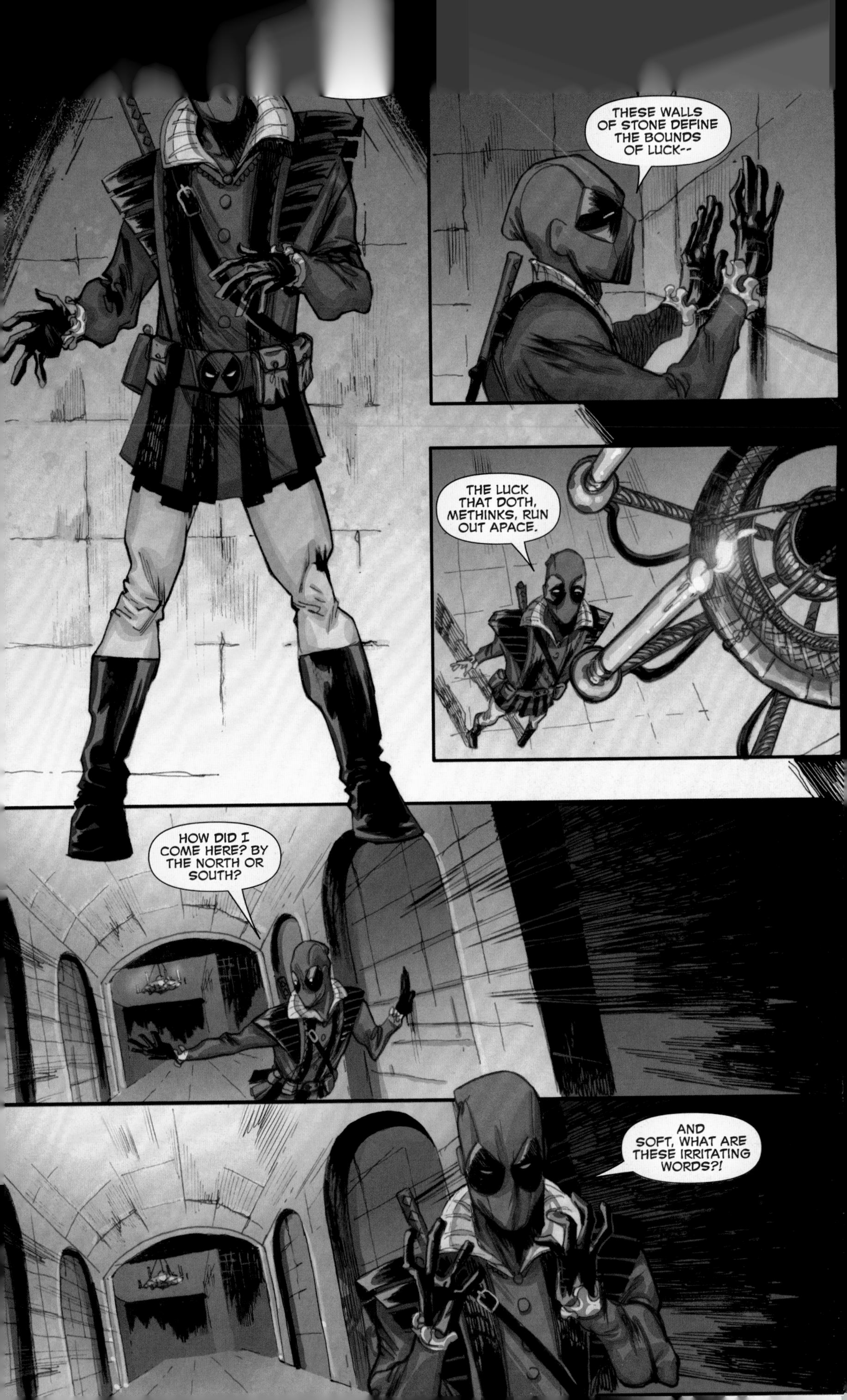
THESE WALLS OF STONE DEFINE THE BOUNDS OF LUCK--
THE LUCK THAT DOTH, METHINKS, RUN OUT APACE.
HOW DID I COME HERE? BY THE NORTH OR SOUTH?
AND SOFT, WHAT ARE THESE IRRITATING WORDS?!

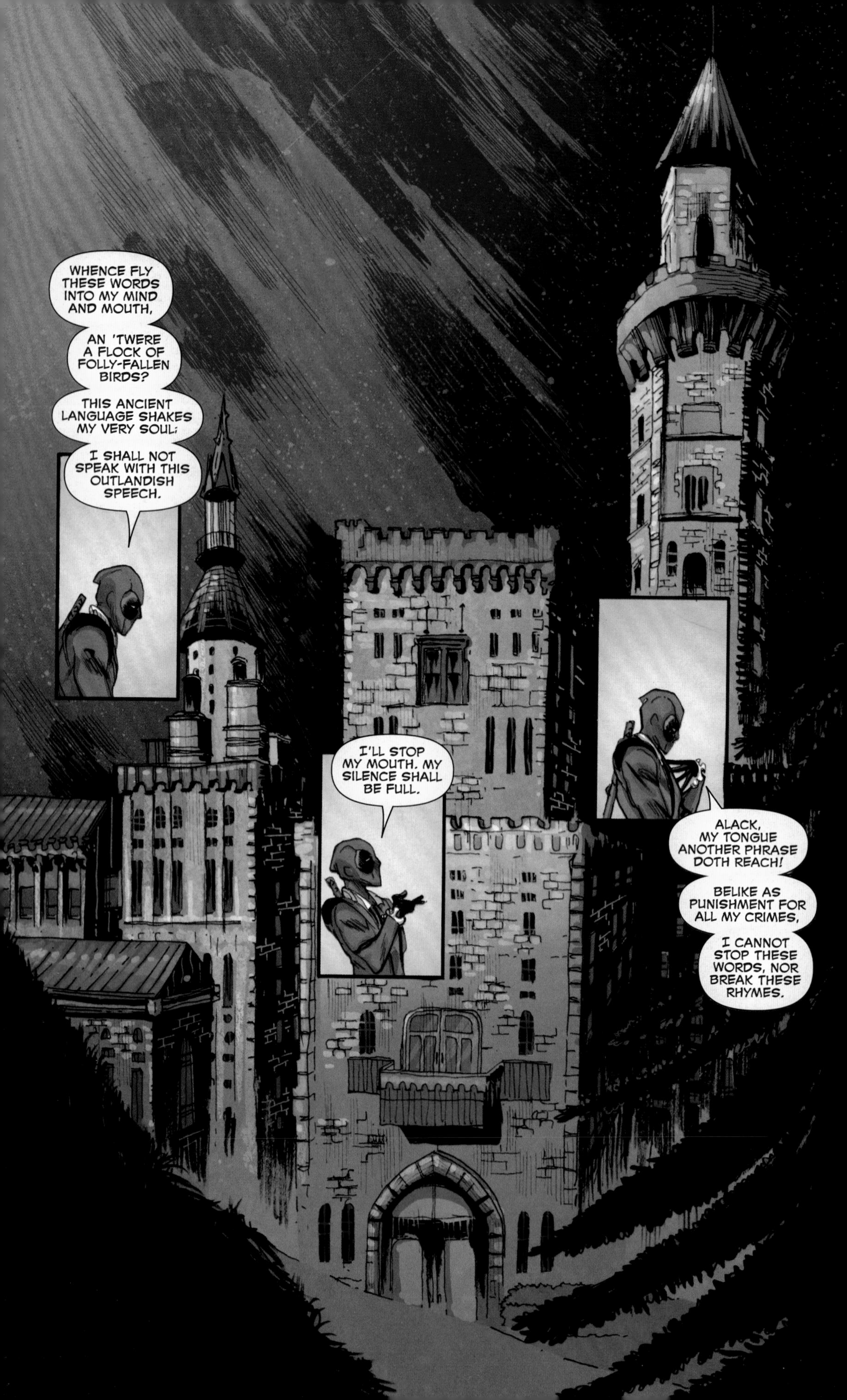
WHENCE FLY THESE WORDS INTO MY MIND AND MOUTH,
AN 'TWERE A FLOCK OF FOLLY-FALLEN BIRDS?
THIS ANCIENT LANGUAGE SHAKES MY VERY SOUL;
I SHALL NOT SPEAK WITH THIS OUTLANDISH SPEECH.
I'LL STOP MY MOUTH. MY SILENCE SHALL BE FULL.
ALACK, MY TONGUE ANOTHER PHRASE DOTH REACH!
BELIKE AS PUNISHMENT FOR ALL MY CRIMES,
I CANNOT STOP THESE WORDS, NOR BREAK THESE RHYMES.

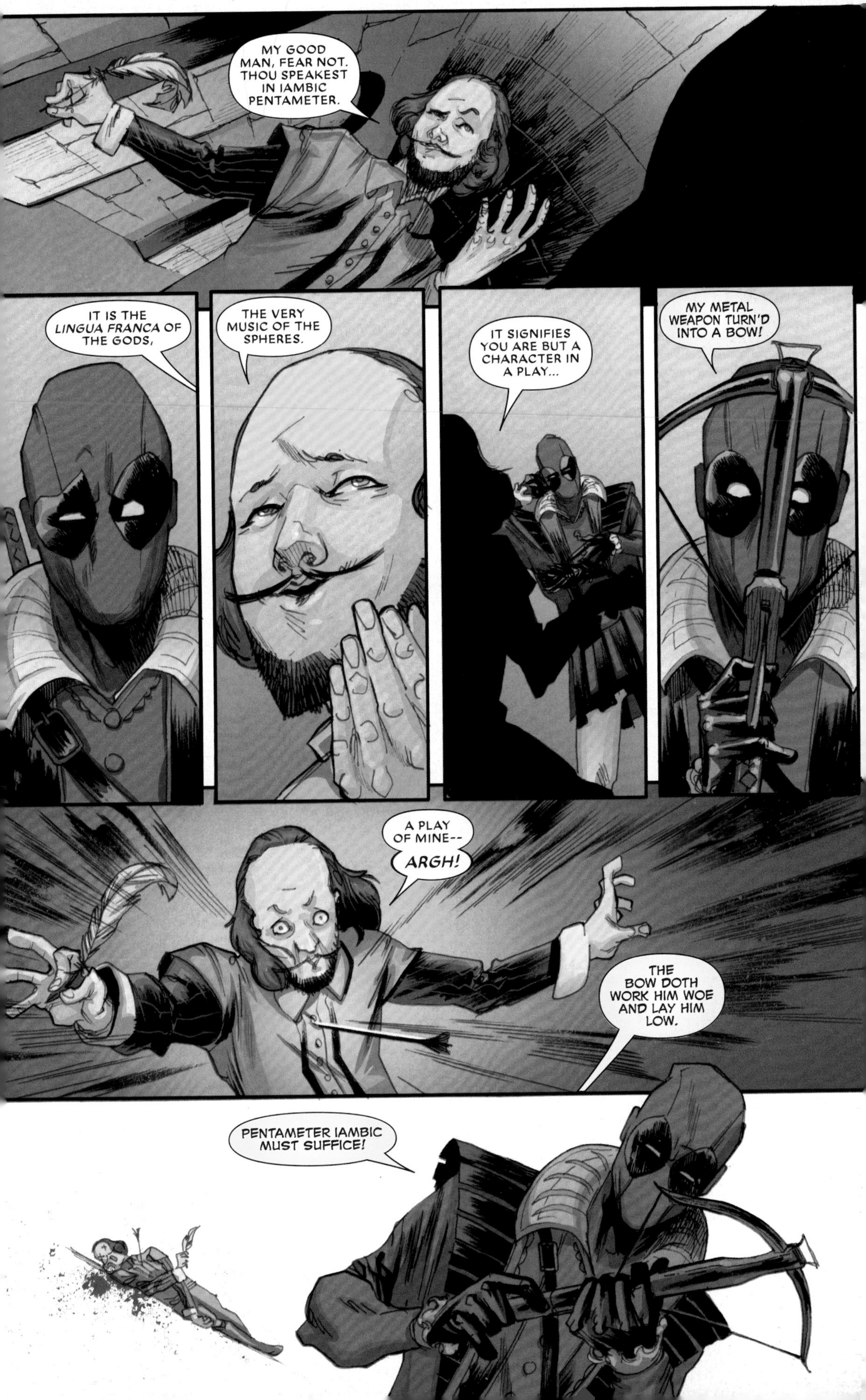
MY GOOD MAN, FEAR NOT. THOU SPEAKEST IN IAMBIC PENTAMETER.
IT IS THE *LINGUA FRANCA* OF THE GODS,
THE VERY MUSIC OF THE SPHERES.
IT SIGNIFIES YOU ARE BUT A CHARACTER IN A PLAY...
MY METAL WEAPON TURN'D INTO A BOW!
A PLAY OF MINE--
ARGH!
THE BOW DOTH WORK HIM WOE AND LAY HIM LOW.
PENTAMETER IAMBIC MUST SUFFICE!

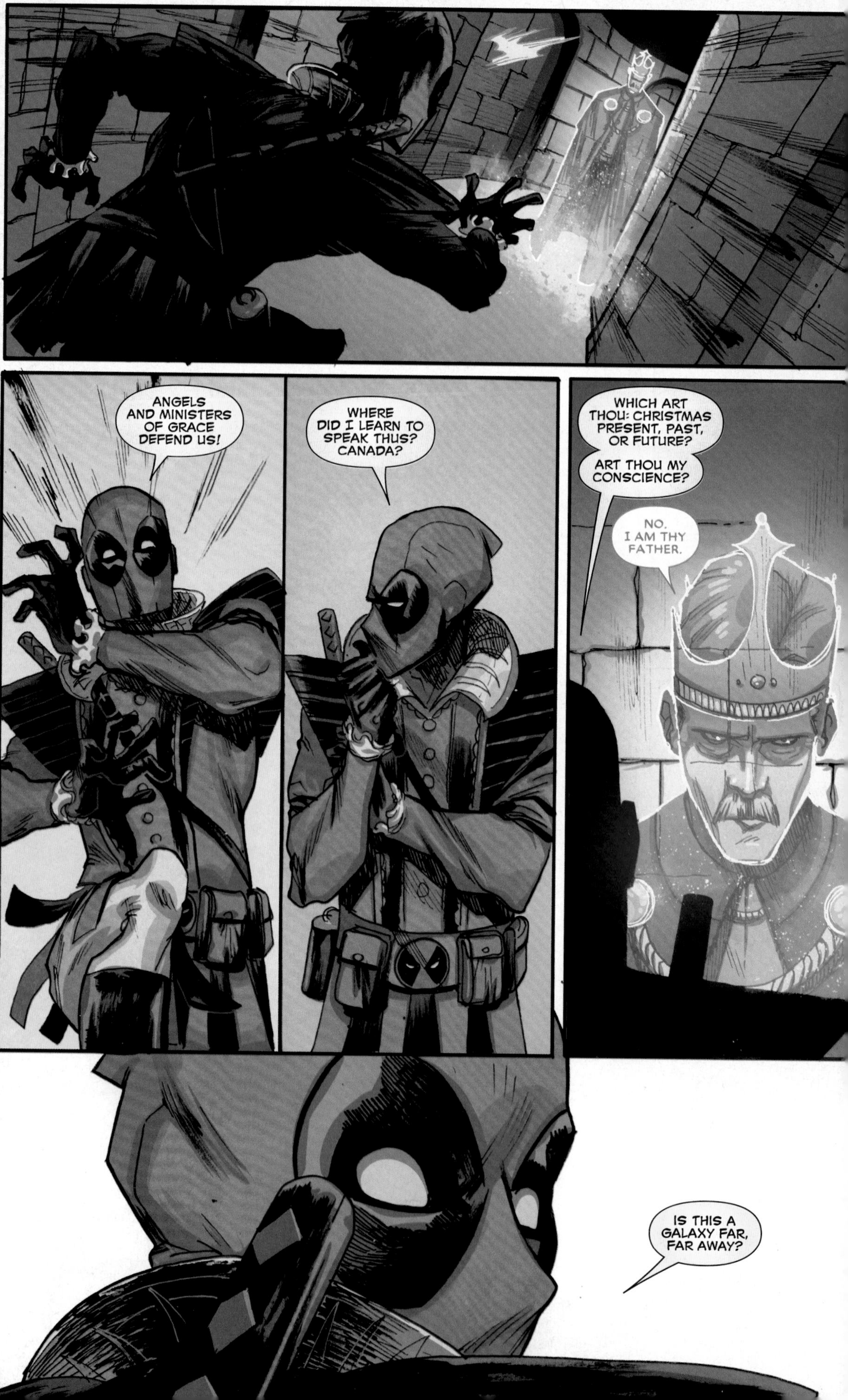
ANGELS AND MINISTERS OF GRACE DEFEND US!
WHERE DID I LEARN TO SPEAK THUS? CANADA?
WHICH ART THOU: CHRISTMAS PRESENT, PAST, OR FUTURE?
ART THOU MY CONSCIENCE?
NO. I AM THY FATHER.
IS THIS A GALAXY FAR, FAR AWAY?

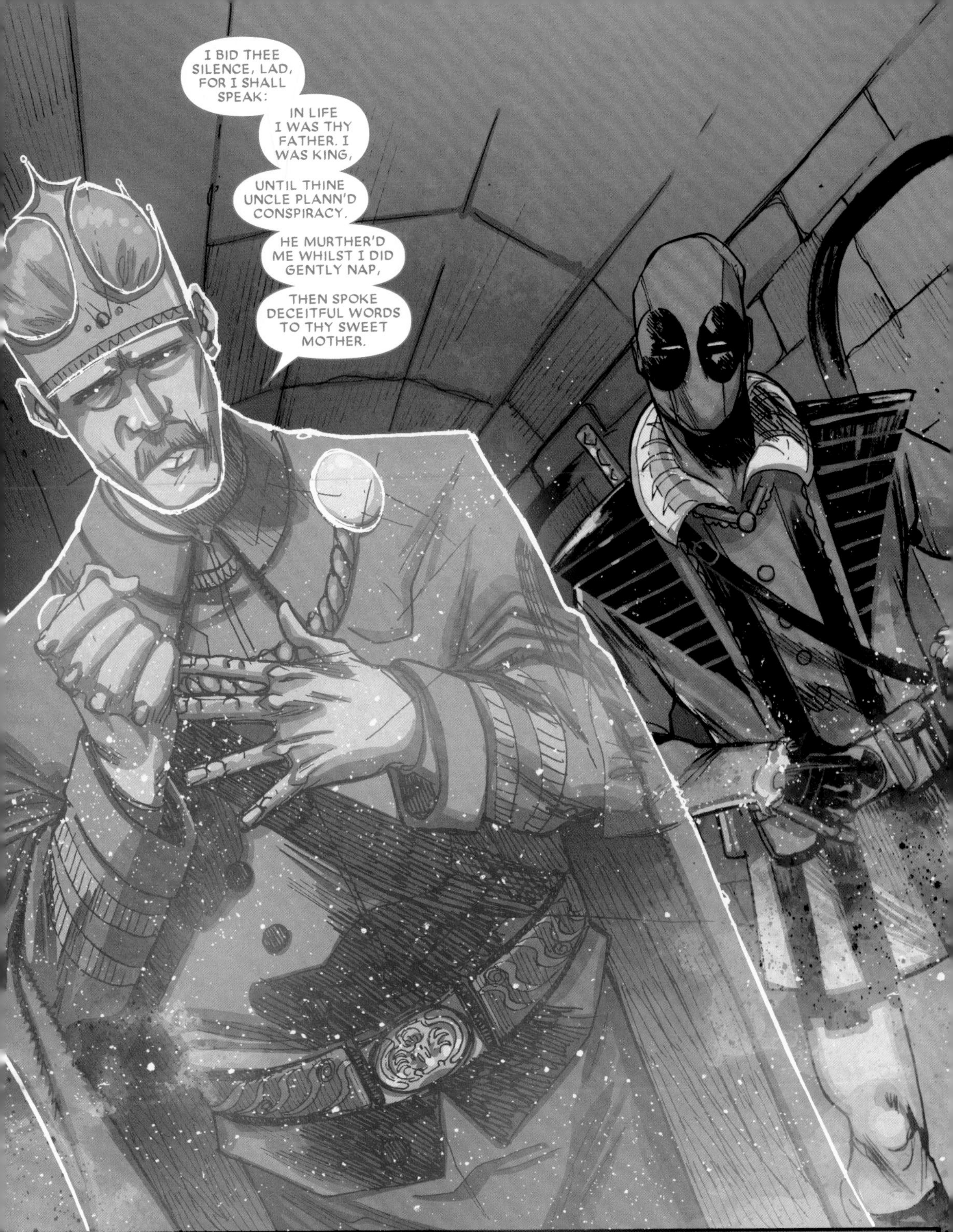
I BID THEE SILENCE, LAD, FOR I SHALL SPEAK:
IN LIFE I WAS THY FATHER. I WAS KING,
UNTIL THINE UNCLE PLANN'D CONSPIRACY.
HE MURTHER'D ME WHILST I DID GENTLY NAP,
THEN SPOKE DECEITFUL WORDS TO THY SWEET MOTHER.

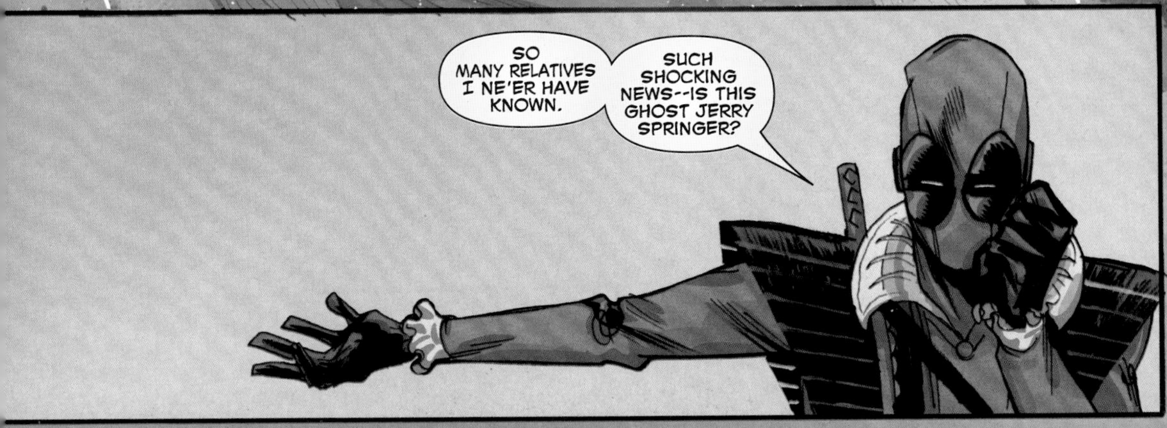
SO MANY RELATIVES I NE'ER HAVE KNOWN.
SUCH SHOCKING NEWS--IS THIS GHOST JERRY SPRINGER?

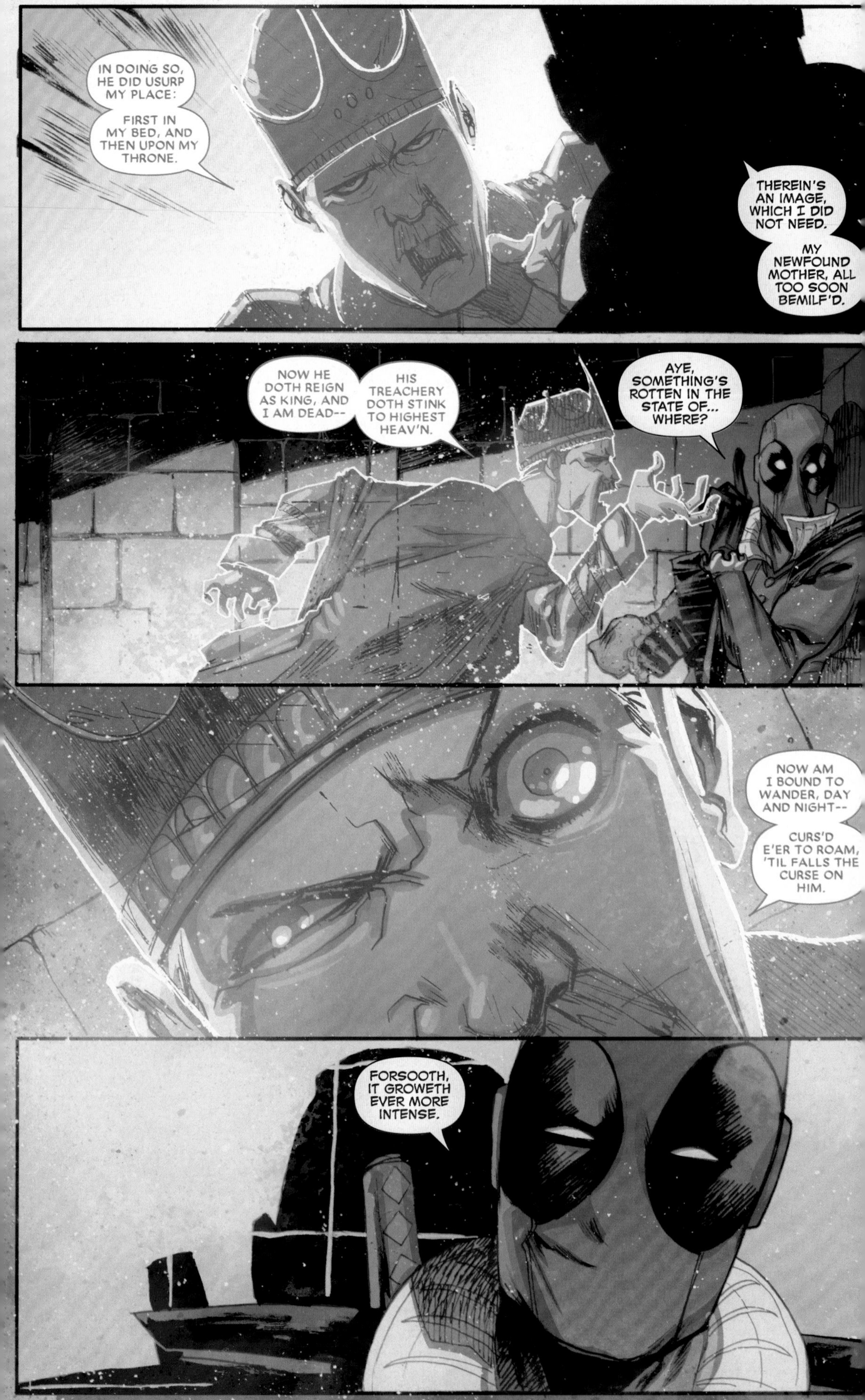
IN DOING SO, HE DID USURP MY PLACE:
FIRST IN MY BED, AND THEN UPON MY THRONE.
THEREIN'S AN IMAGE, WHICH I DID NOT NEED.
MY NEWFOUND MOTHER, ALL TOO SOON BEMILF'D.
NOW HE DOTH REIGN AS KING, AND I AM DEAD--
HIS TREACHERY DOTH STINK TO HIGHEST HEAV'N.
AYE, SOMETHING'S ROTTEN IN THE STATE OF... WHERE?
NOW AM I BOUND TO WANDER, DAY AND NIGHT--
CURS'D E'ER TO ROAM, 'TIL FALLS THE CURSE ON HIM.
FORSOOTH, IT GROWETH EVER MORE INTENSE.

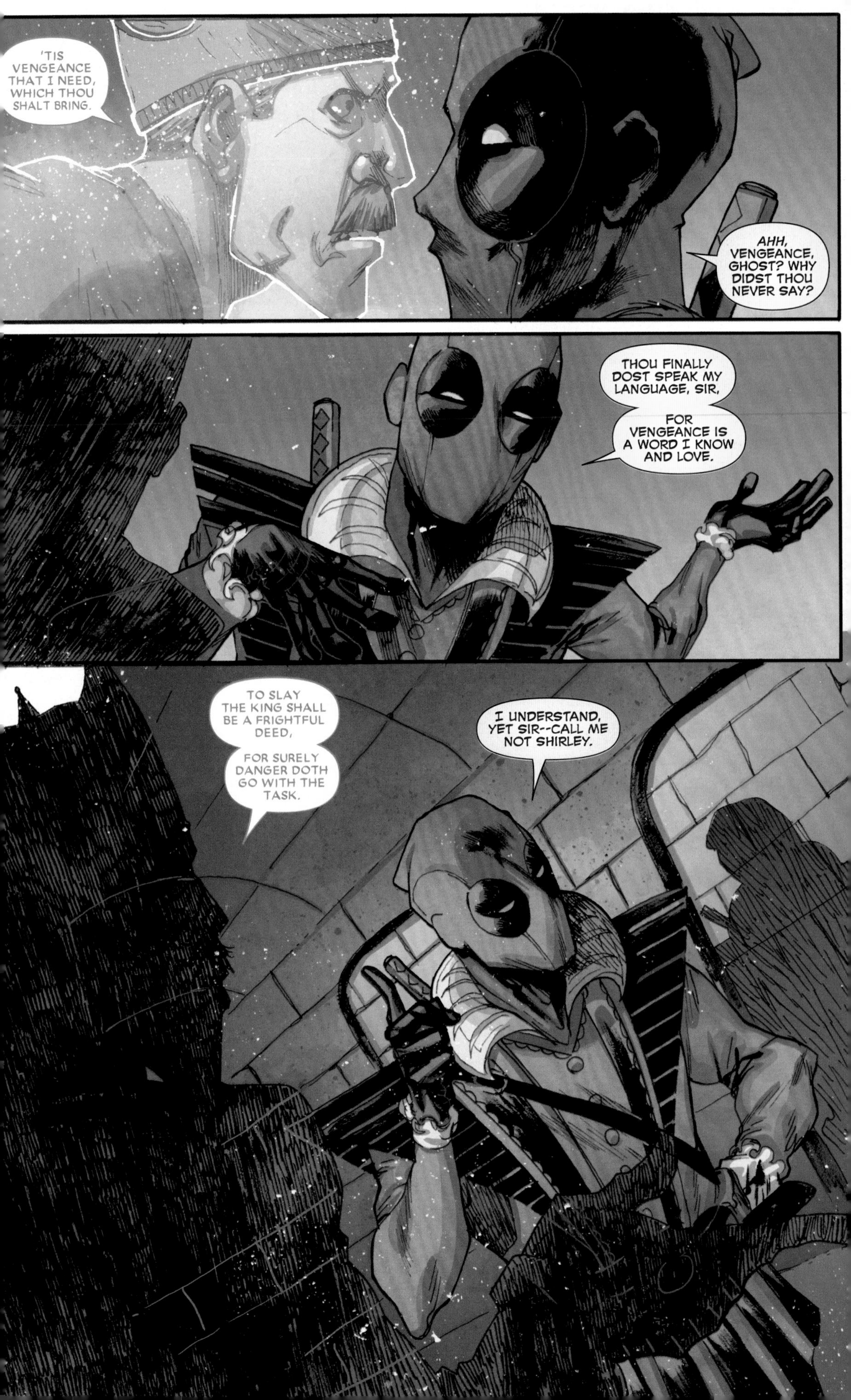
'TIS VENGEANCE THAT I NEED, WHICH THOU SHALT BRING.
AHH, VENGEANCE, GHOST? WHY DIDST THOU NEVER SAY?
THOU FINALLY DOST SPEAK MY LANGUAGE, SIR,
FOR VENGEANCE IS A WORD I KNOW AND LOVE.
TO SLAY THE KING SHALL BE A FRIGHTFUL DEED,
FOR SURELY DANGER DOTH GO WITH THE TASK.
I UNDERSTAND, YET SIR--CALL ME NOT SHIRLEY.

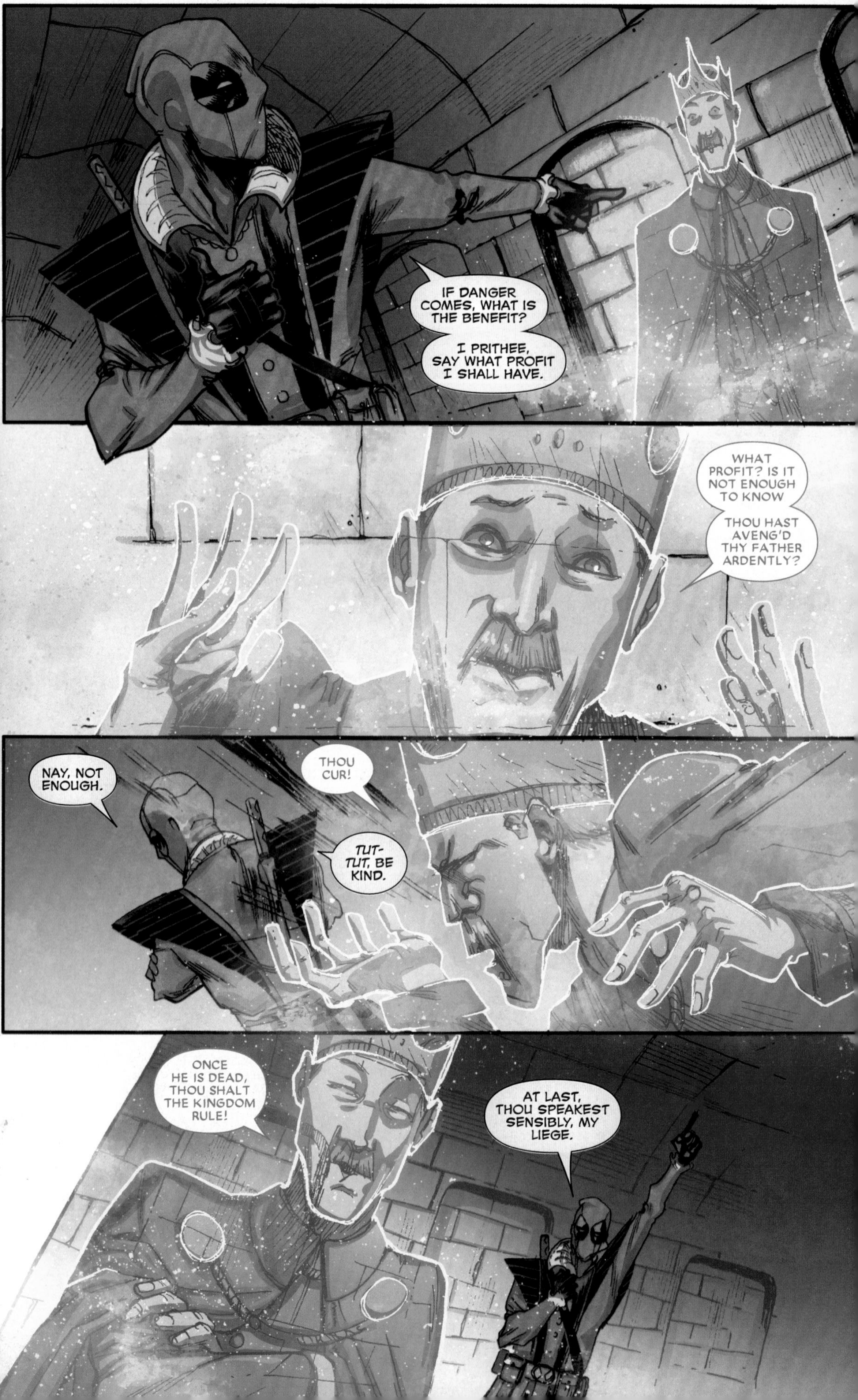
IF DANGER COMES, WHAT IS THE BENEFIT?
I PRITHEE, SAY WHAT PROFIT I SHALL HAVE.
WHAT PROFIT? IS IT NOT ENOUGH TO KNOW
THOU HAST AVENG'D THY FATHER ARDENTLY?
NAY, NOT ENOUGH.
THOU CUR!
TUT-TUT, BE KIND.
ONCE HE IS DEAD, THOU SHALT THE KINGDOM RULE!
AT LAST, THOU SPEAKEST SENSIBLY, MY LIEGE.

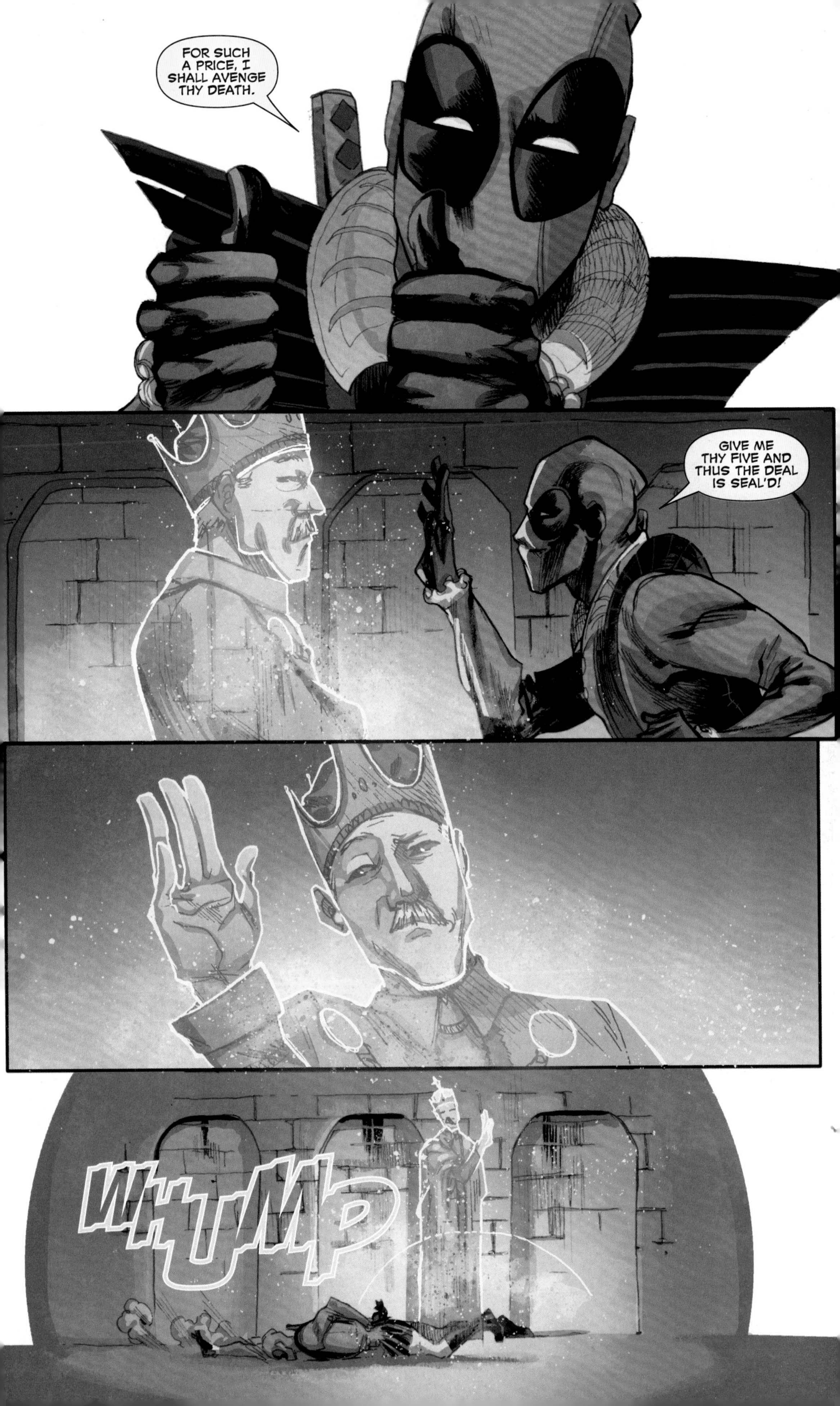
FOR SUCH A PRICE, I SHALL AVENGE THY DEATH.
GIVE ME THY FIVE AND THUS THE DEAL IS SEAL'D!
WHUMP

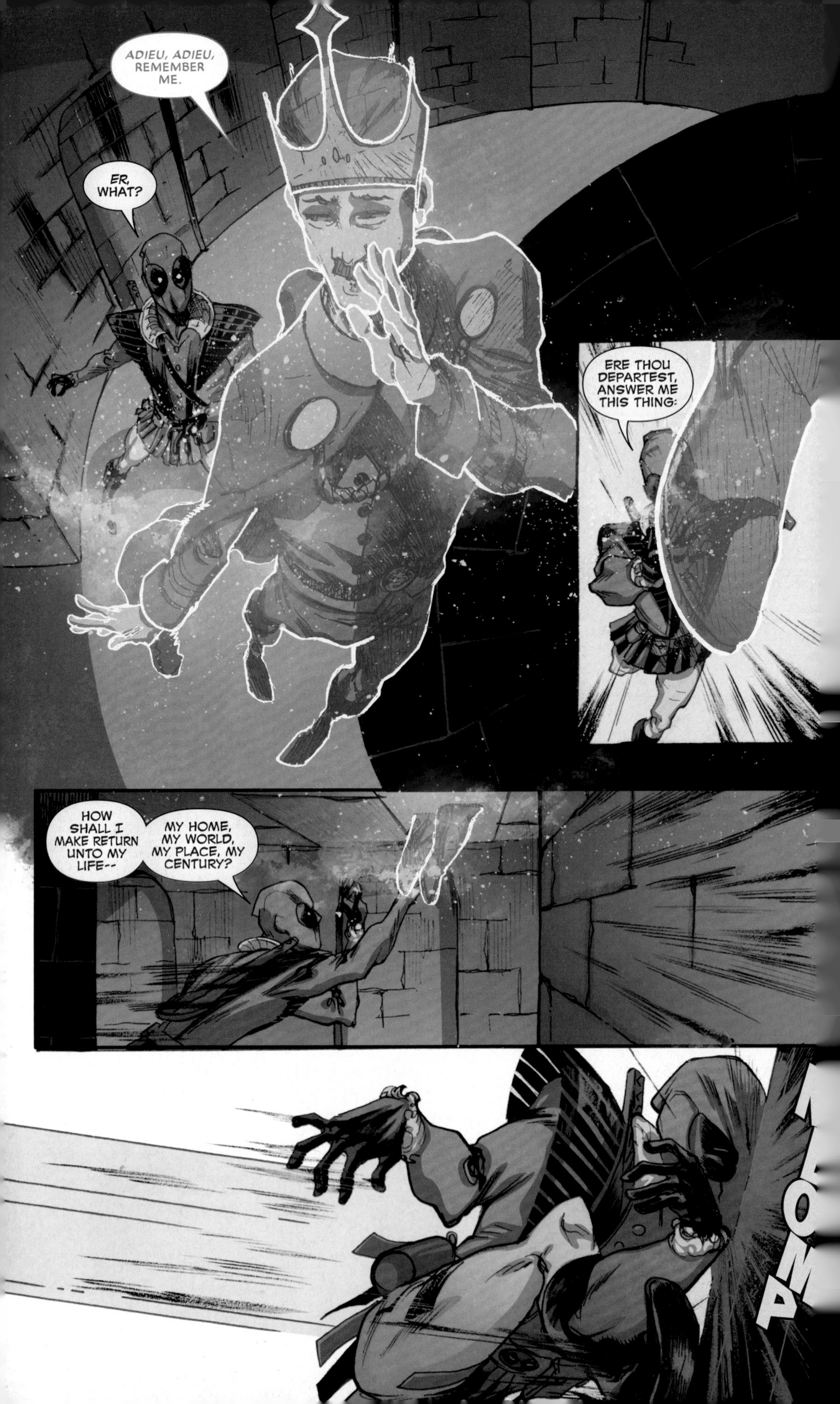
ADIEU, ADIEU, REMEMBER ME.
ER, WHAT?
ERE THOU DEPARTEST, ANSWER ME THIS THING:
HOW SHALL I MAKE RETURN UNTO MY LIFE--
MY HOME, MY WORLD, MY PLACE, MY CENTURY?
MOMP

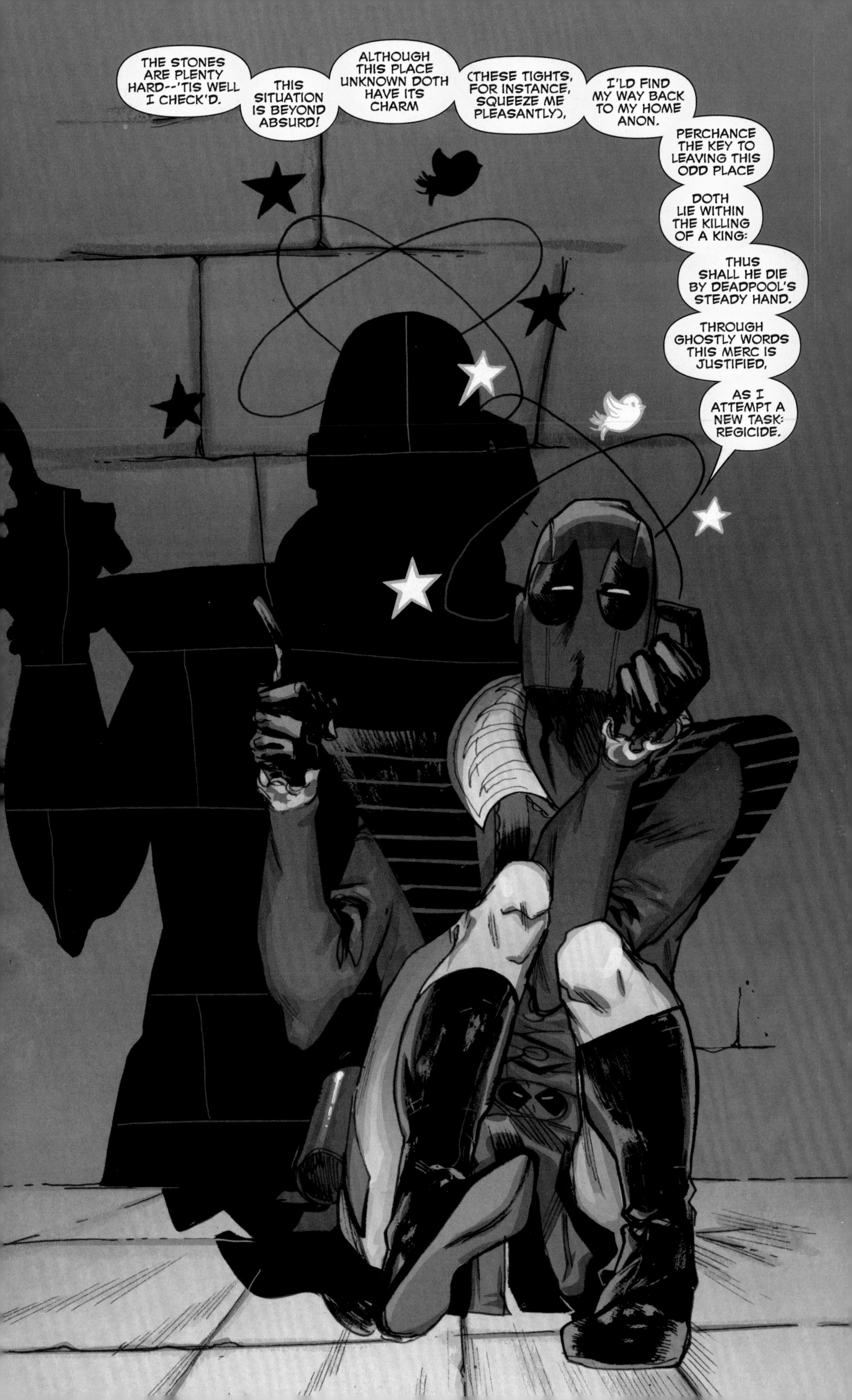
THE STONES ARE PLENTY HARD--'TIS WELL I CHECK'D.
THIS SITUATION IS BEYOND ABSURD!
ALTHOUGH THIS PLACE UNKNOWN DOTH HAVE ITS CHARM
(THESE TIGHTS, FOR INSTANCE, SQUEEZE ME PLEASANTLY),
I'LD FIND MY WAY BACK TO MY HOME ANON.
PERCHANCE THE KEY TO LEAVING THIS ODD PLACE
DOTH LIE WITHIN THE KILLING OF A KING:
THUS SHALL HE DIE BY DEADPOOL'S STEADY HAND.
THROUGH GHOSTLY WORDS THIS MERC IS JUSTIFIED,
AS I ATTEMPT A NEW TASK: REGICIDE.

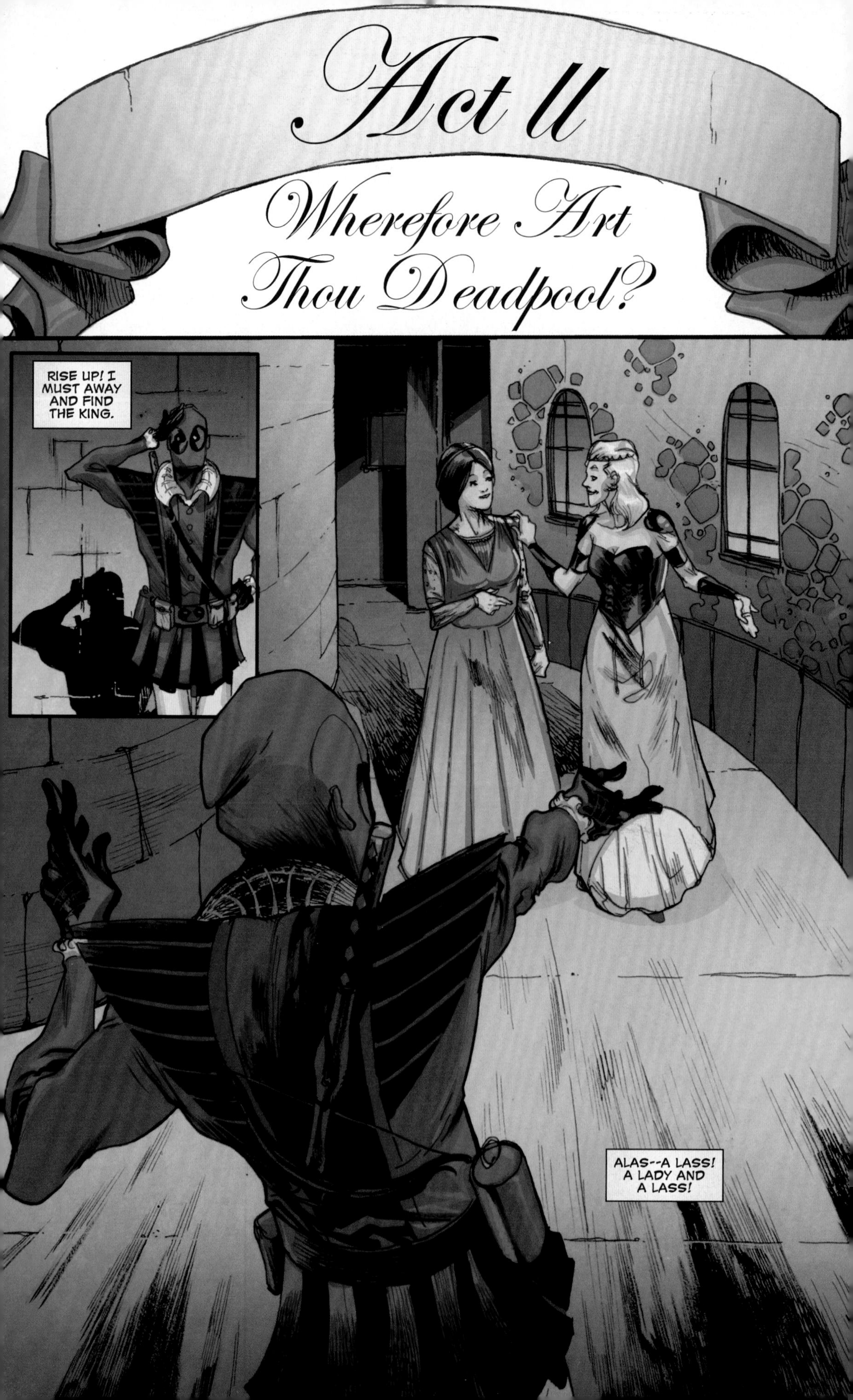
Act II
Wherefore Art Thou Deadpool?
RISE UP! I MUST AWAY AND FIND THE KING.
ALAS--A LASS! A LADY AND A LASS!

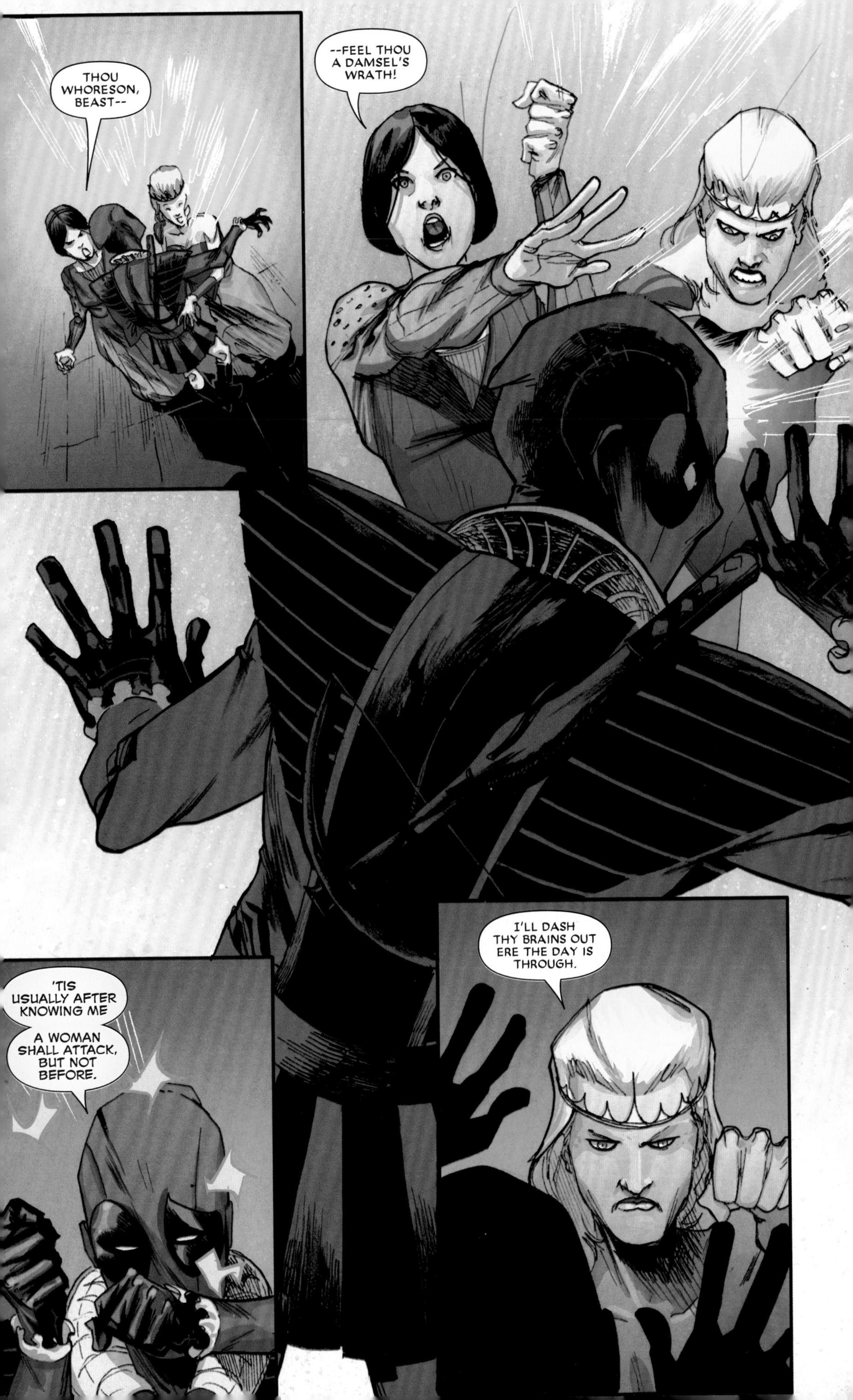
THOU WHORESON, BEAST--
--FEEL THOU A DAMSEL'S WRATH!
'TIS USUALLY AFTER KNOWING ME
A WOMAN SHALL ATTACK, BUT NOT BEFORE.
I'LL DASH THY BRAINS OUT ERE THE DAY IS THROUGH.

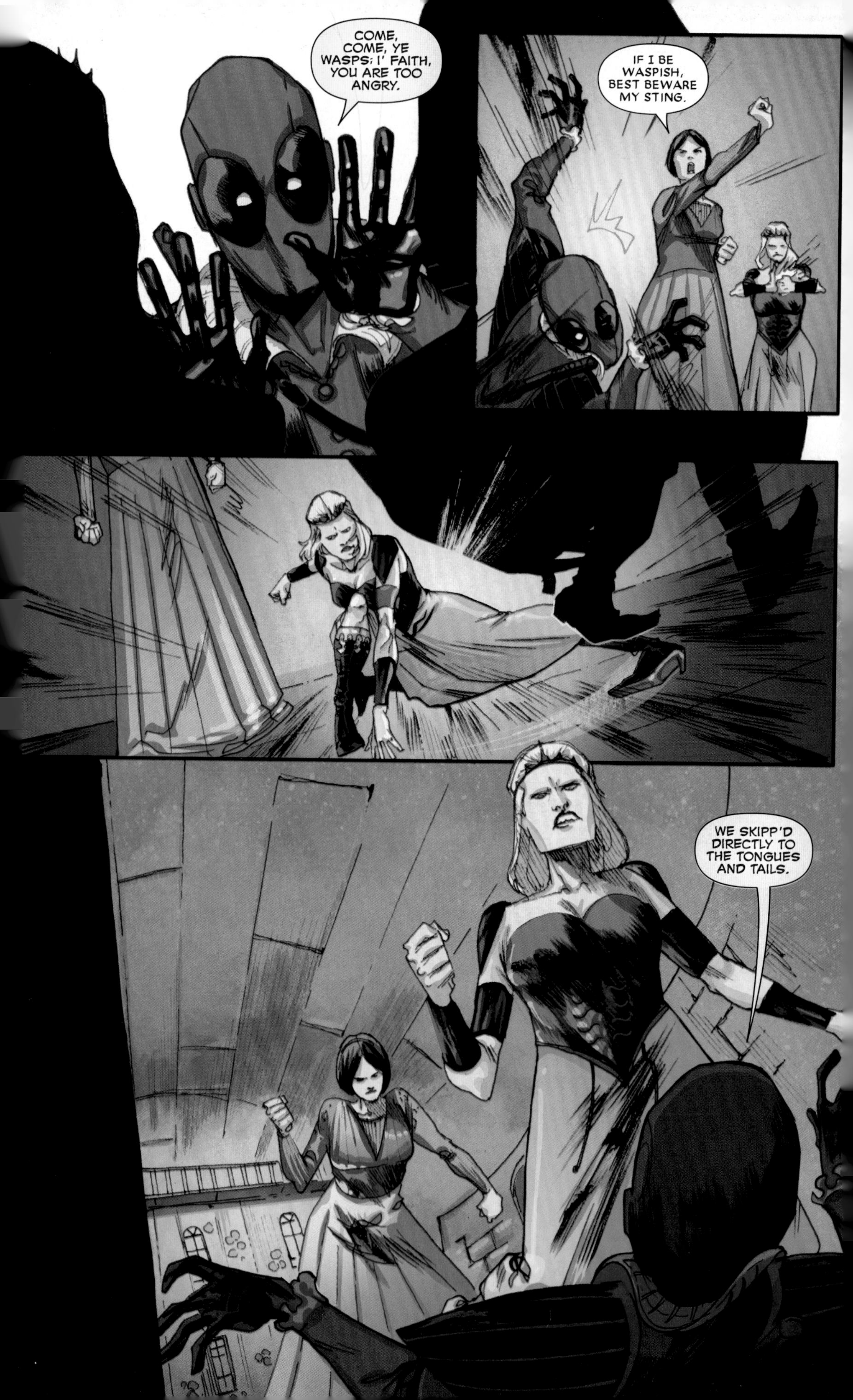
COME, COME, YE WASPS; I' FAITH, YOU ARE TOO ANGRY.
IF I BE WASPISH, BEST BEWARE MY STING.
WE SKIPP'D DIRECTLY TO THE TONGUES AND TAILS.

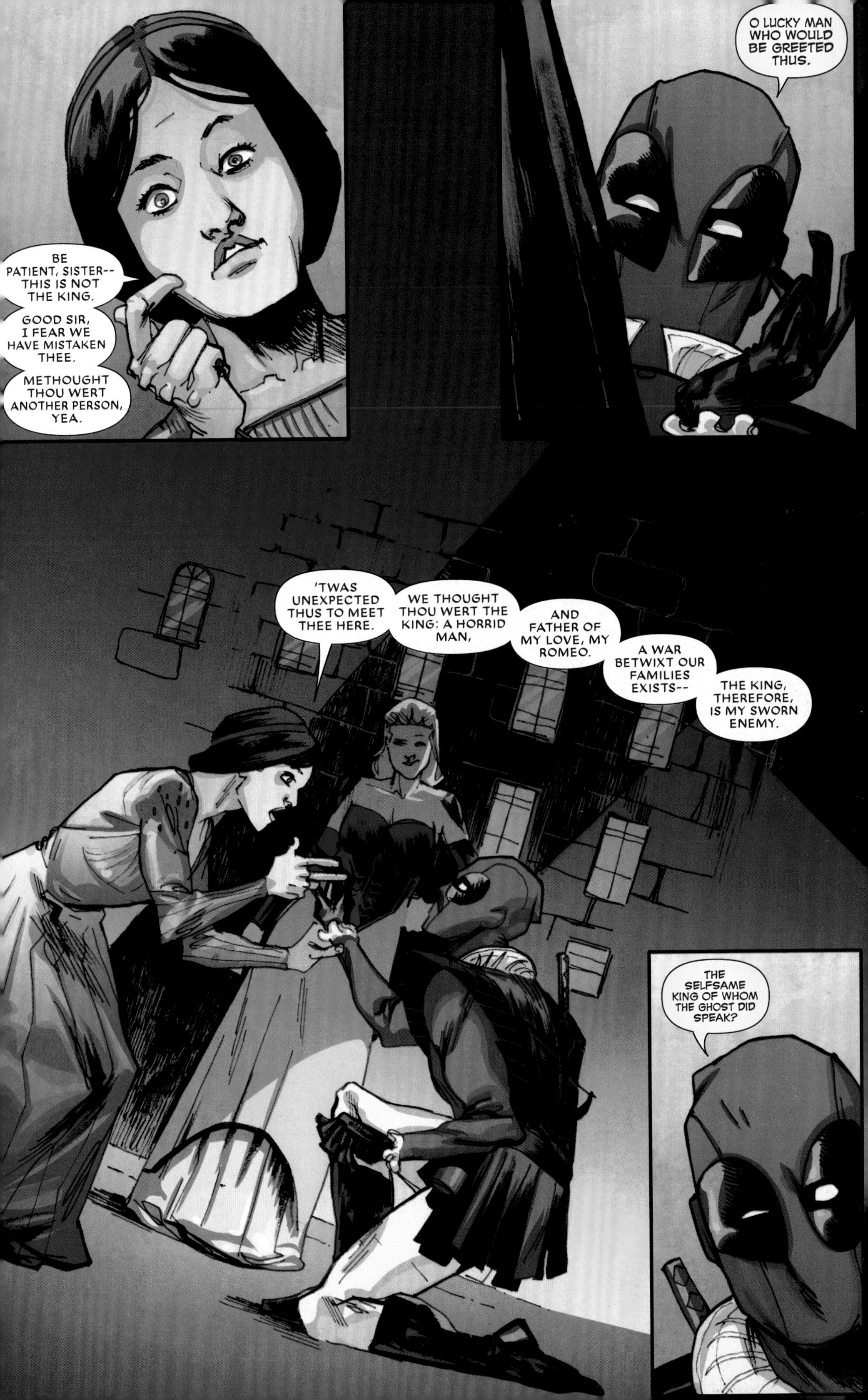
BE PATIENT, SISTER-- THIS IS NOT THE KING.
GOOD SIR, I FEAR WE HAVE MISTAKEN THEE.
METHOUGHT THOU WERT ANOTHER PERSON, YEA.
O LUCKY MAN WHO WOULD BE GREETED THUS.
'TWAS UNEXPECTED THUS TO MEET THEE HERE.
WE THOUGHT THOU WERT THE KING: A HORRID MAN,
AND FATHER OF MY LOVE, MY ROMEO.
A WAR BETWIXT OUR FAMILIES EXISTS--
THE KING, THEREFORE, IS MY SWORN ENEMY.
THE SELFSAME KING OF WHOM THE GHOST DID SPEAK?

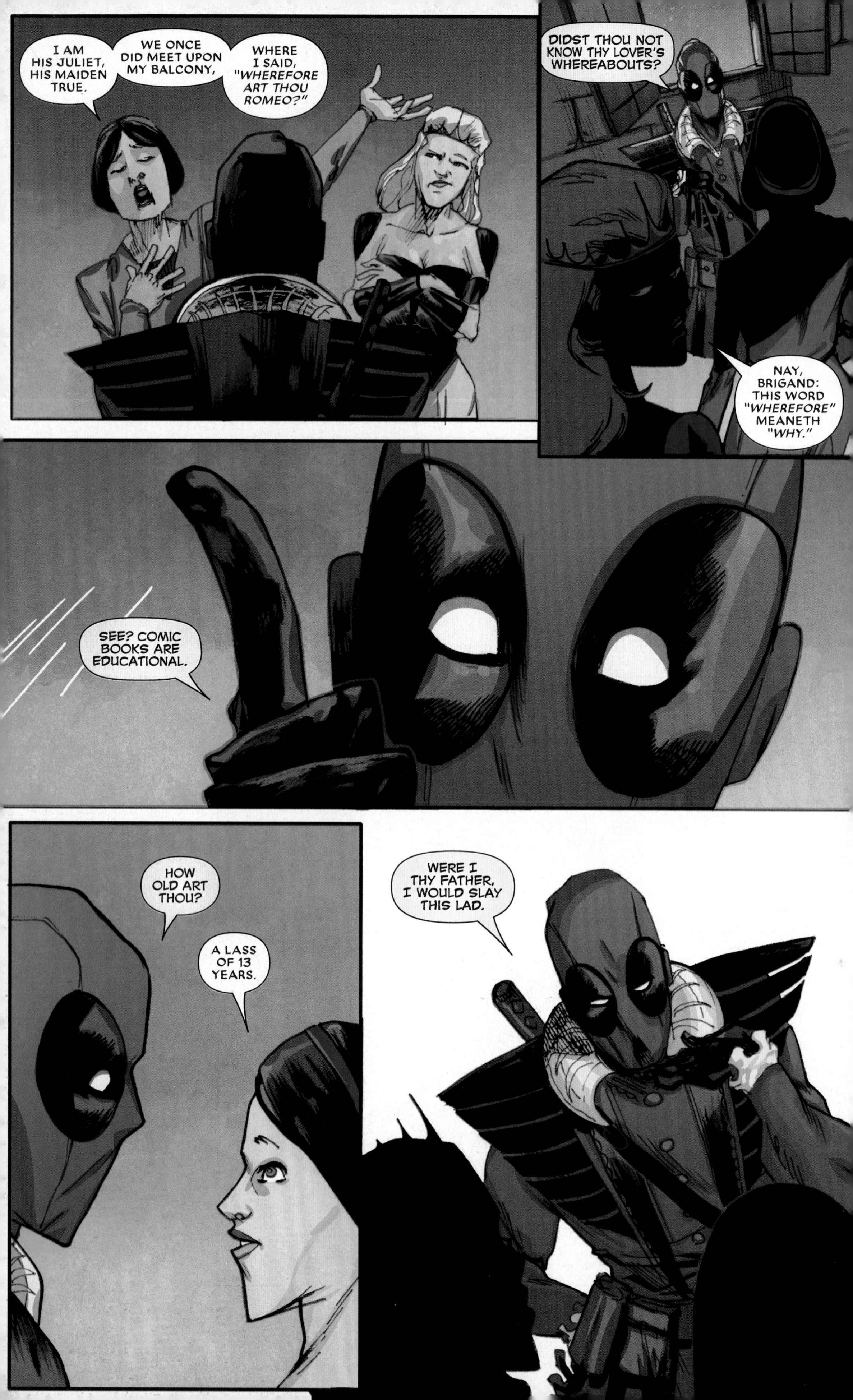

I AM HIS JULIET, HIS MAIDEN TRUE.
WE ONCE DID MEET UPON MY BALCONY,
WHERE I SAID, "WHEREFORE ART THOU ROMEO?"
DIDST THOU NOT KNOW THY LOVER'S WHEREABOUTS?
NAY, BRIGAND: THIS WORD "WHEREFORE" MEANETH "WHY."
SEE? COMIC BOOKS ARE EDUCATIONAL.
HOW OLD ART THOU?
A LASS OF 13 YEARS.
WERE I THY FATHER, I WOULD SLAY THIS LAD.

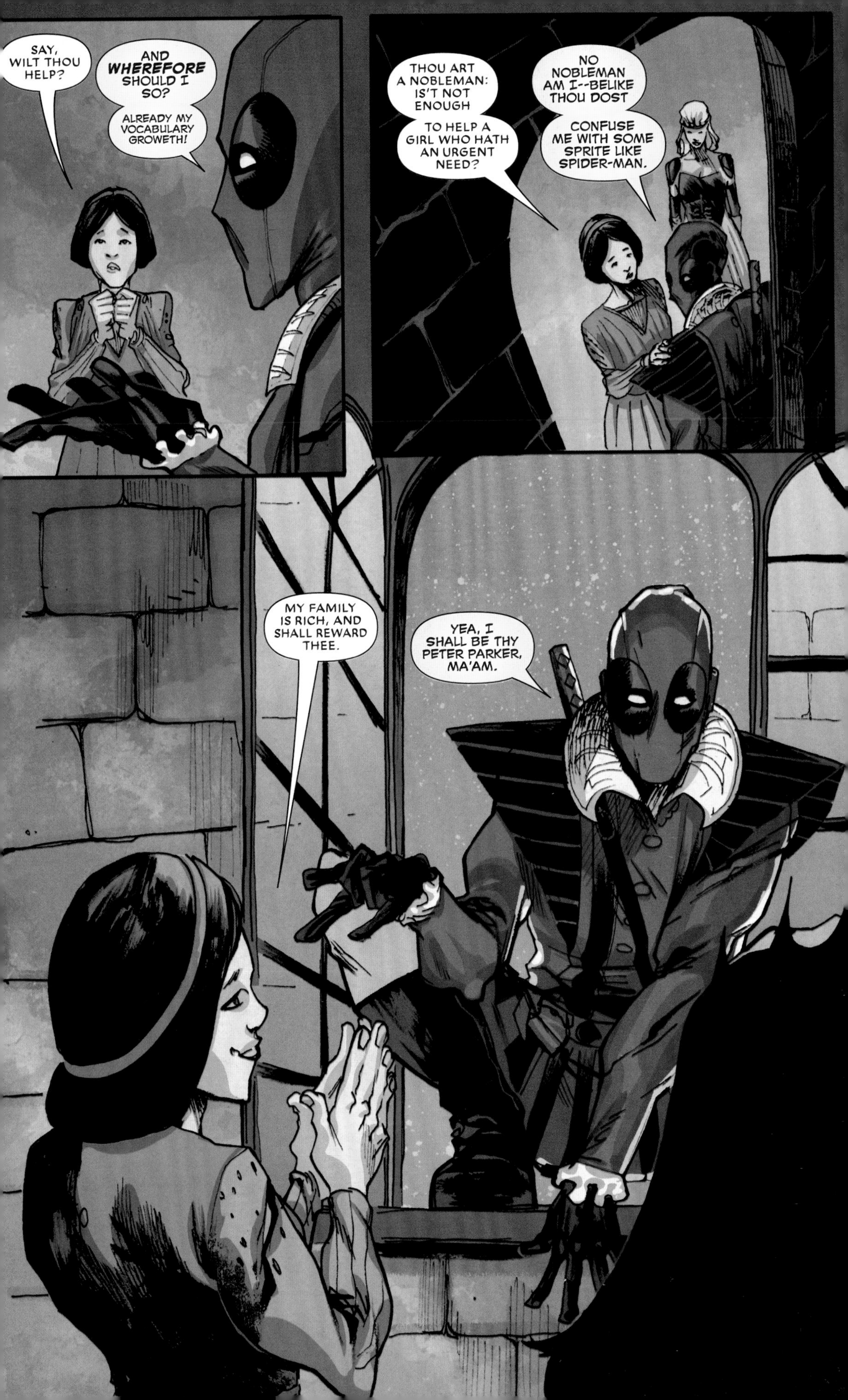
SAY, WILT THOU HELP?
AND *WHEREFORE* SHOULD I SO?
ALREADY MY VOCABULARY GROWETH!
THOU ART A NOBLEMAN: IS'T NOT ENOUGH
TO HELP A GIRL WHO HATH AN URGENT NEED?
NO NOBLEMAN AM I--BELIKE THOU DOST
CONFUSE ME WITH SOME SPRITE LIKE SPIDER-MAN.
MY FAMILY IS RICH, AND SHALL REWARD THEE.
YEA, I SHALL BE THY PETER PARKER, MA'AM.

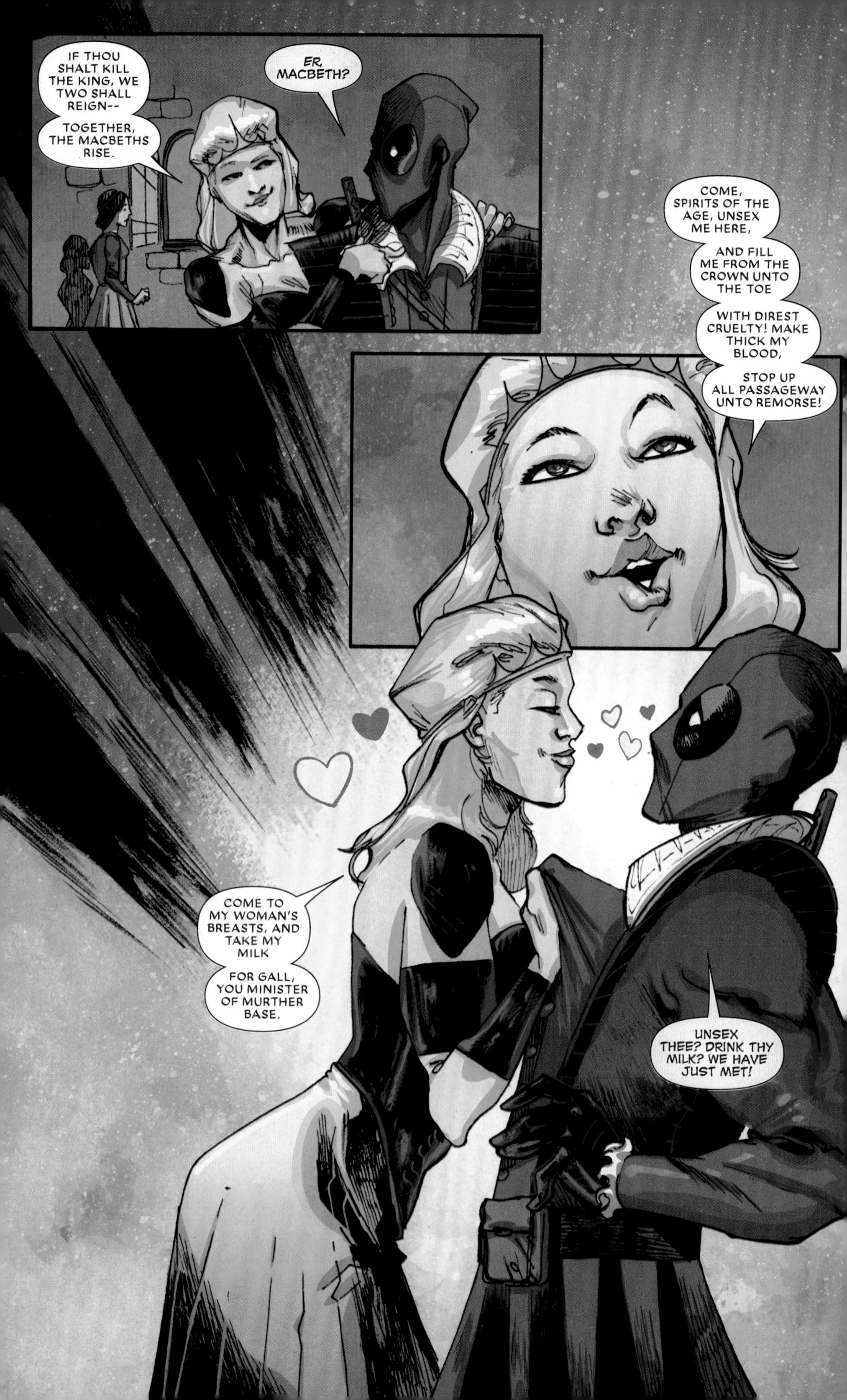
IF THOU SHALT KILL THE KING, WE TWO SHALL REIGN--
TOGETHER, THE MACBETHS RISE.
ER, MACBETH?
COME, SPIRITS OF THE AGE, UNSEX ME HERE,
AND FILL ME FROM THE CROWN UNTO THE TOE
WITH DIREST CRUELTY! MAKE THICK MY BLOOD,
STOP UP ALL PASSAGEWAY UNTO REMORSE!
COME TO MY WOMAN'S BREASTS, AND TAKE MY MILK
FOR GALL, YOU MINISTER OF MURTHER BASE.
UNSEX THEE? DRINK THY MILK? WE HAVE JUST MET!

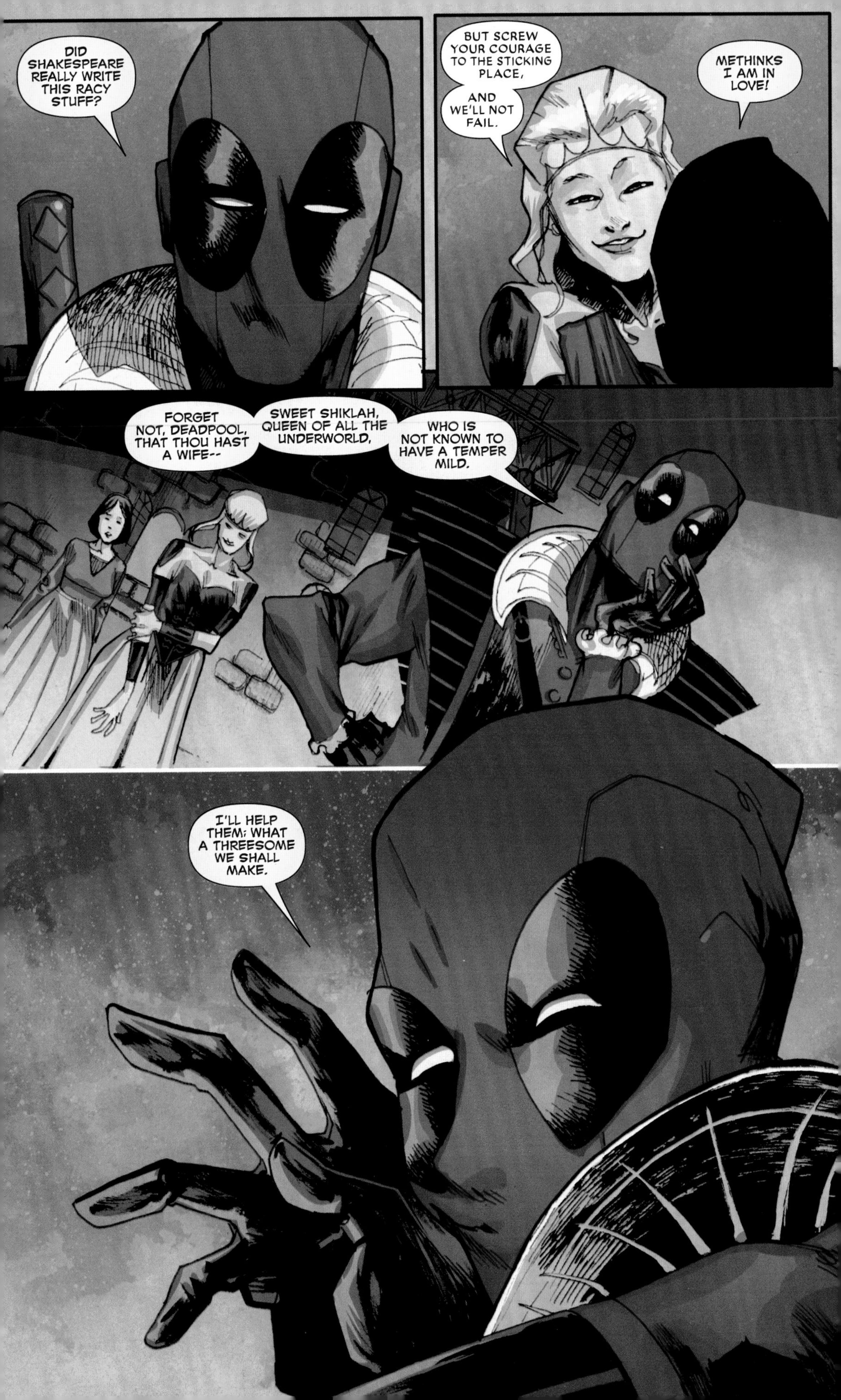
DID SHAKESPEARE REALLY WRITE THIS RACY STUFF?
BUT SCREW YOUR COURAGE TO THE STICKING PLACE,
AND WE'LL NOT FAIL.
METHINKS I AM IN LOVE!
FORGET NOT, DEADPOOL, THAT THOU HAST A WIFE--
SWEET SHIKLAH, QUEEN OF ALL THE UNDERWORLD,
WHO IS NOT KNOWN TO HAVE A TEMPER MILD.
I'LL HELP THEM; WHAT A THREESOME WE SHALL MAKE.

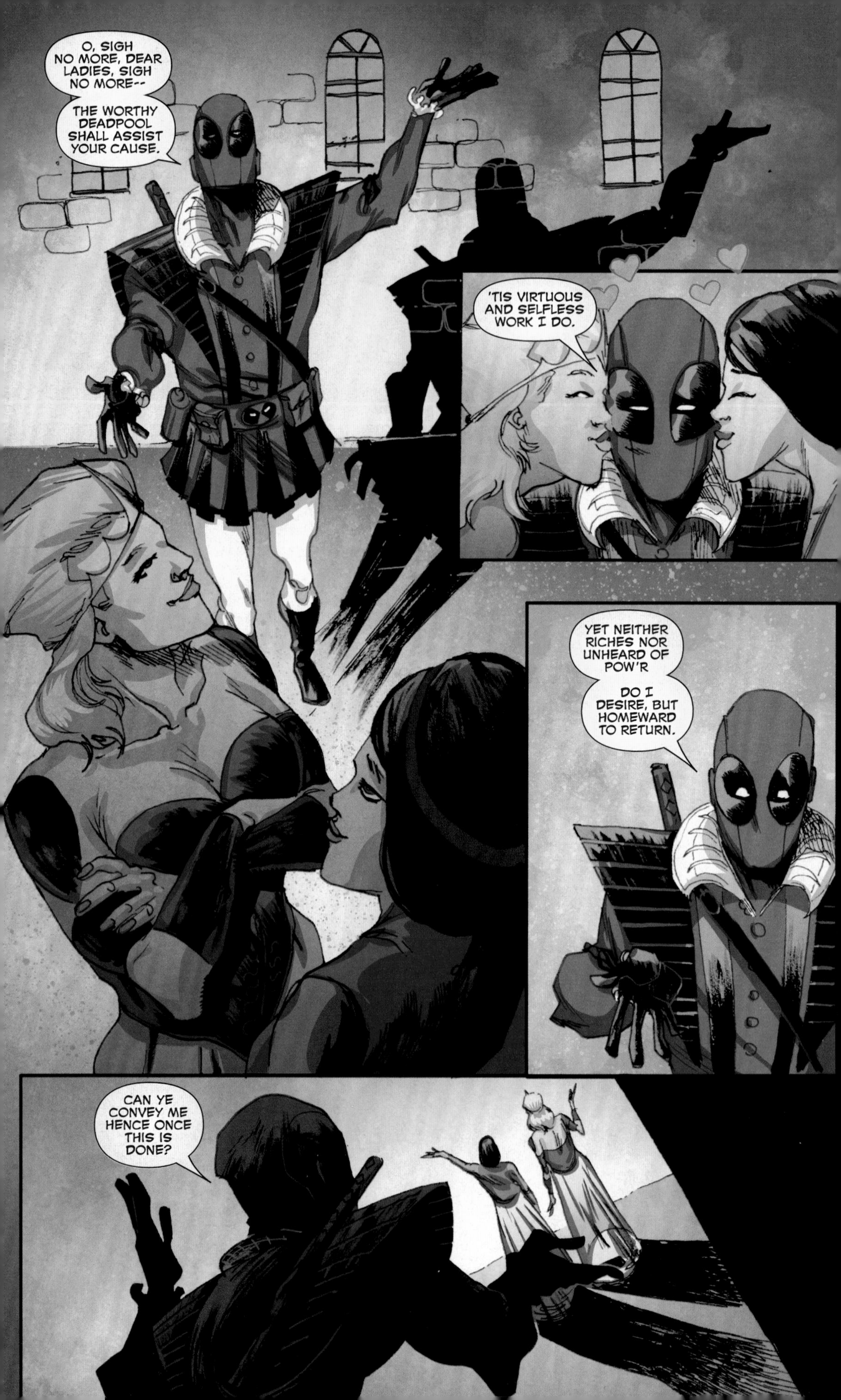

O, SIGH NO MORE, DEAR LADIES, SIGH NO MORE--
THE WORTHY DEADPOOL SHALL ASSIST YOUR CAUSE.
'TIS VIRTUOUS AND SELFLESS WORK I DO.
YET NEITHER RICHES NOR UNHEARD OF POW'R
DO I DESIRE, BUT HOMEWARD TO RETURN.
CAN YE CONVEY ME HENCE ONCE THIS IS DONE?

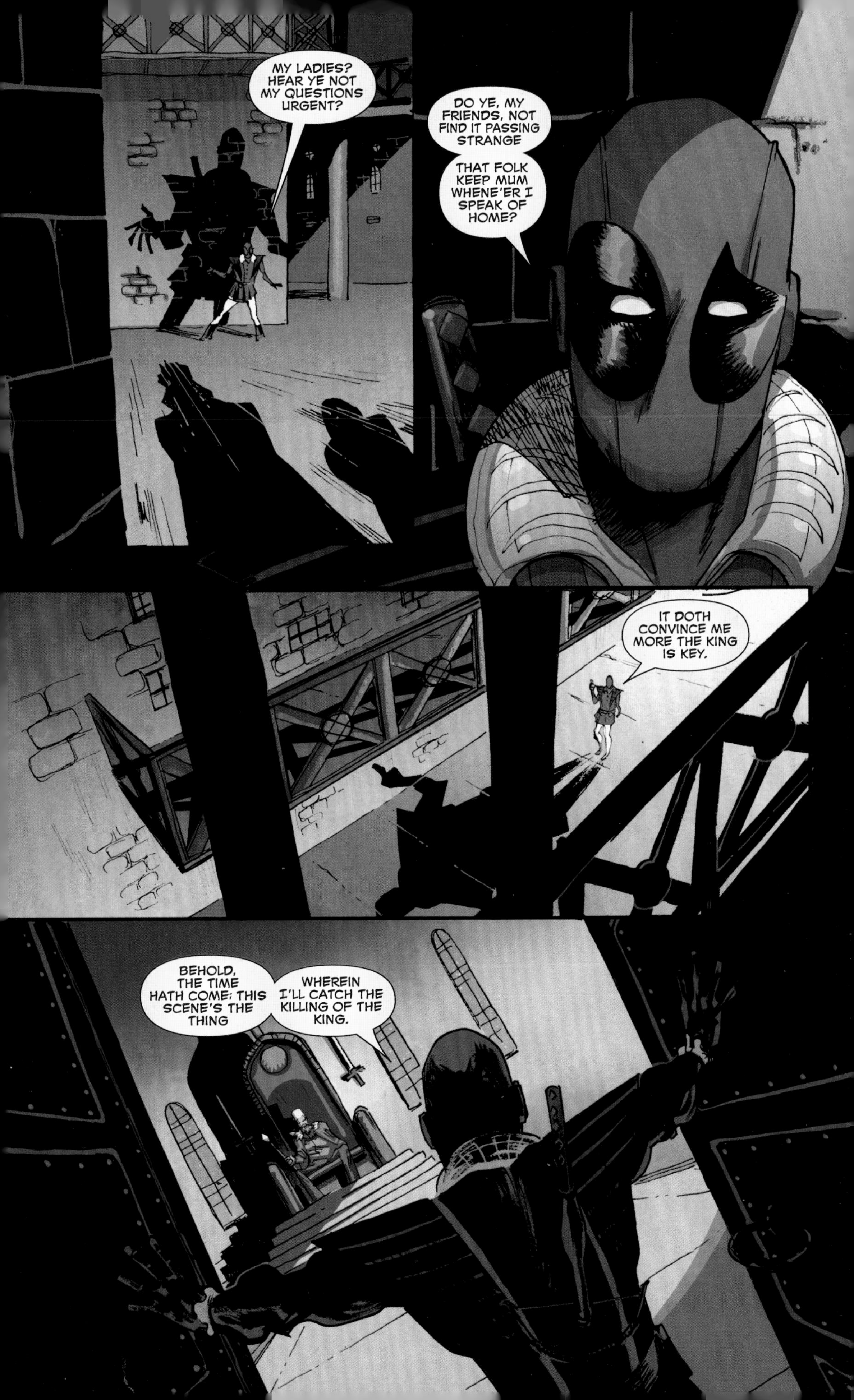
MY LADIES? HEAR YE NOT MY QUESTIONS URGENT?
DO YE, MY FRIENDS, NOT FIND IT PASSING STRANGE
THAT FOLK KEEP MUM WHENE'ER I SPEAK OF HOME?
IT DOTH CONVINCE ME MORE THE KING IS KEY.
BEHOLD, THE TIME HATH COME; THIS SCENE'S THE THING
WHEREIN I'LL CATCH THE KILLING OF THE KING.

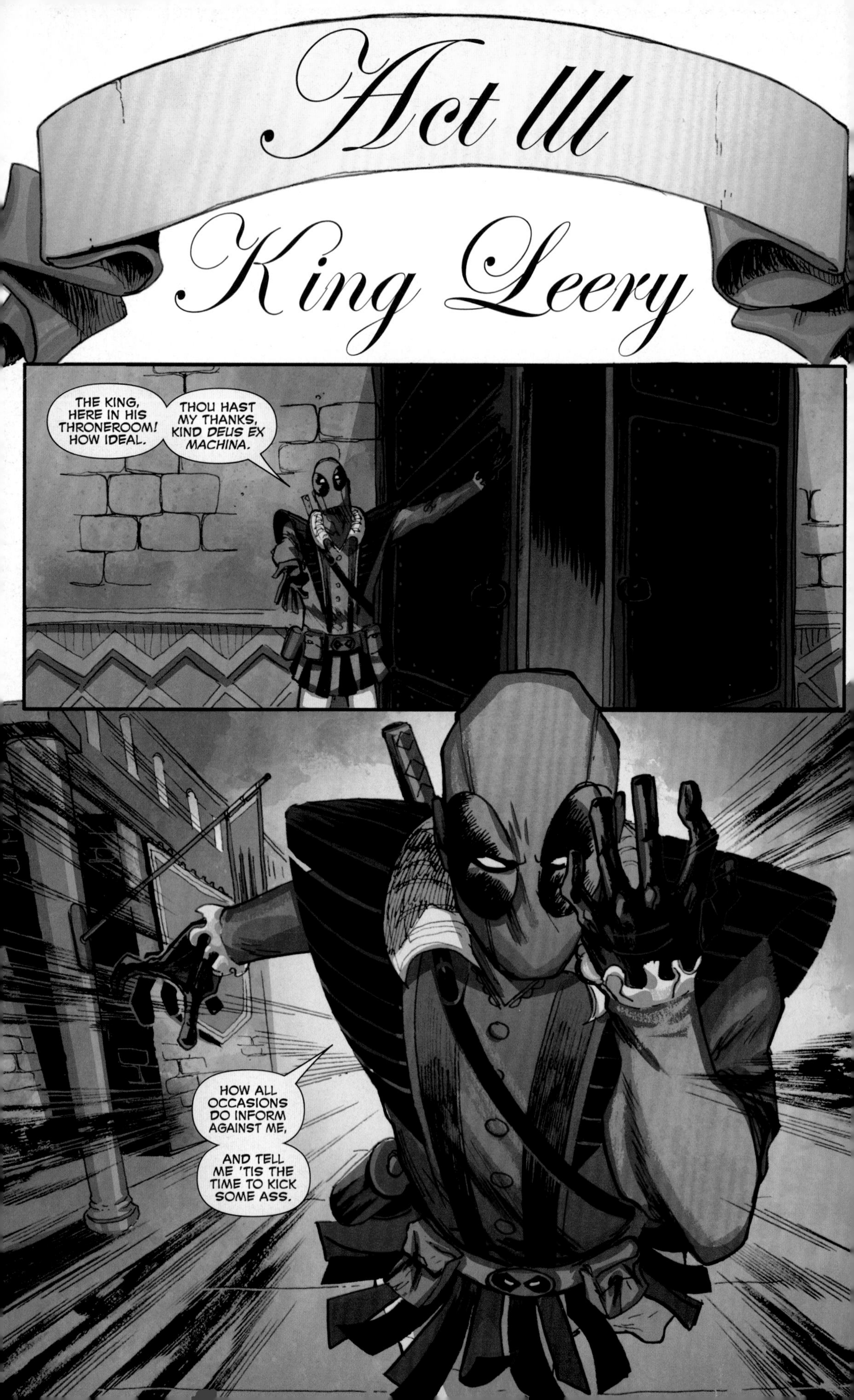
Act III
King Leery
THE KING, HERE IN HIS THRONEROOM! HOW IDEAL.
THOU HAST MY THANKS, KIND DEUS EX MACHINA.
HOW ALL OCCASIONS DO INFORM AGAINST ME,
AND TELL ME 'TIS THE TIME TO KICK SOME ASS.

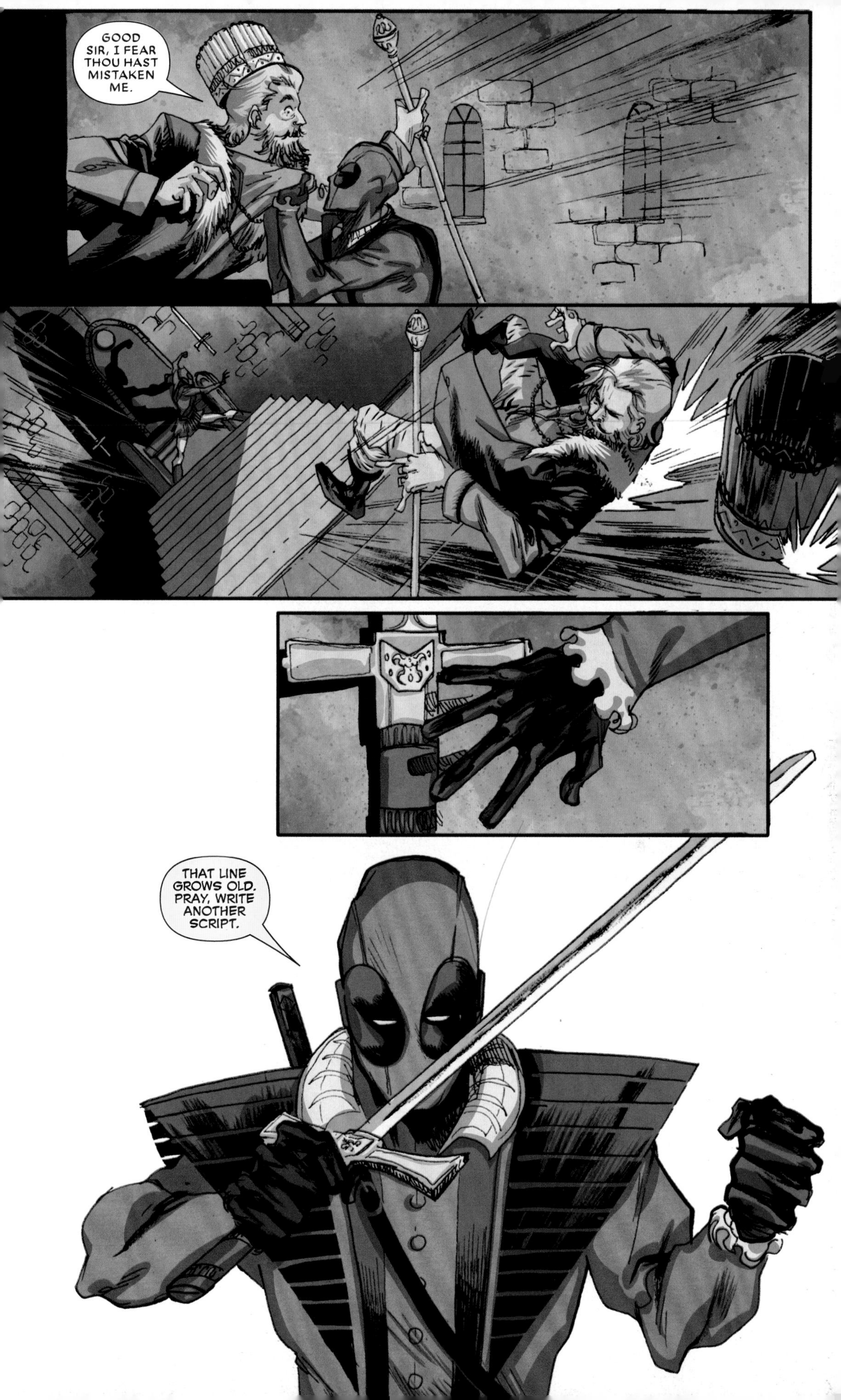
GOOD SIR, I FEAR THOU HAST MISTAKEN ME.
THAT LINE GROWS OLD. PRAY, WRITE ANOTHER SCRIPT.

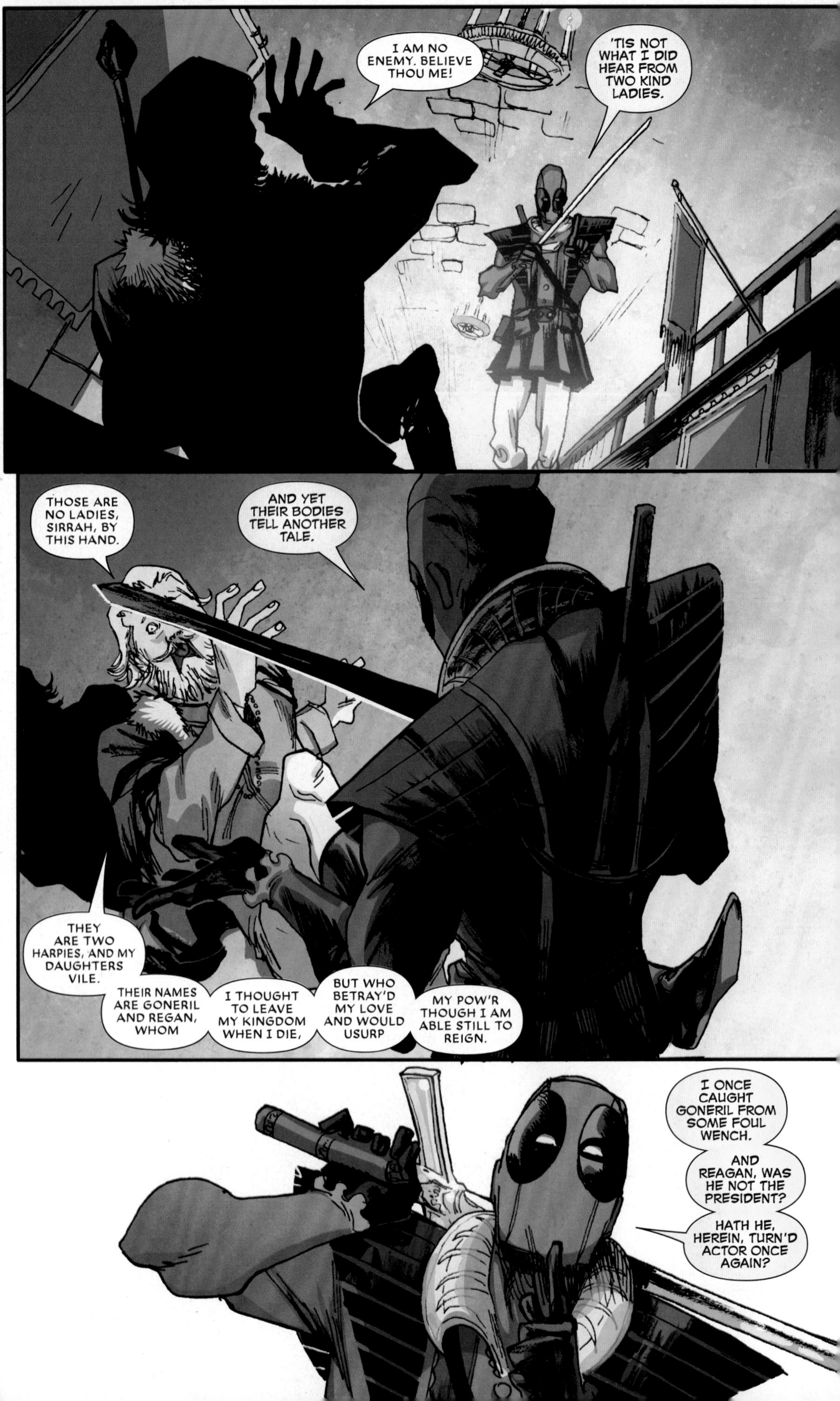
I AM NO ENEMY. BELIEVE THOU ME!
'TIS NOT WHAT I DID HEAR FROM TWO KIND LADIES.
THOSE ARE NO LADIES, SIRRAH, BY THIS HAND.
AND YET THEIR BODIES TELL ANOTHER TALE.
THEY ARE TWO HARPIES, AND MY DAUGHTERS VILE.
THEIR NAMES ARE GONERIL AND REGAN, WHOM
I THOUGHT TO LEAVE MY KINGDOM WHEN I DIE,
BUT WHO BETRAY'D MY LOVE AND WOULD USURP
MY POW'R THOUGH I AM ABLE STILL TO REIGN.
I ONCE CAUGHT GONERIL FROM SOME FOUL WENCH.
AND REAGAN, WAS HE NOT THE PRESIDENT?
HATH HE, HEREIN, TURN'D ACTOR ONCE AGAIN?

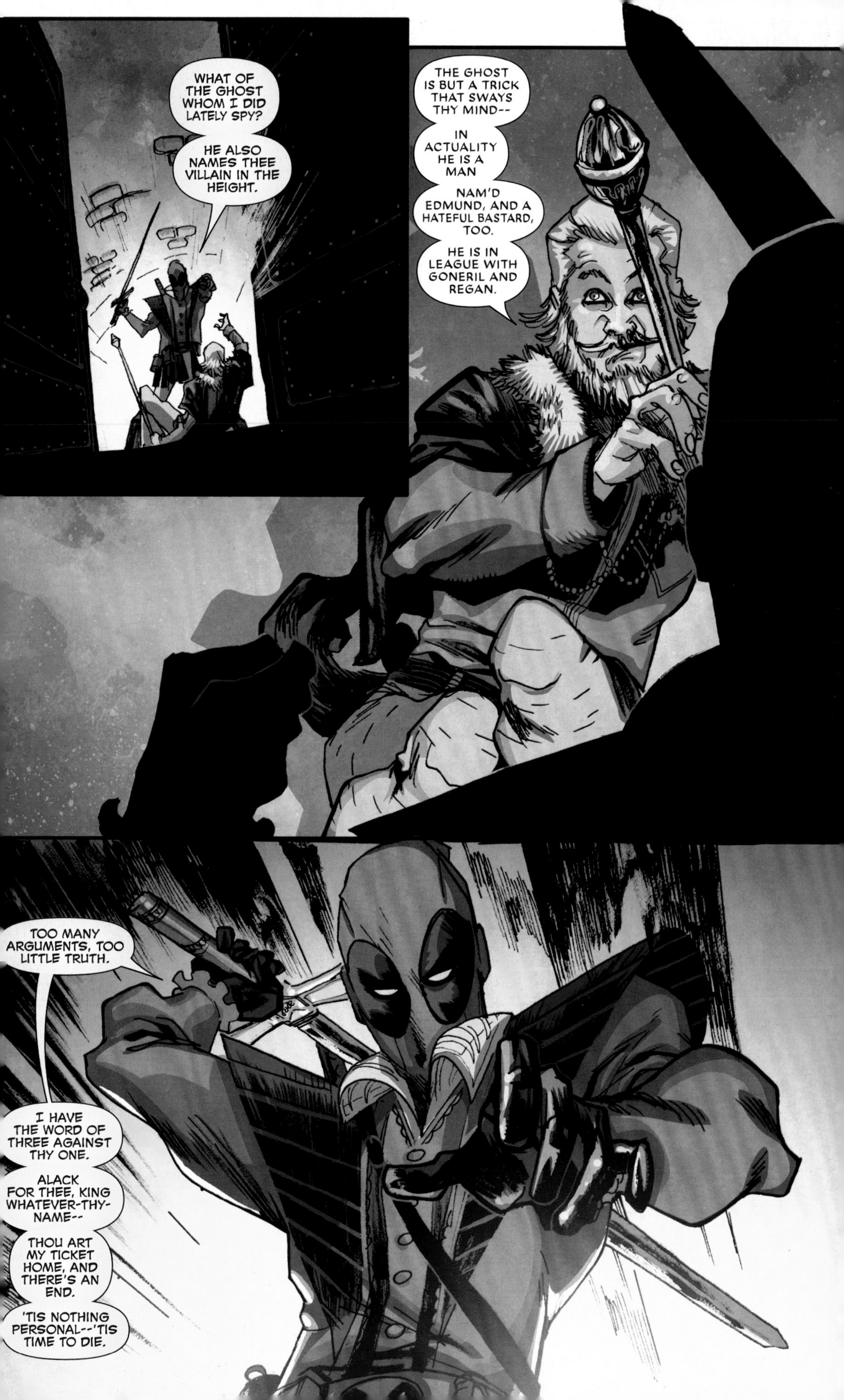
WHAT OF THE GHOST WHOM I DID LATELY SPY?
HE ALSO NAMES THEE VILLAIN IN THE HEIGHT.
THE GHOST IS BUT A TRICK THAT SWAYS THY MIND--
IN ACTUALITY HE IS A MAN
NAM'D EDMUND, AND A HATEFUL BASTARD, TOO.
HE IS IN LEAGUE WITH GONERIL AND REGAN.
TOO MANY ARGUMENTS, TOO LITTLE TRUTH.
I HAVE THE WORD OF THREE AGAINST THY ONE.
ALACK FOR THEE, KING WHATEVER-THY-NAME--
THOU ART MY TICKET HOME, AND THERE'S AN END.
'TIS NOTHING PERSONAL--'TIS TIME TO DIE.

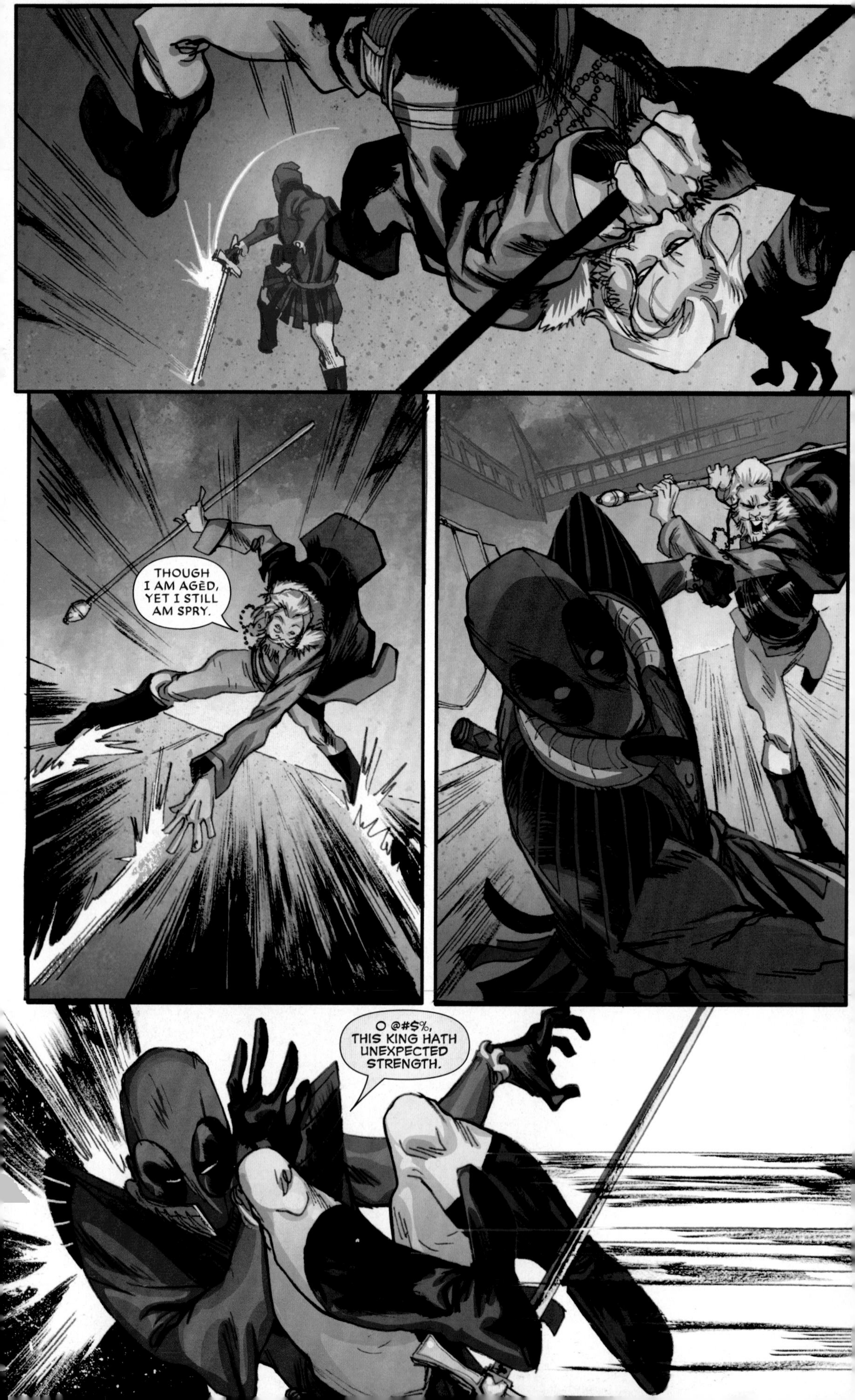
THOUGH I AM AGED, YET I STILL AM SPRY.
O @#$%, THIS KING HATH UNEXPECTED STRENGTH.

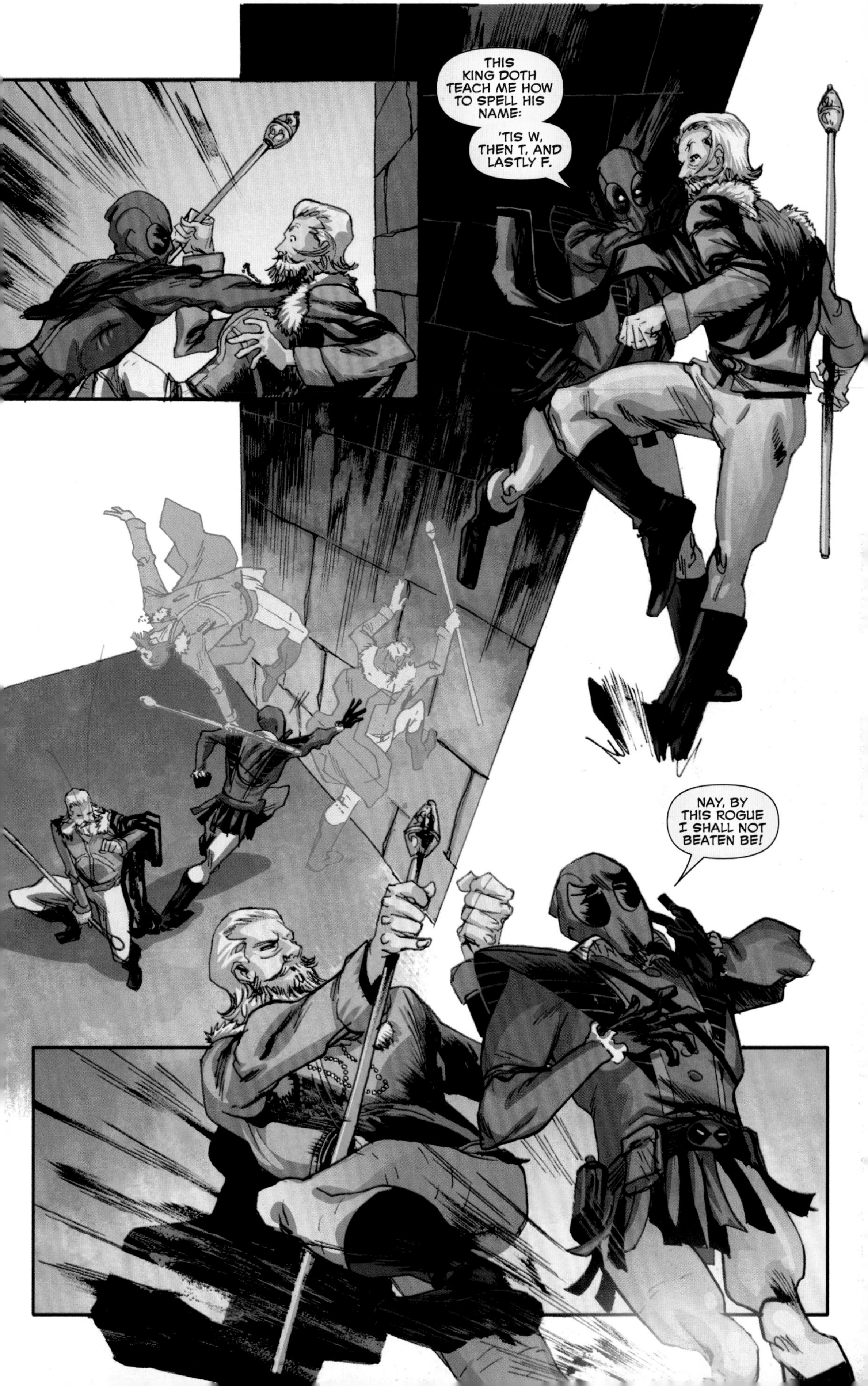
THIS KING DOTH TEACH ME HOW TO SPELL HIS NAME:
'TIS W, THEN T, AND LASTLY F.
NAY, BY THIS ROGUE I SHALL NOT BEATEN BE!

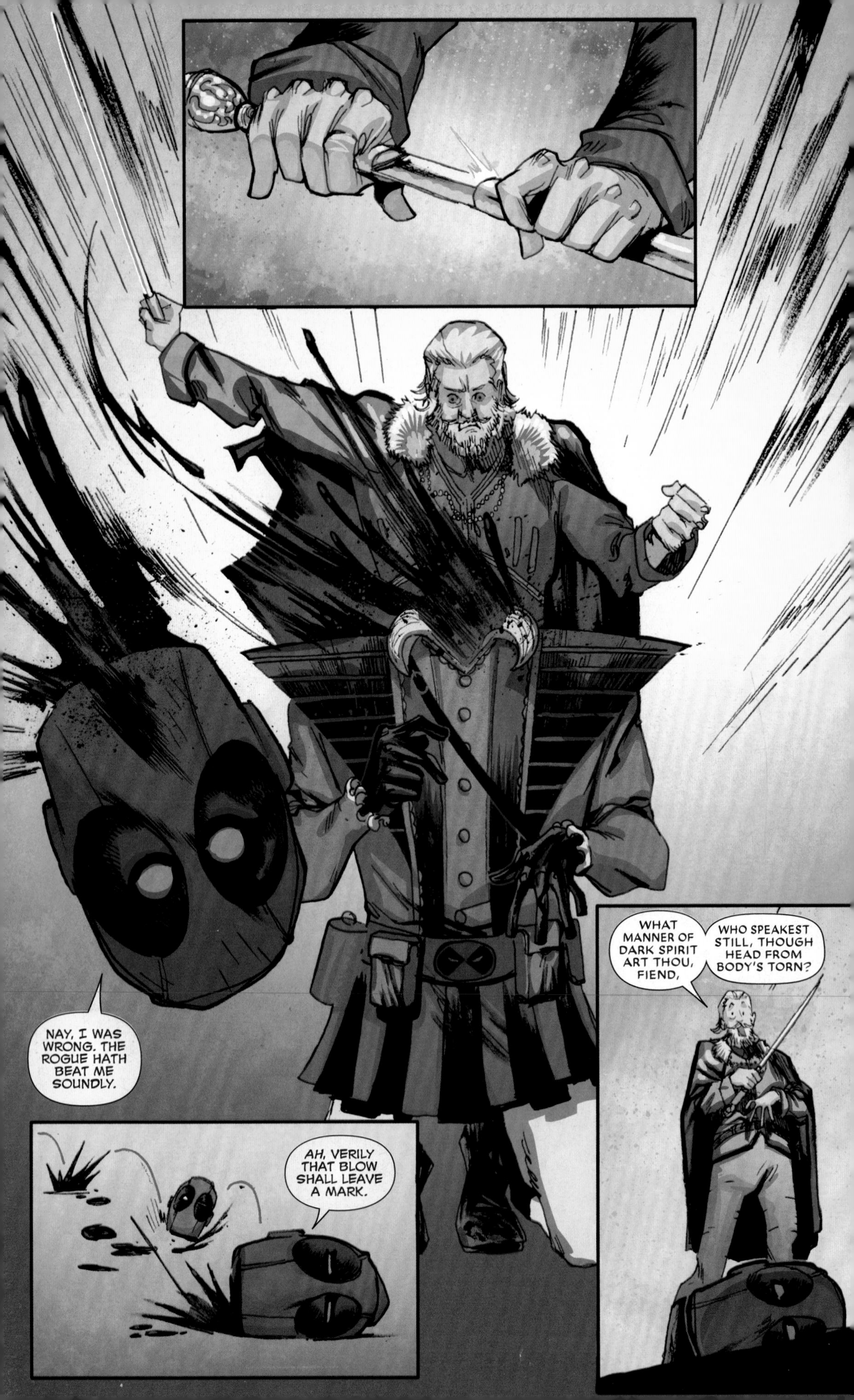
NAY, I WAS WRONG. THE ROGUE HATH BEAT ME SOUNDLY.
AH, VERILY THAT BLOW SHALL LEAVE A MARK.
WHAT MANNER OF DARK SPIRIT ART THOU, FIEND,
WHO SPEAKEST STILL, THOUGH HEAD FROM BODY'S TORN?

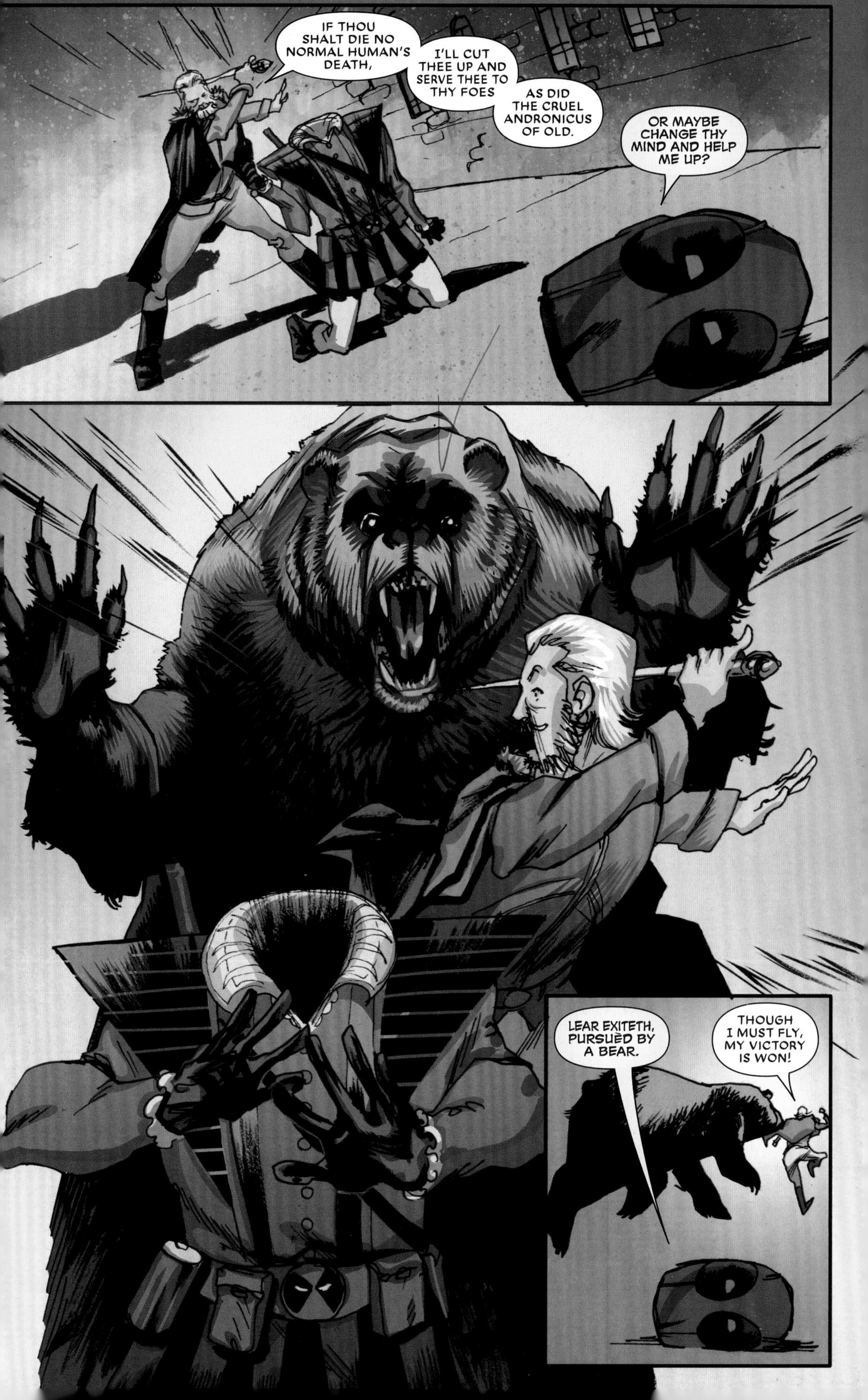
IF THOU SHALT DIE NO NORMAL HUMAN'S DEATH,
I'LL CUT THEE UP AND SERVE THEE TO THY FOES
AS DID THE CRUEL ANDRONICUS OF OLD.
OR MAYBE CHANGE THY MIND AND HELP ME UP?
LEAR EXITETH, PURSUÈD BY A BEAR.
THOUGH I MUST FLY, MY VICTORY IS WON!

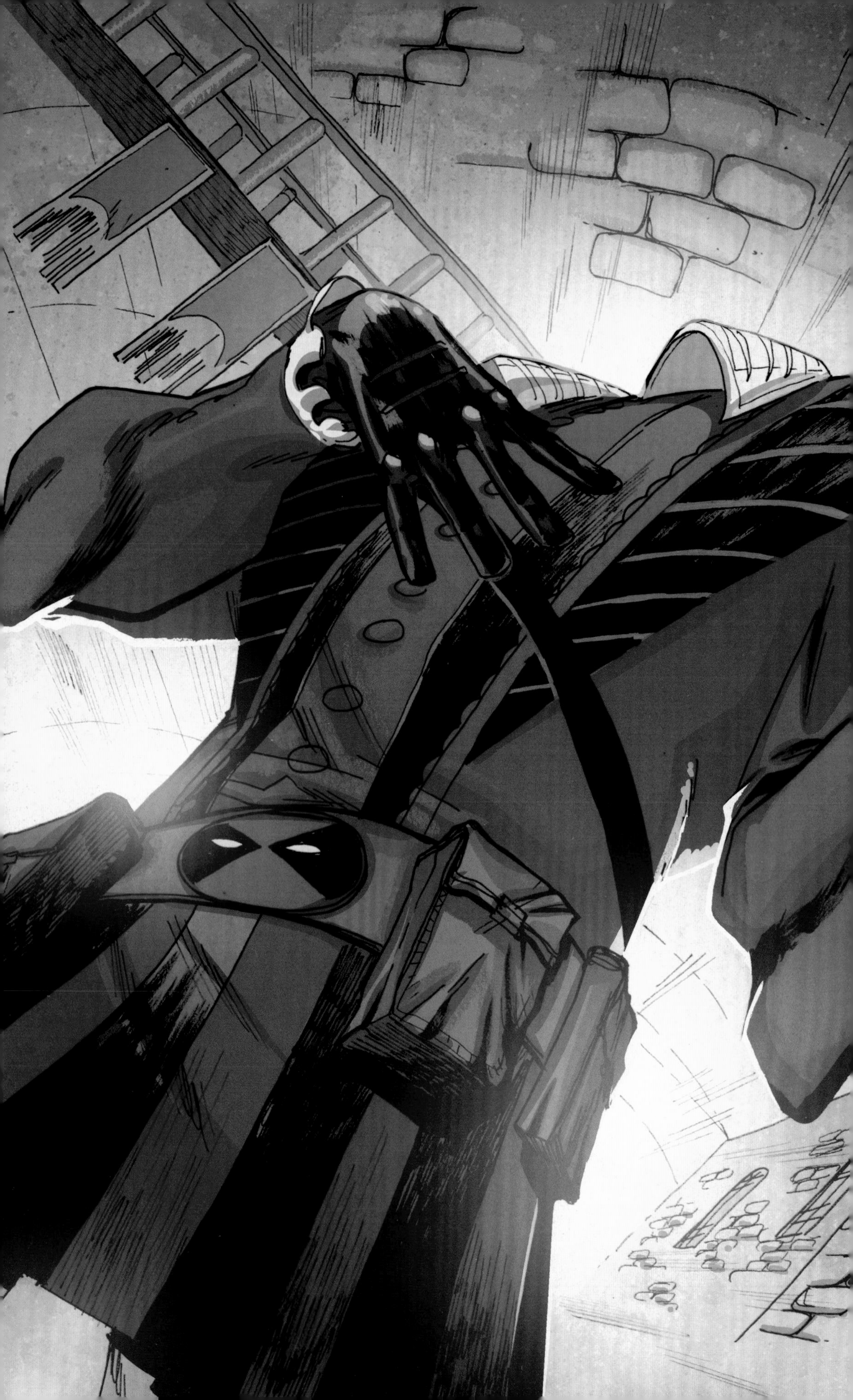

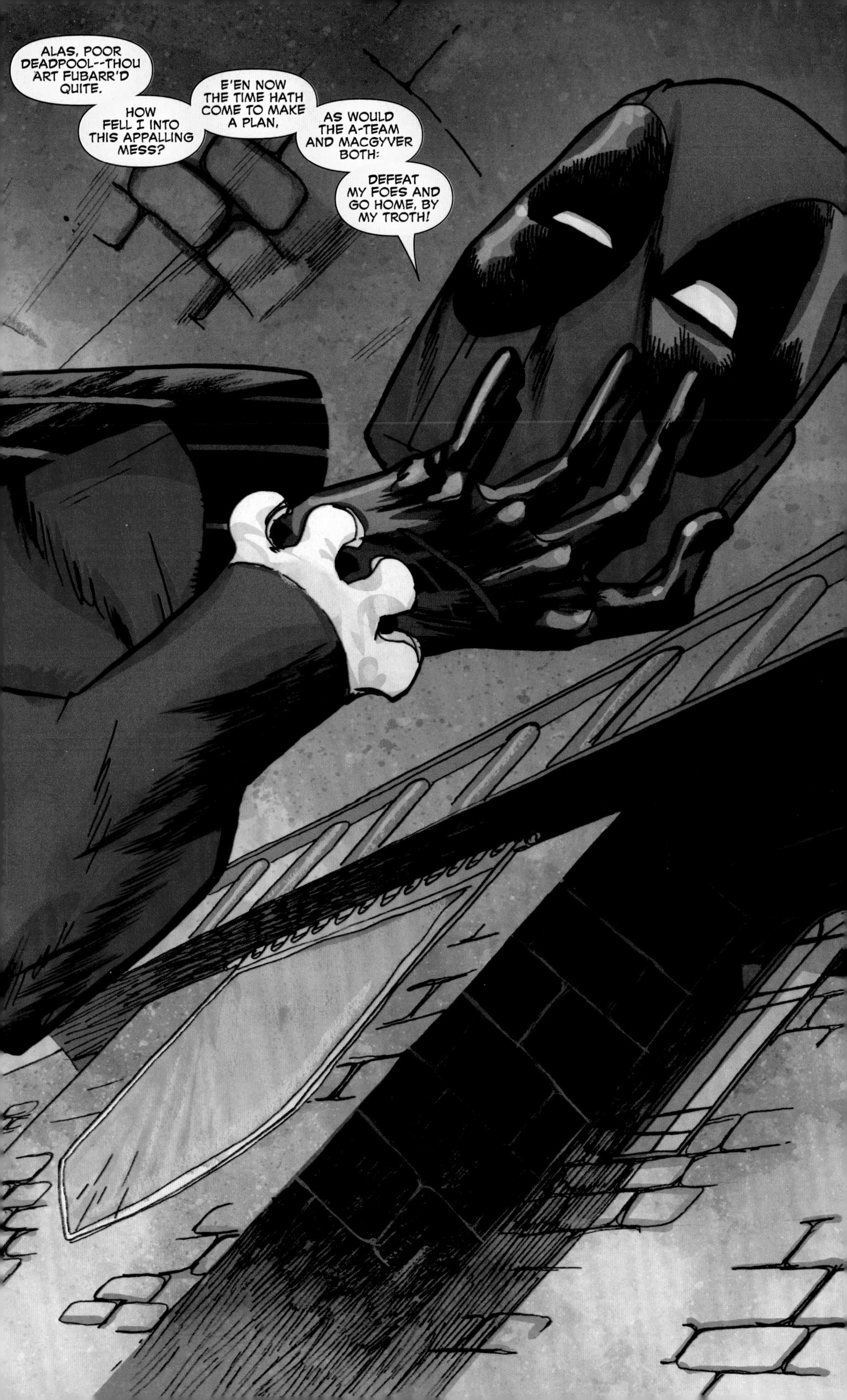
ALAS, POOR DEADPOOL--THOU ART FUBARR'D QUITE.
HOW FELL I INTO THIS APPALLING MESS?
E'EN NOW THE TIME HATH COME TO MAKE A PLAN,
AS WOULD THE A-TEAM AND MACGYVER BOTH:
DEFEAT MY FOES AND GO HOME, BY MY TROTH!

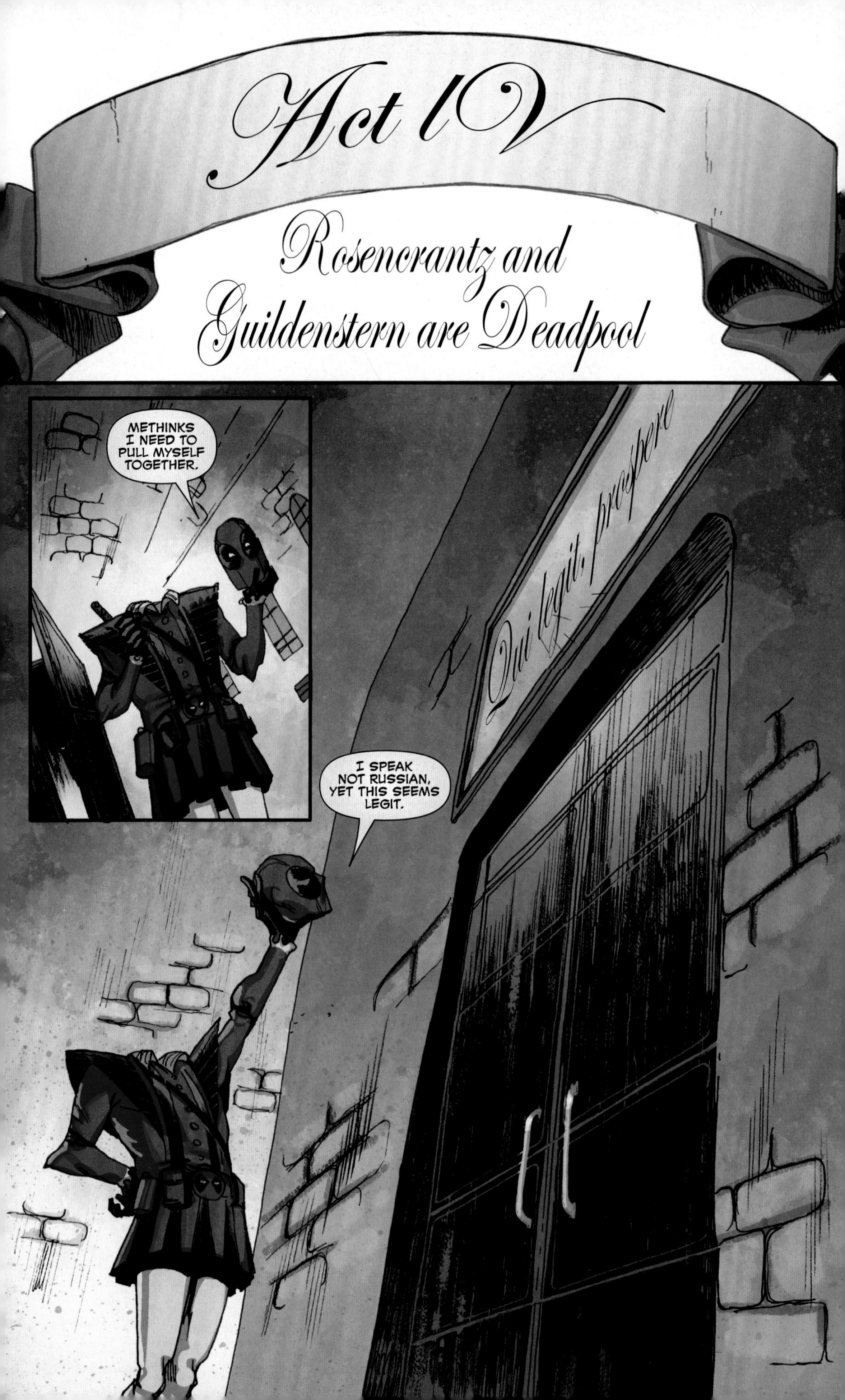
Act IV
Rosencrantz and Guildenstern are Deadpool
METHINKS I NEED TO PULL MYSELF TOGETHER.
Qui legit, prospere
I SPEAK NOT RUSSIAN, YET THIS SEEMS LEGIT.

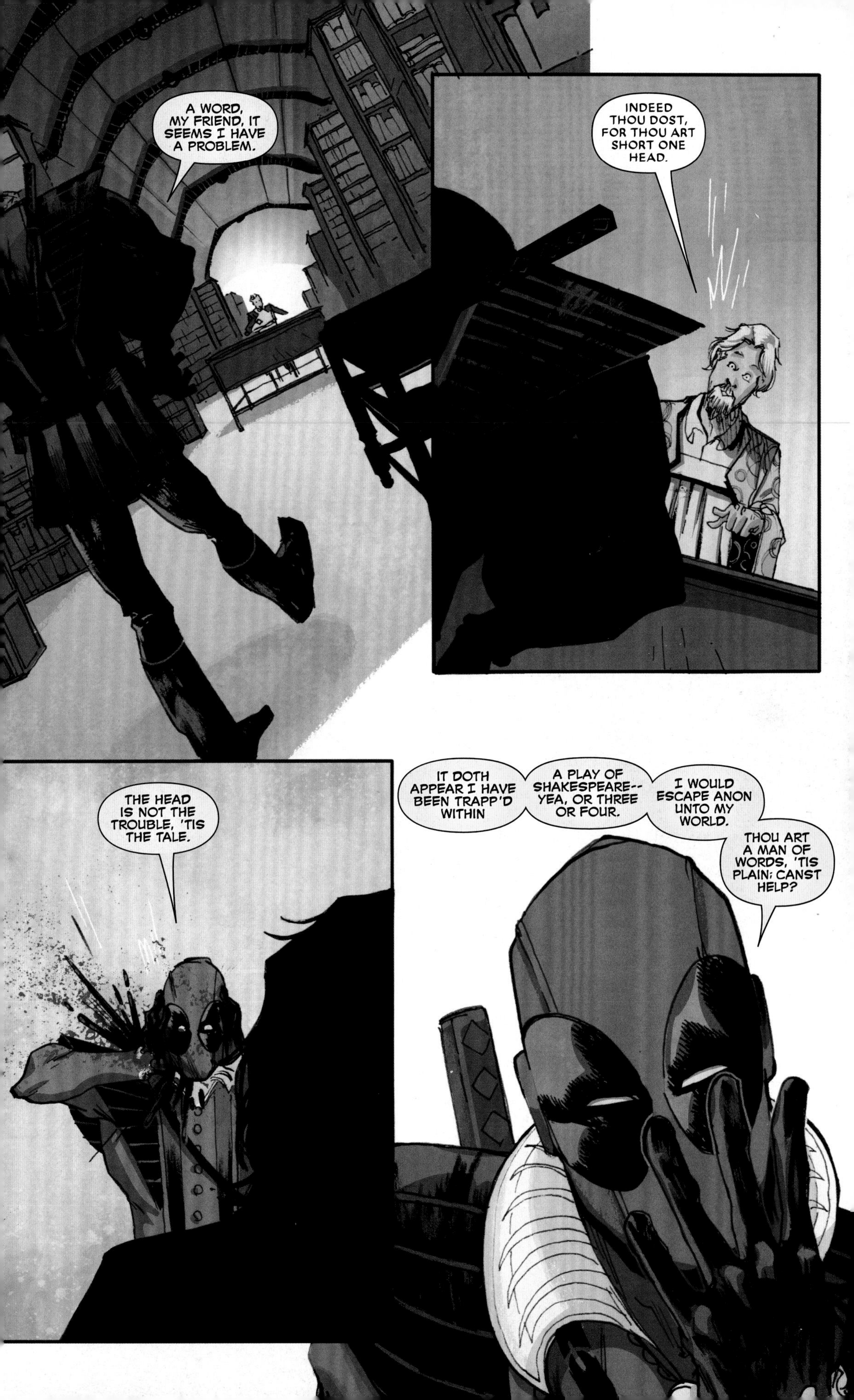
A WORD, MY FRIEND, IT SEEMS I HAVE A PROBLEM.
INDEED THOU DOST, FOR THOU ART SHORT ONE HEAD.
THE HEAD IS NOT THE TROUBLE, 'TIS THE TALE.
IT DOTH APPEAR I HAVE BEEN TRAPP'D WITHIN
A PLAY OF SHAKESPEARE-- YEA, OR THREE OR FOUR.
I WOULD ESCAPE ANON UNTO MY WORLD.
THOU ART A MAN OF WORDS, 'TIS PLAIN; CANST HELP?

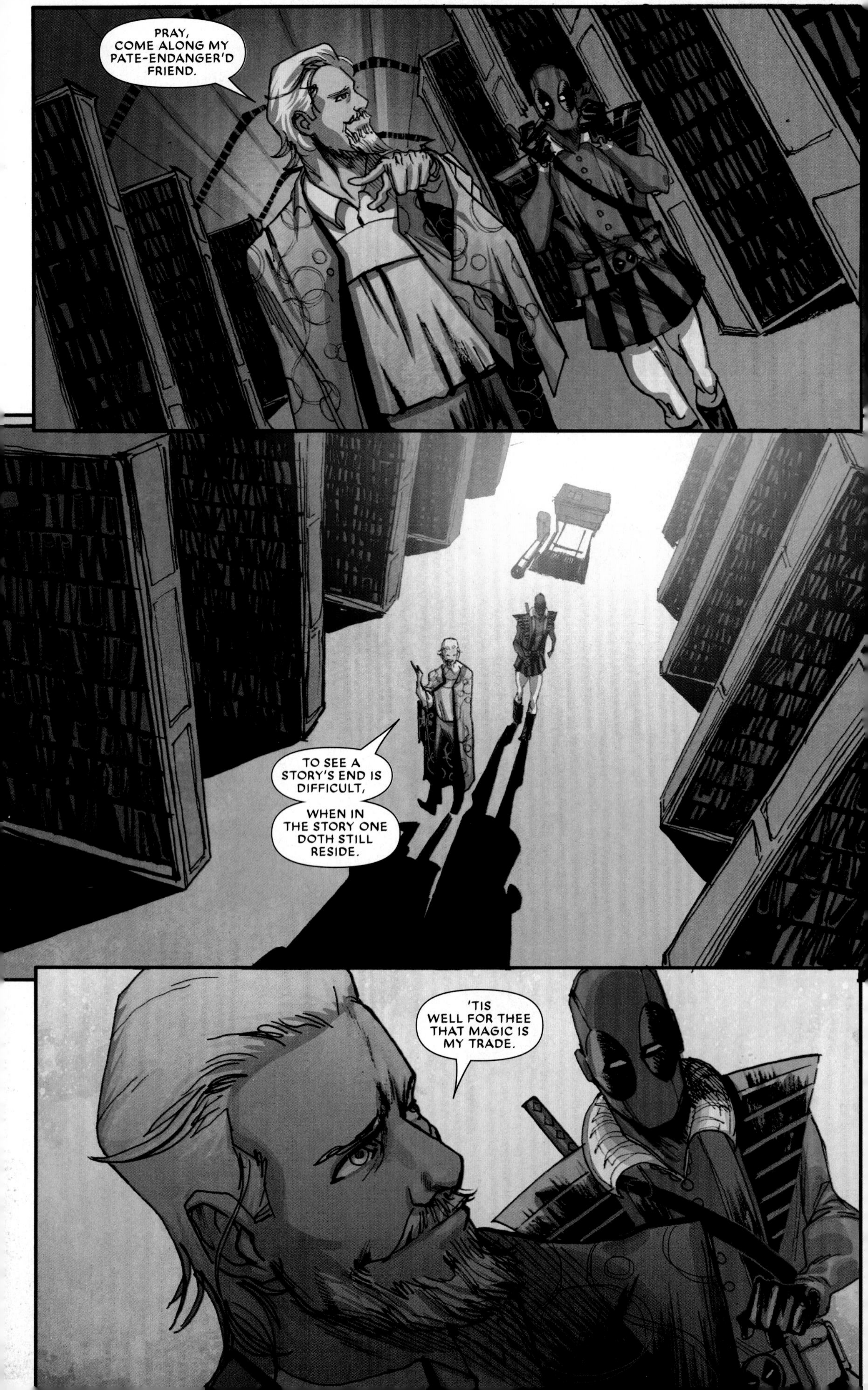
PRAY, COME ALONG MY PATE-ENDANGER'D FRIEND.
TO SEE A STORY'S END IS DIFFICULT,
WHEN IN THE STORY ONE DOTH STILL RESIDE.
'TIS WELL FOR THEE THAT MAGIC IS MY TRADE.

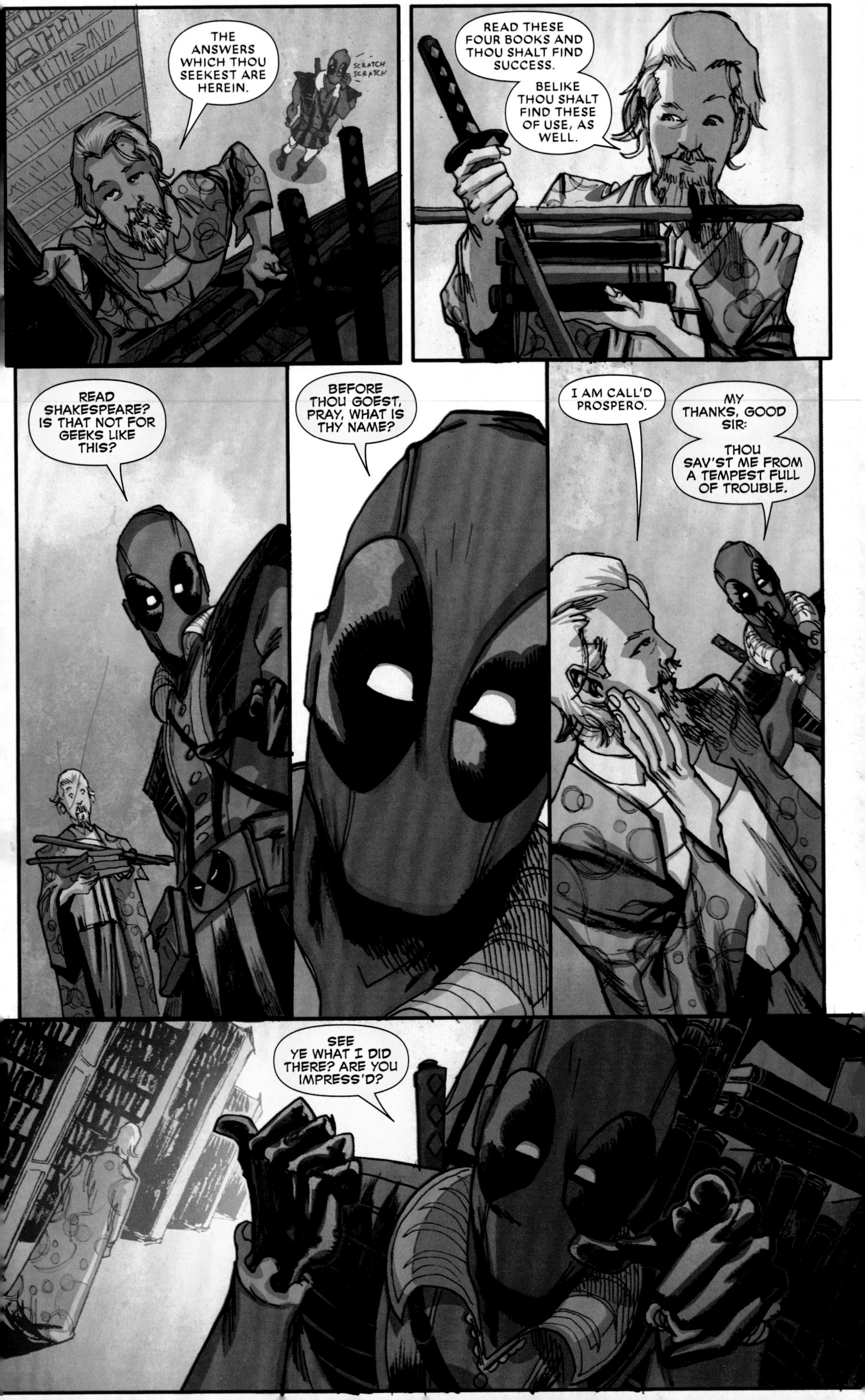
THE ANSWERS WHICH THOU SEEKEST ARE HEREIN.
SCRATCH SCRATCH
READ THESE FOUR BOOKS AND THOU SHALT FIND SUCCESS.
BELIKE THOU SHALT FIND THESE OF USE, AS WELL.
READ SHAKESPEARE? IS THAT NOT FOR GEEKS LIKE THIS?
BEFORE THOU GOEST, PRAY, WHAT IS THY NAME?
I AM CALL'D PROSPERO.
MY THANKS, GOOD SIR:
THOU SAV'ST ME FROM A TEMPEST FULL OF TROUBLE.
SEE YE WHAT I DID THERE? ARE YOU IMPRESS'D?

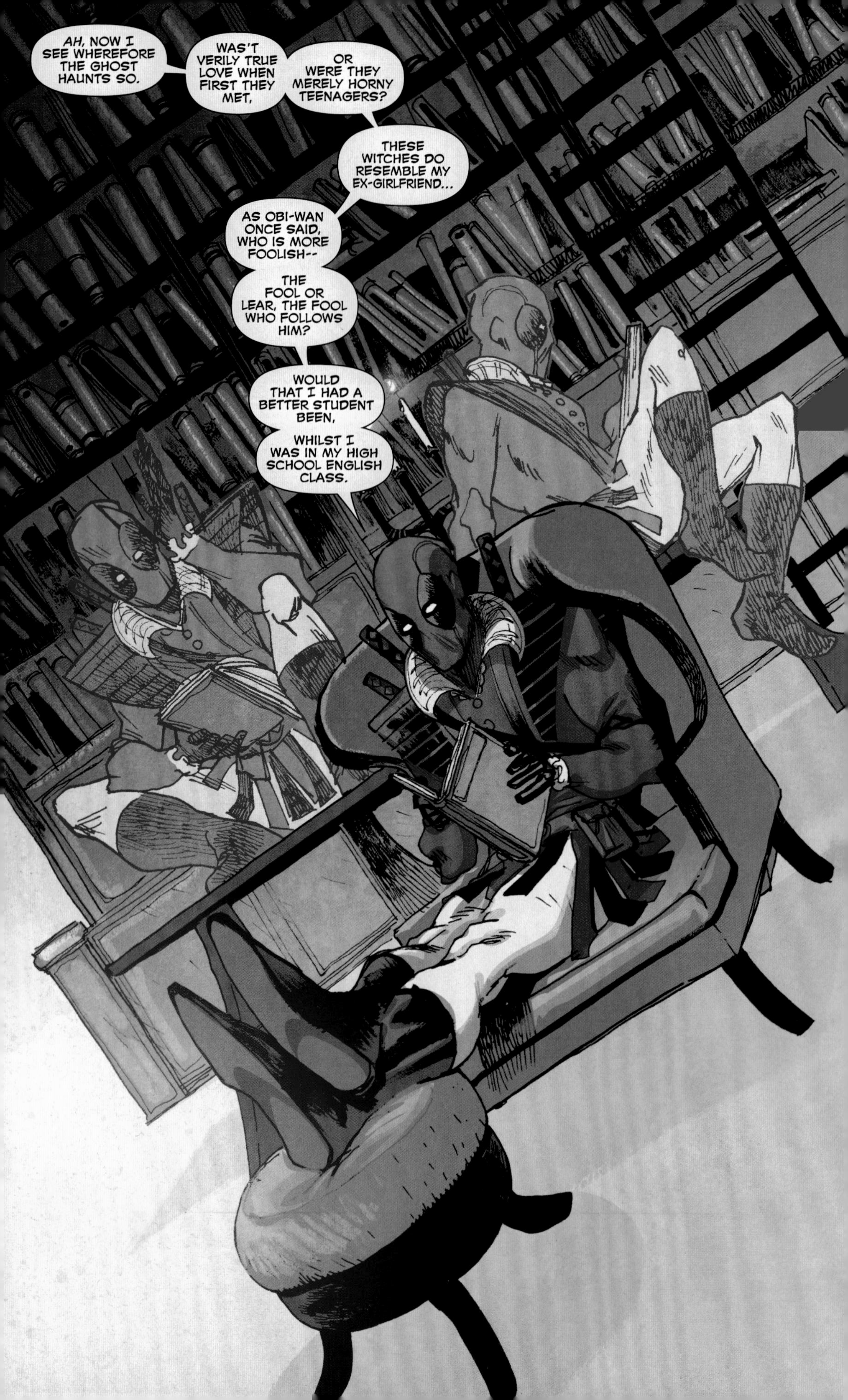
AH, NOW I SEE WHEREFORE THE GHOST HAUNTS SO.
WAS'T VERILY TRUE LOVE WHEN FIRST THEY MET,
OR WERE THEY MERELY HORNY TEENAGERS?
THESE WITCHES DO RESEMBLE MY EX-GIRLFRIEND...
AS OBI-WAN ONCE SAID, WHO IS MORE FOOLISH--
THE FOOL OR LEAR, THE FOOL WHO FOLLOWS HIM?
WOULD THAT I HAD A BETTER STUDENT BEEN,
WHILST I WAS IN MY HIGH SCHOOL ENGLISH CLASS.

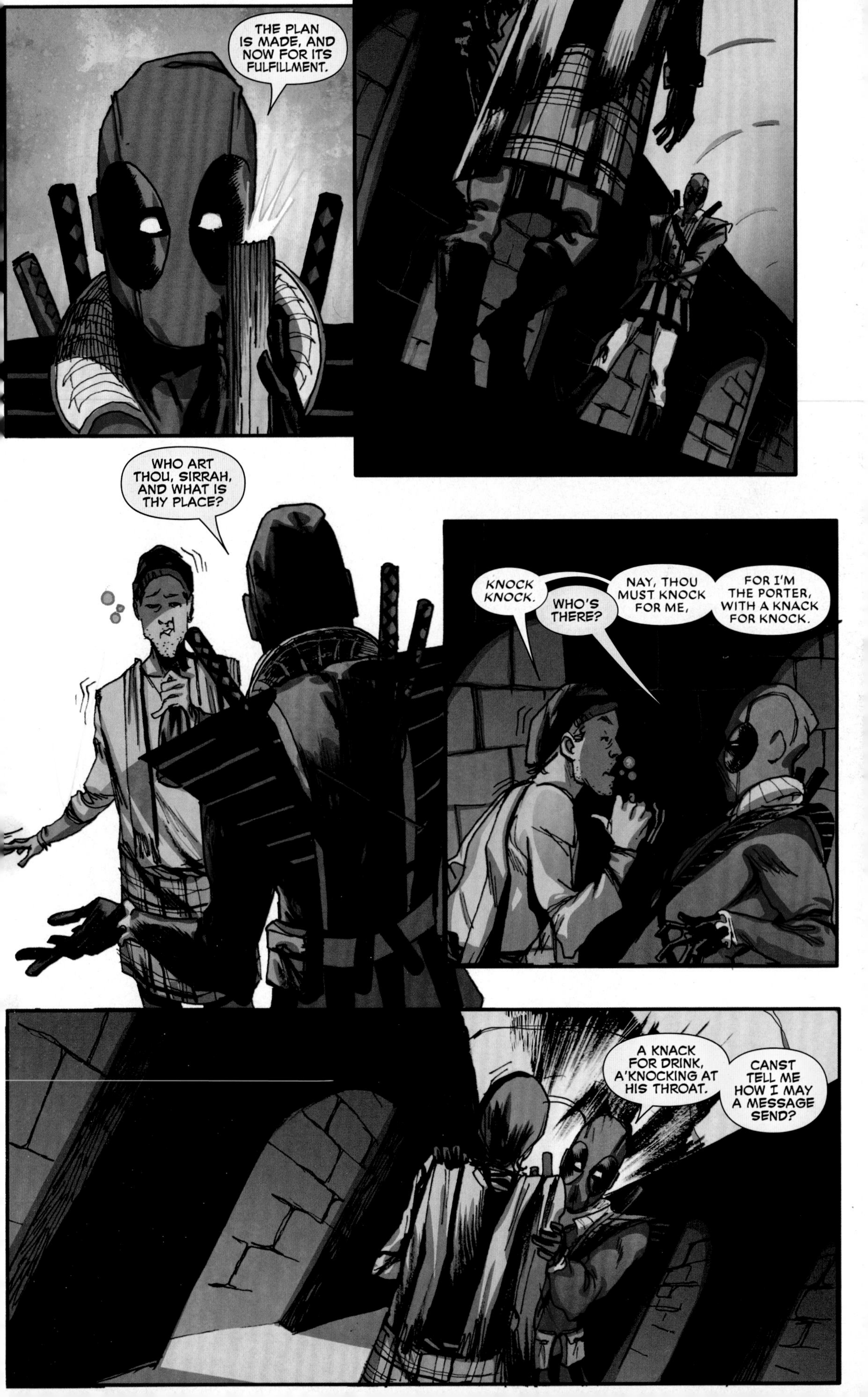
THE PLAN IS MADE, AND NOW FOR ITS FULFILLMENT.
WHO ART THOU, SIRRAH, AND WHAT IS THY PLACE?
KNOCK KNOCK.
WHO'S THERE?
NAY, THOU MUST KNOCK FOR ME,
FOR I'M THE PORTER, WITH A KNACK FOR KNOCK.
A KNACK FOR DRINK, A'KNOCKING AT HIS THROAT.
CANST TELL ME HOW I MAY A MESSAGE SEND?

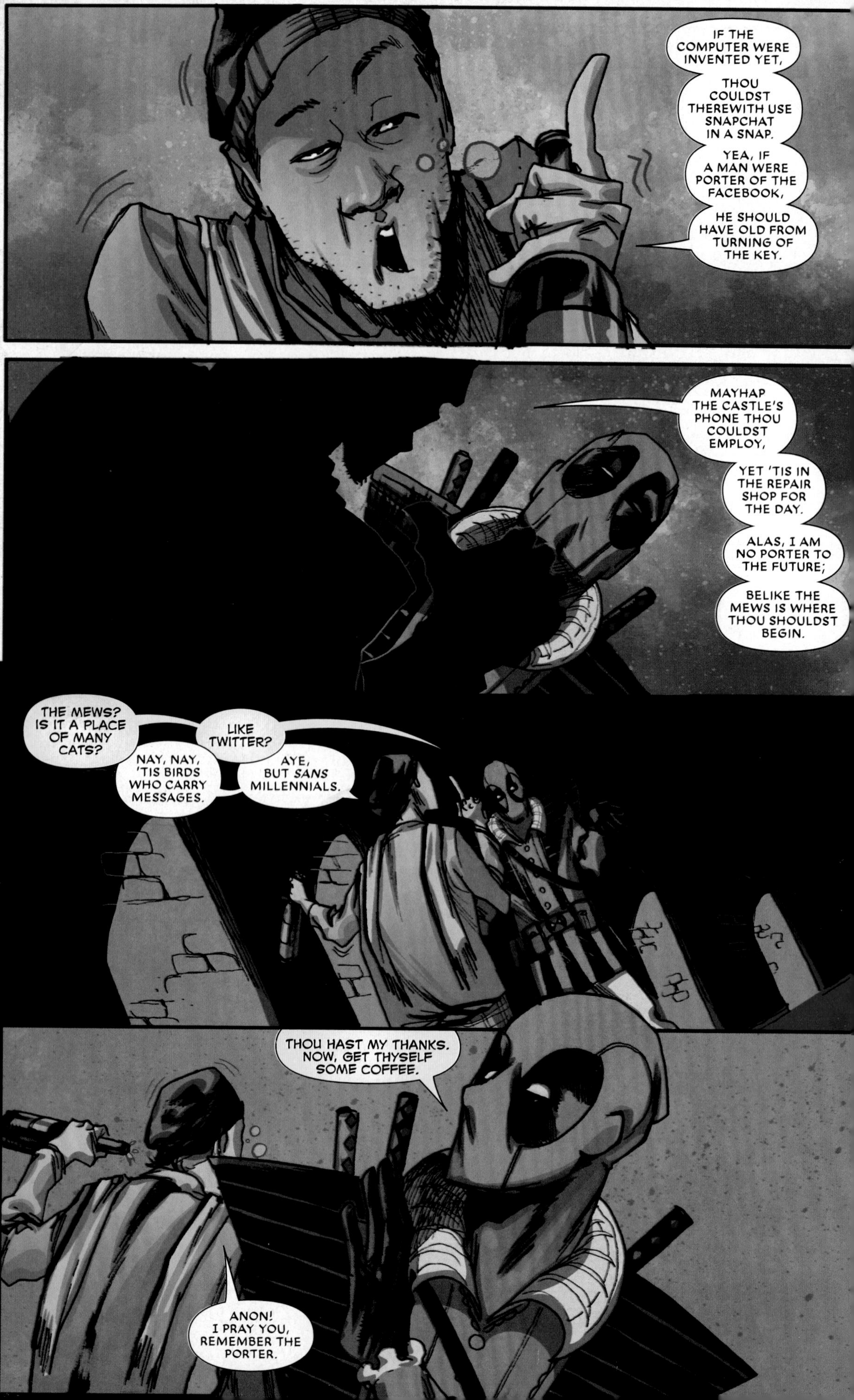
IF THE COMPUTER WERE INVENTED YET,
THOU COULDST THEREWITH USE SNAPCHAT IN A SNAP.
YEA, IF A MAN WERE PORTER OF THE FACEBOOK,
HE SHOULD HAVE OLD FROM TURNING OF THE KEY.
MAYHAP THE CASTLE'S PHONE THOU COULDST EMPLOY,
YET 'TIS IN THE REPAIR SHOP FOR THE DAY.
ALAS, I AM NO PORTER TO THE FUTURE;
BELIKE THE MEWS IS WHERE THOU SHOULDST BEGIN.
THE MEWS? IS IT A PLACE OF MANY CATS?
NAY, NAY, 'TIS BIRDS WHO CARRY MESSAGES.
LIKE TWITTER?
AYE, BUT *SANS* MILLENNIALS.
THOU HAST MY THANKS. NOW, GET THYSELF SOME COFFEE.
ANON! I PRAY YOU, REMEMBER THE PORTER.

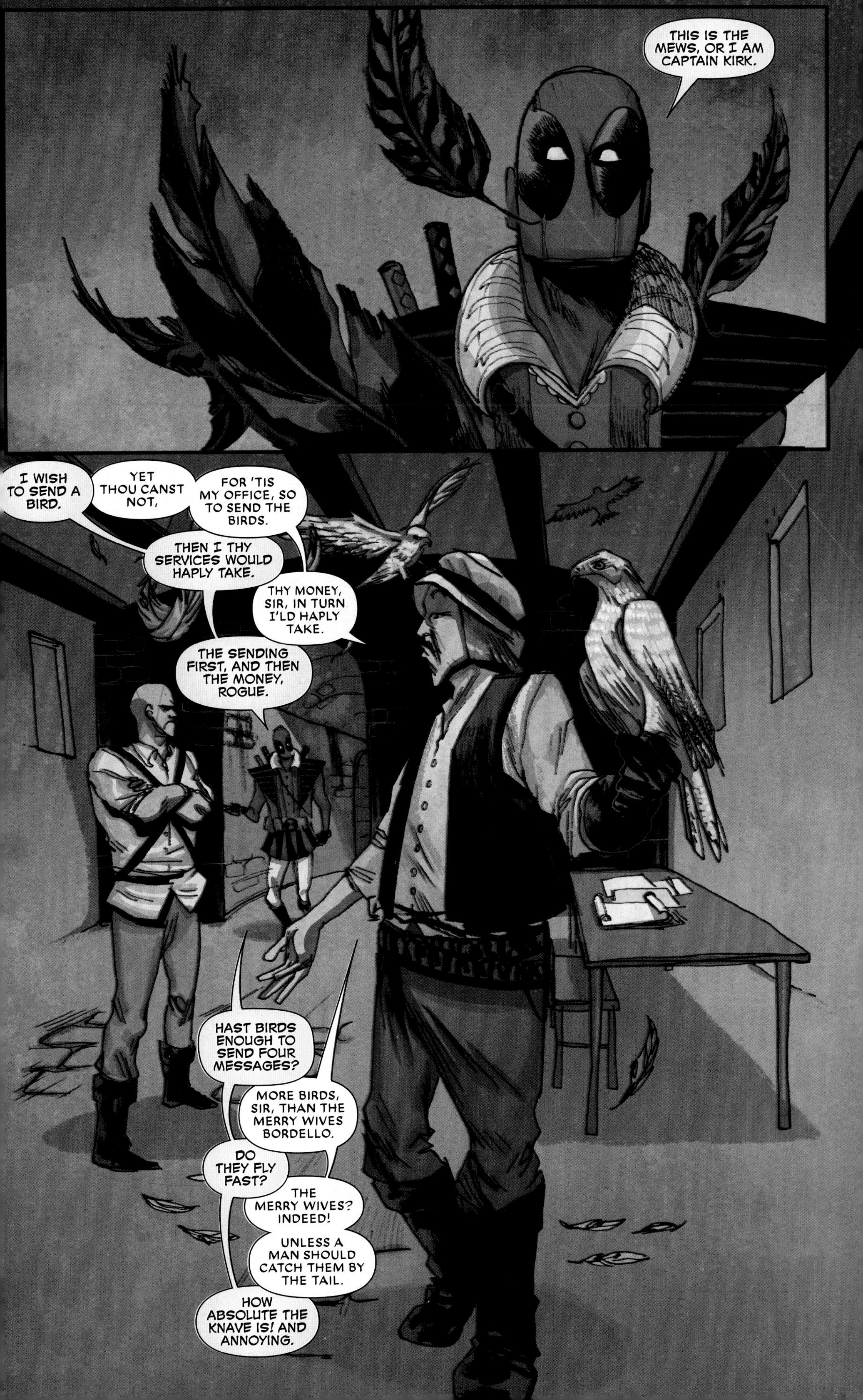
THIS IS THE MEWS, OR I AM CAPTAIN KIRK.
I WISH TO SEND A BIRD.
YET THOU CANST NOT,
FOR 'TIS MY OFFICE, SO TO SEND THE BIRDS.
THEN I THY SERVICES WOULD HAPLY TAKE.
THY MONEY, SIR, IN TURN I'LD HAPLY TAKE.
THE SENDING FIRST, AND THEN THE MONEY, ROGUE.
HAST BIRDS ENOUGH TO SEND FOUR MESSAGES?
MORE BIRDS, SIR, THAN THE MERRY WIVES BORDELLO.
DO THEY FLY FAST?
THE MERRY WIVES? INDEED!
UNLESS A MAN SHOULD CATCH THEM BY THE TAIL.
HOW ABSOLUTE THE KNAVE IS! AND ANNOYING.

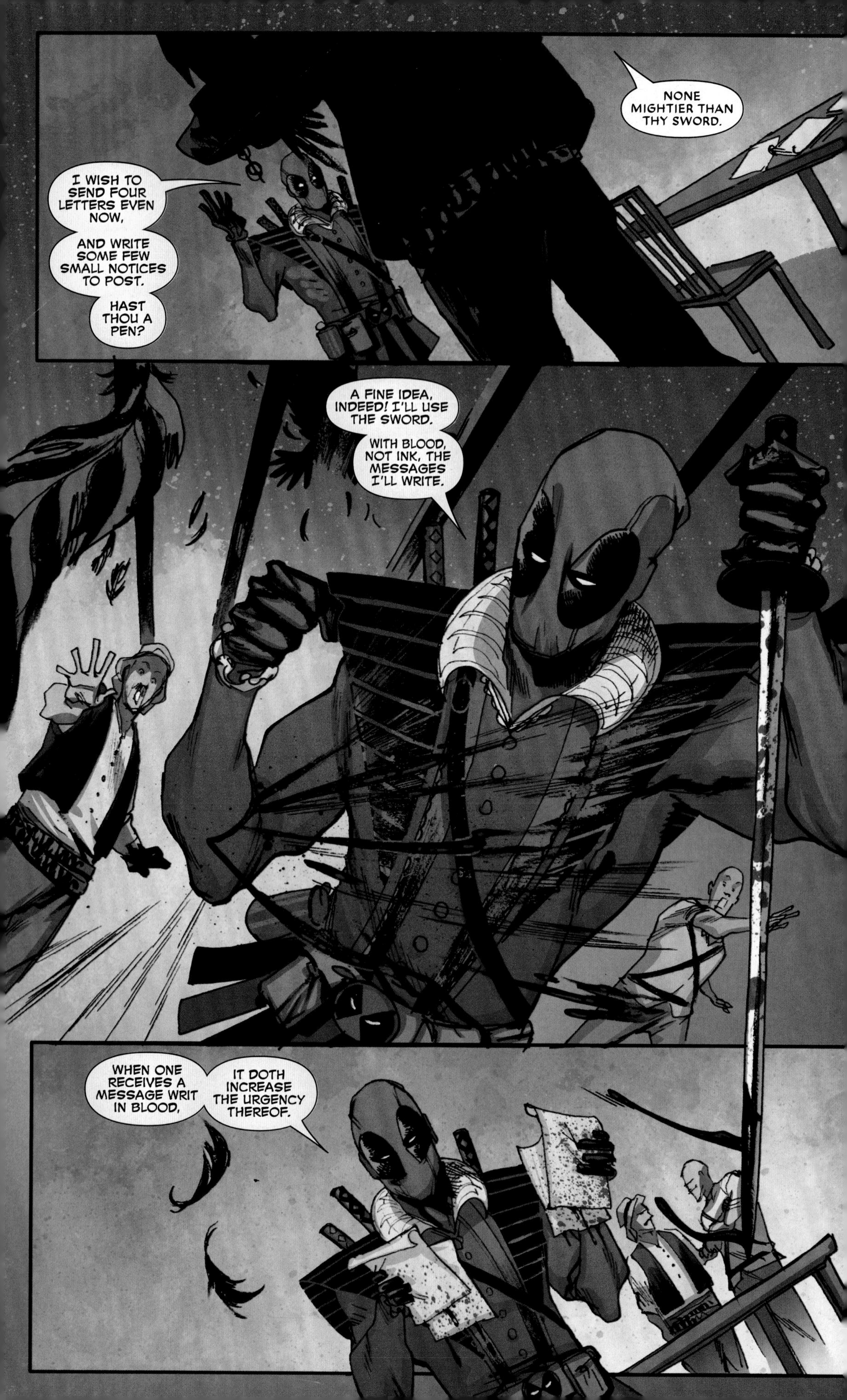
NONE MIGHTIER THAN THY SWORD.
I WISH TO SEND FOUR LETTERS EVEN NOW,
AND WRITE SOME FEW SMALL NOTICES TO POST.
HAST THOU A PEN?
A FINE IDEA, INDEED! I'LL USE THE SWORD.
WITH BLOOD, NOT INK, THE MESSAGES I'LL WRITE.
WHEN ONE RECEIVES A MESSAGE WRIT IN BLOOD,
IT DOTH INCREASE THE URGENCY THEREOF.

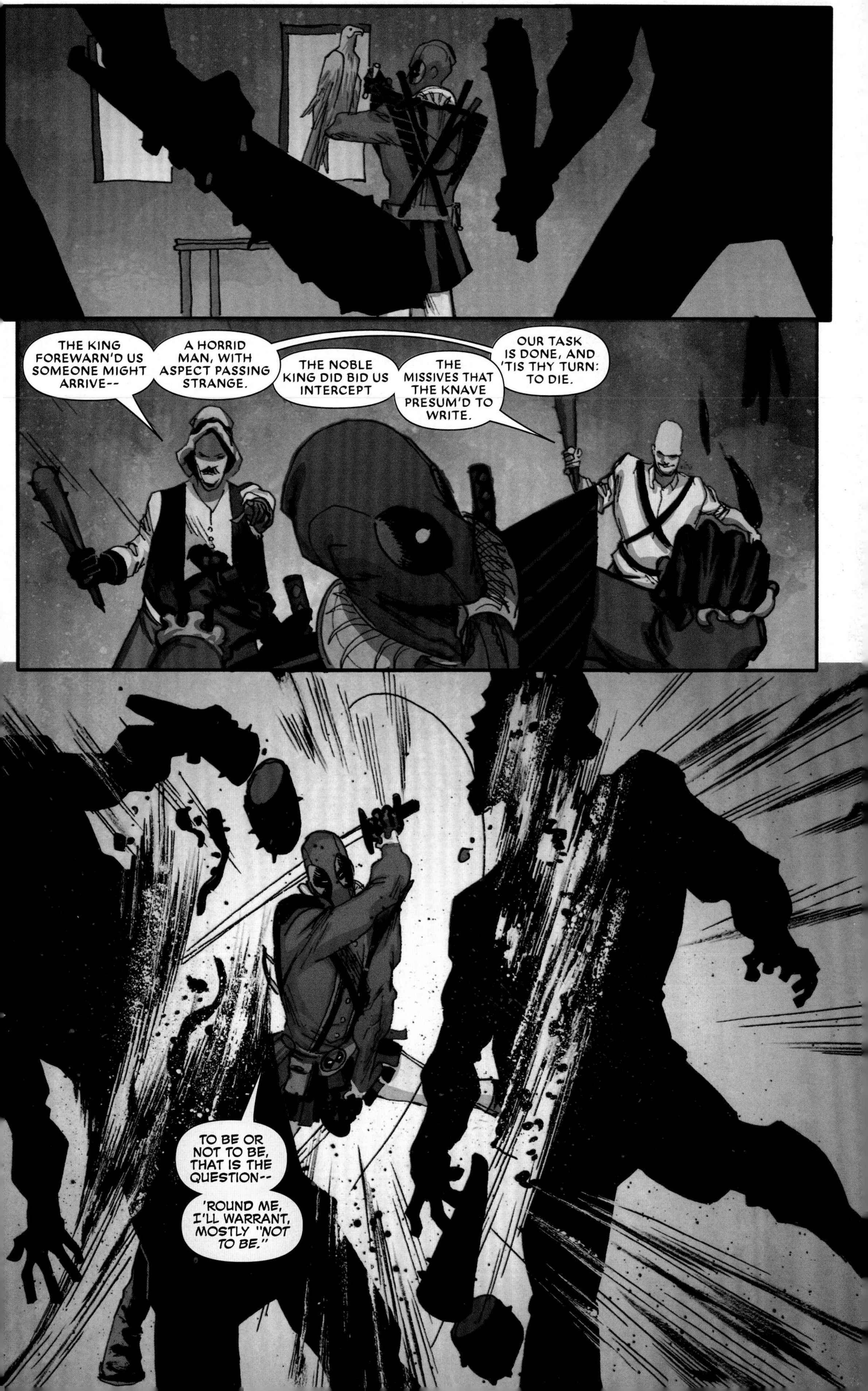
THE KING FOREWARN'D US SOMEONE MIGHT ARRIVE--
A HORRID MAN, WITH ASPECT PASSING STRANGE.
THE NOBLE KING DID BID US INTERCEPT
THE MISSIVES THAT THE KNAVE PRESUM'D TO WRITE.
OUR TASK IS DONE, AND 'TIS THY TURN: TO DIE.
TO BE OR NOT TO BE, THAT IS THE QUESTION--
'ROUND ME, I'LL WARRANT, MOSTLY "NOT TO BE."

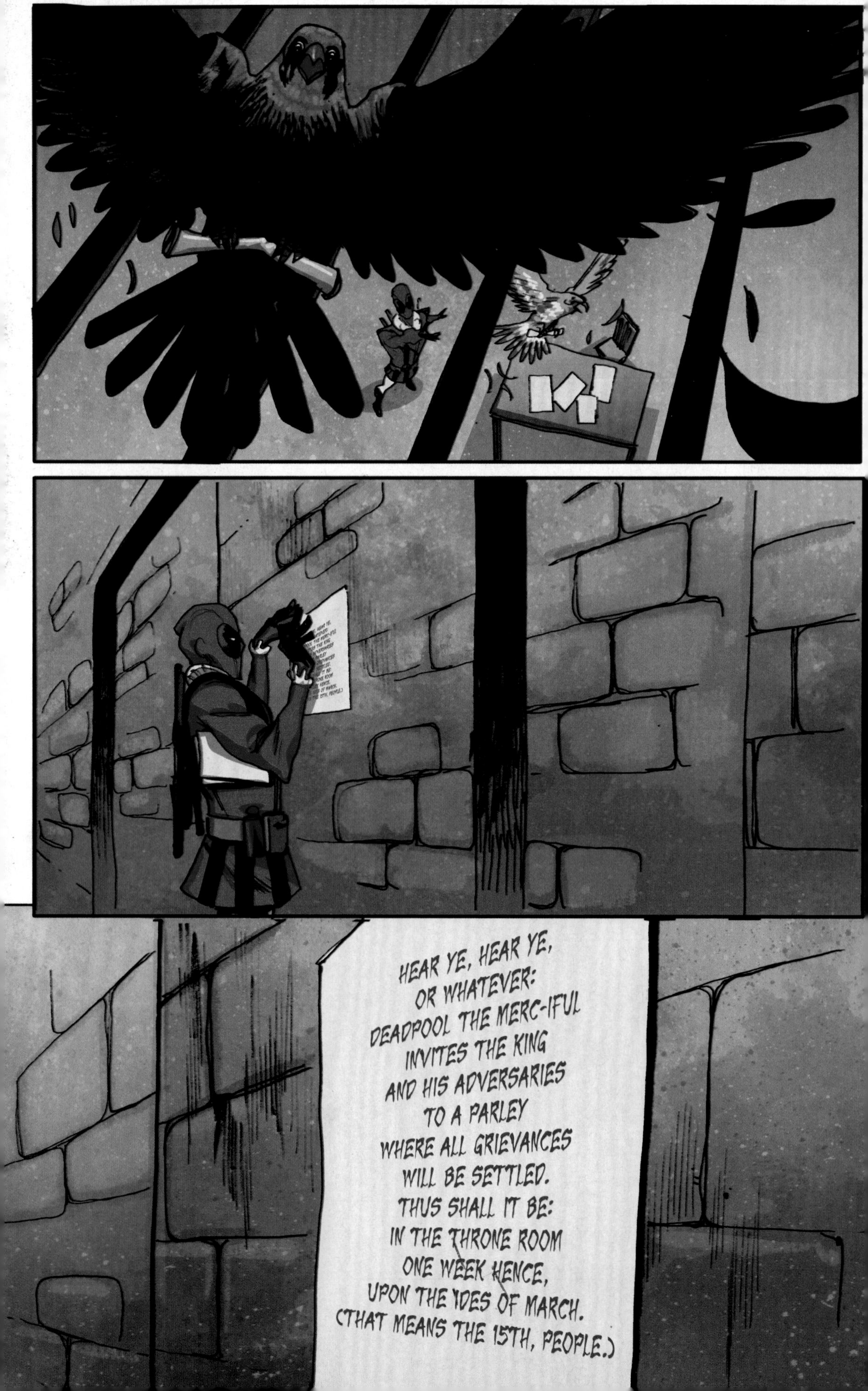
HEAR YE, HEAR YE,
OR WHATEVER:
DEADPOOL THE MERC-IFUL
INVITES THE KING
AND HIS ADVERSARIES
TO A PARLEY
WHERE ALL GRIEVANCES
WILL BE SETTLED.
THUS SHALL IT BE:
IN THE THRONE ROOM
ONE WEEK HENCE,
UPON THE IDES OF MARCH.
(THAT MEANS THE 15TH, PEOPLE.)

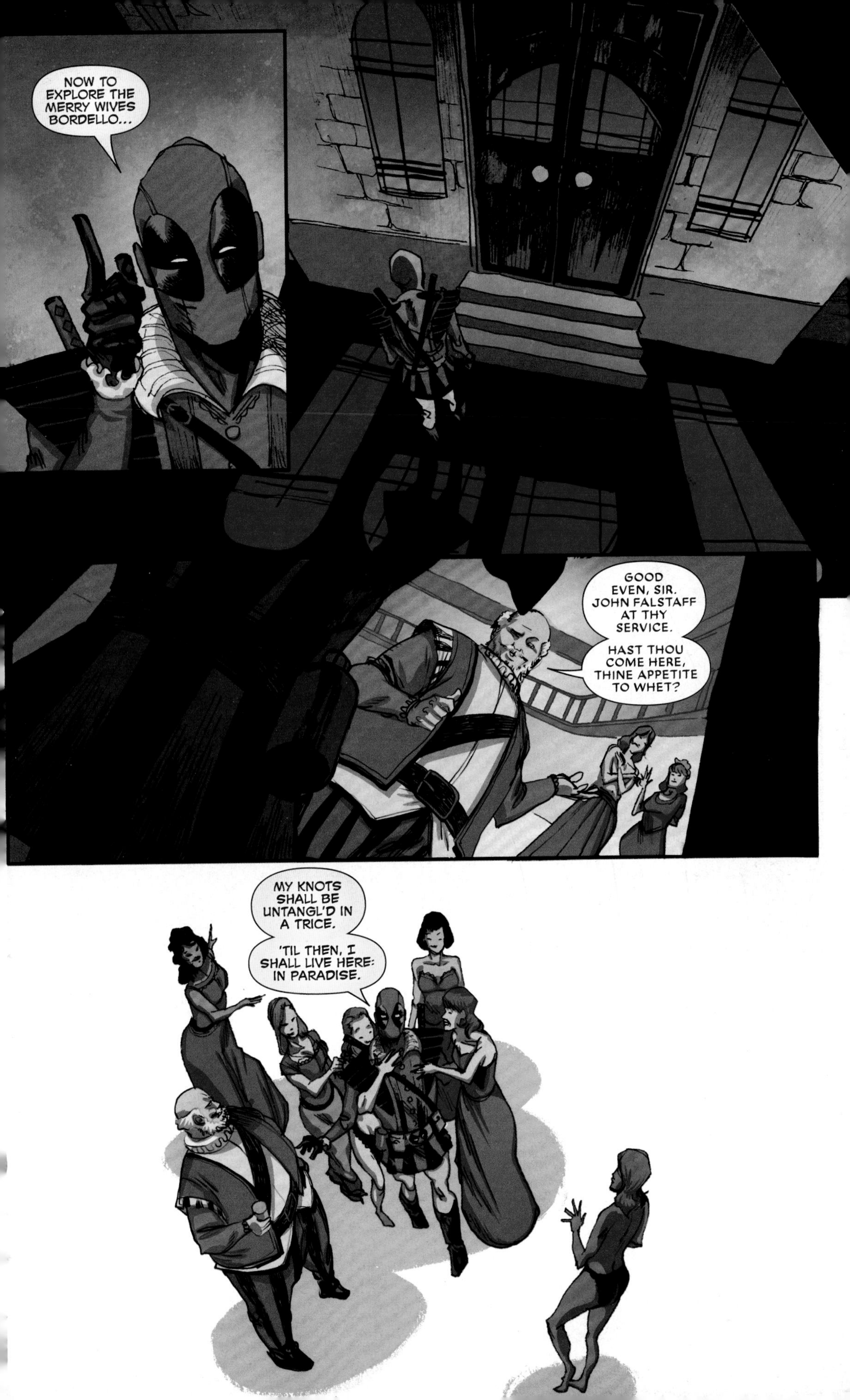
NOW TO EXPLORE THE MERRY WIVES BORDELLO...
GOOD EVEN, SIR. JOHN FALSTAFF AT THY SERVICE.
HAST THOU COME HERE, THINE APPETITE TO WHET?
MY KNOTS SHALL BE UNTANGL'D IN A TRICE.
'TIL THEN, I SHALL LIVE HERE: IN PARADISE.

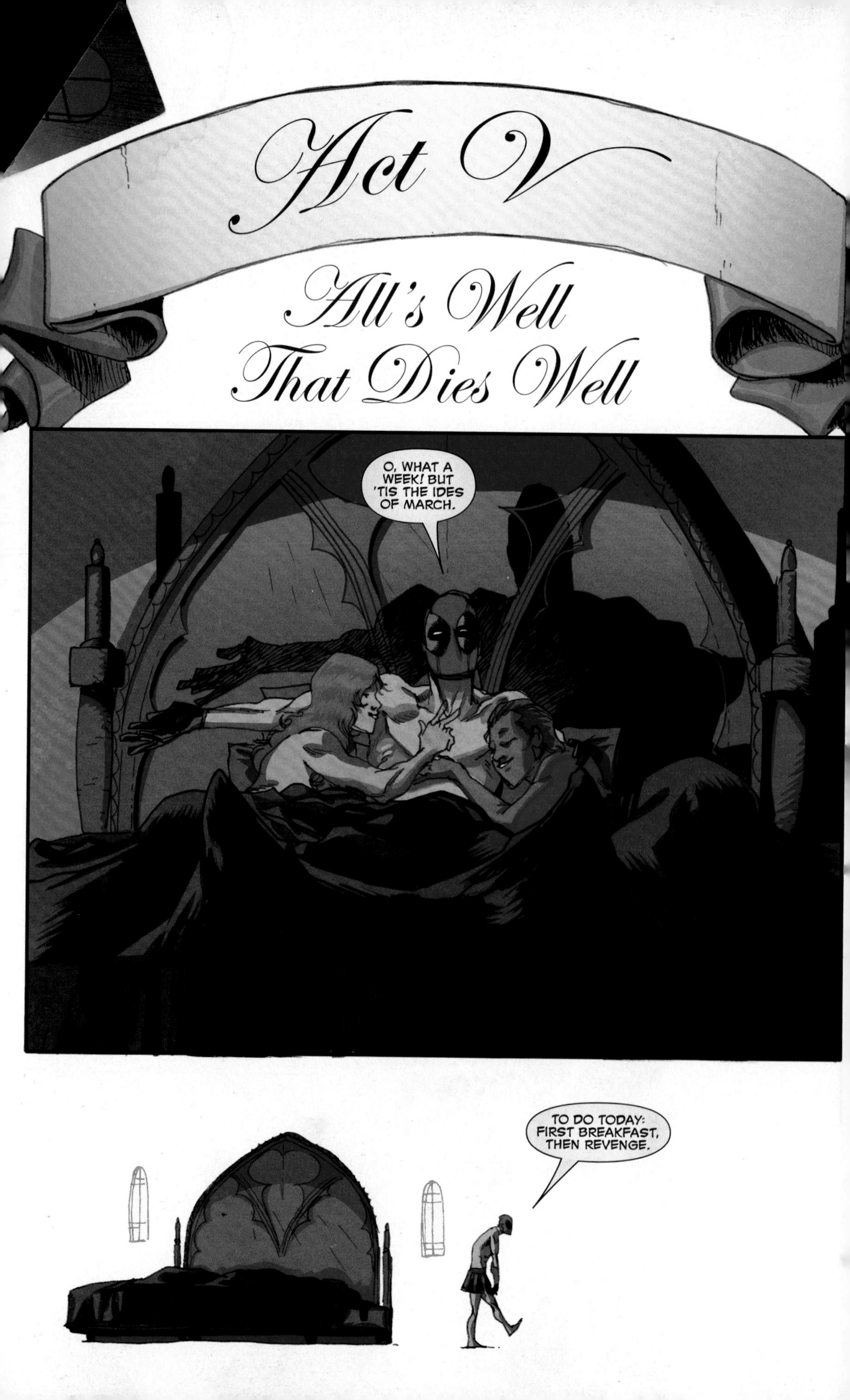
Act V
All's Well That Dies Well
O, WHAT A WEEK! BUT 'TIS THE IDES OF MARCH.
TO DO TODAY: FIRST BREAKFAST, THEN REVENGE.

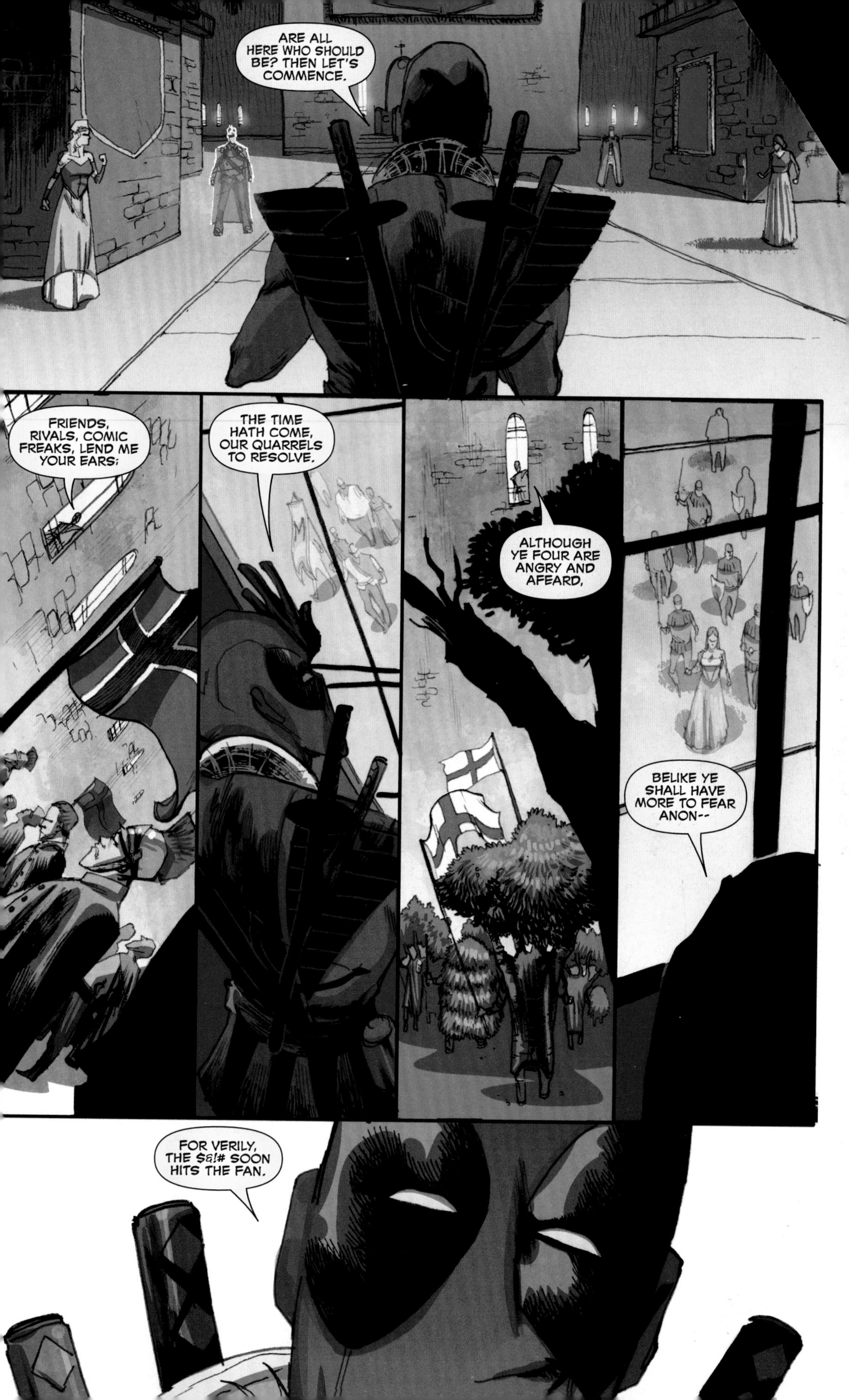
ARE ALL HERE WHO SHOULD BE? THEN LET'S COMMENCE.
FRIENDS, RIVALS, COMIC FREAKS, LEND ME YOUR EARS;
THE TIME HATH COME, OUR QUARRELS TO RESOLVE.
ALTHOUGH YE FOUR ARE ANGRY AND AFEARD,
BELIKE YE SHALL HAVE MORE TO FEAR ANON--
FOR VERILY, THE $&!# SOON HITS THE FAN.

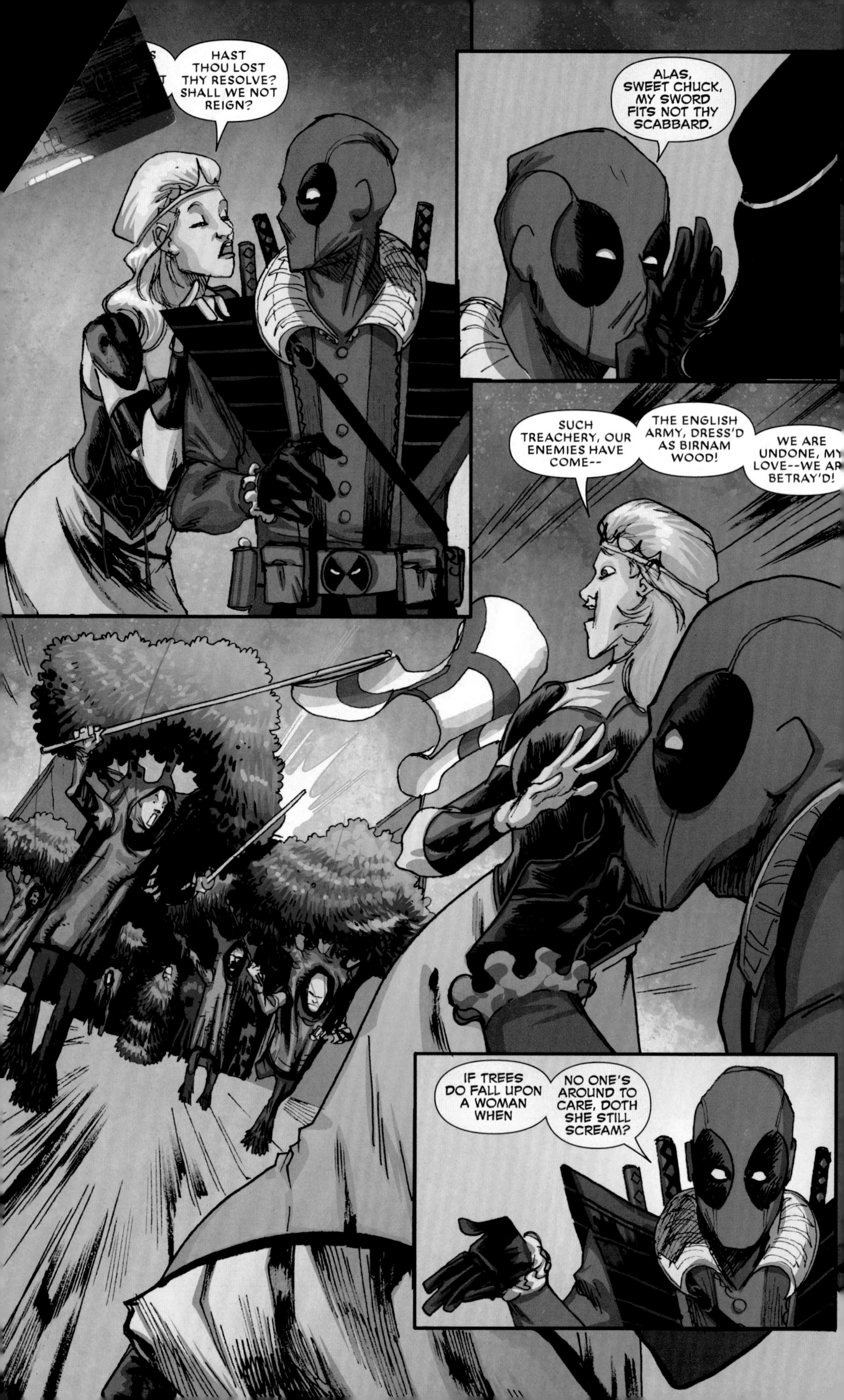

HAST THOU LOST THY RESOLVE? SHALL WE NOT REIGN?
ALAS, SWEET CHUCK, MY SWORD FITS NOT THY SCABBARD.
SUCH TREACHERY, OUR ENEMIES HAVE COME--
THE ENGLISH ARMY, DRESS'D AS BIRNAM WOOD!
WE ARE UNDONE, MY LOVE--WE AR BETRAY'D!
IF TREES DO FALL UPON A WOMAN WHEN
NO ONE'S AROUND TO CARE, DOTH SHE STILL SCREAM?

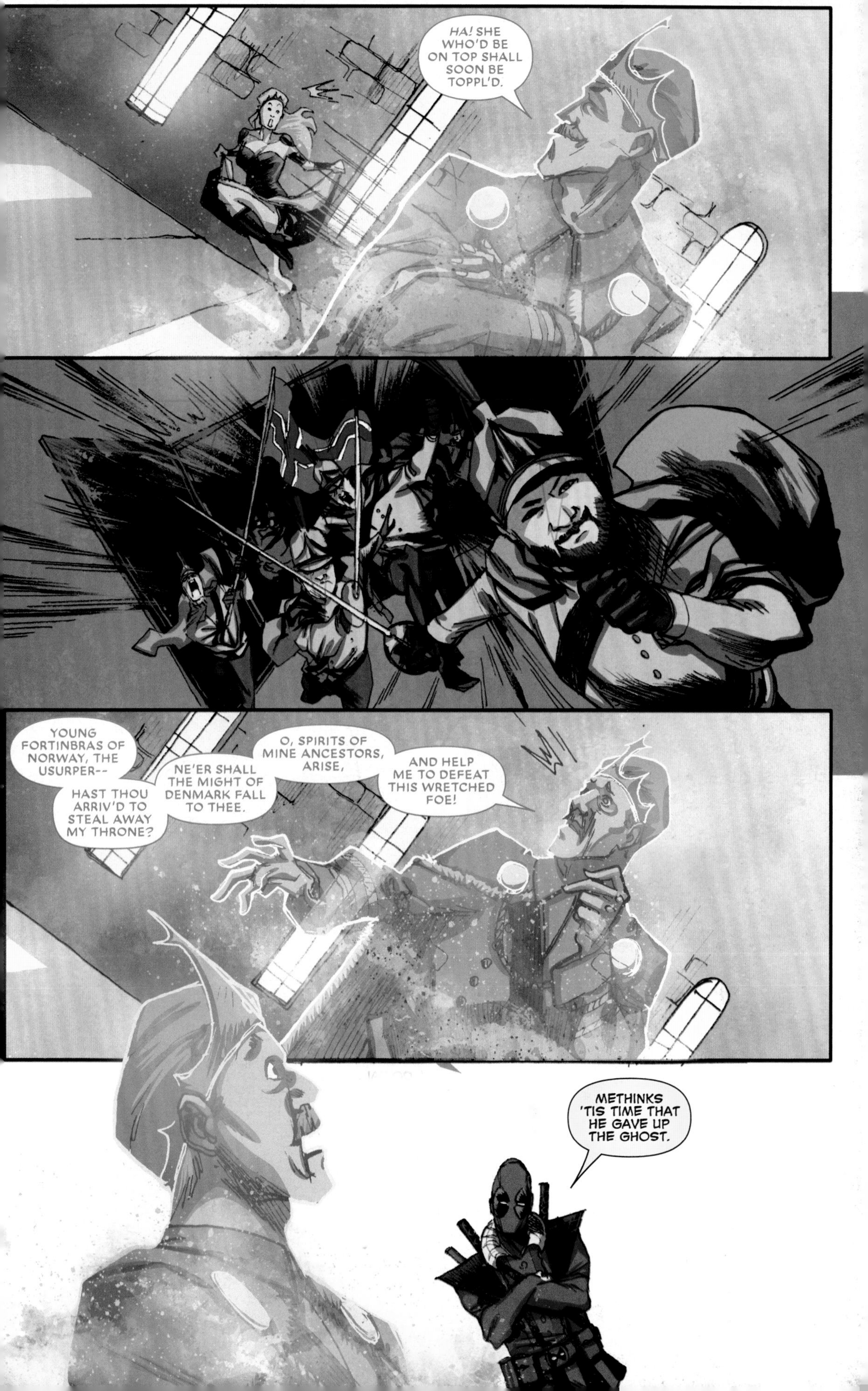
HA! SHE WHO'D BE ON TOP SHALL SOON BE TOPPL'D.
YOUNG FORTINBRAS OF NORWAY, THE USURPER--
HAST THOU ARRIV'D TO STEAL AWAY MY THRONE?
NE'ER SHALL THE MIGHT OF DENMARK FALL TO THEE.
O, SPIRITS OF MINE ANCESTORS, ARISE,
AND HELP ME TO DEFEAT THIS WRETCHED FOE!
METHINKS 'TIS TIME THAT HE GAVE UP THE GHOST.

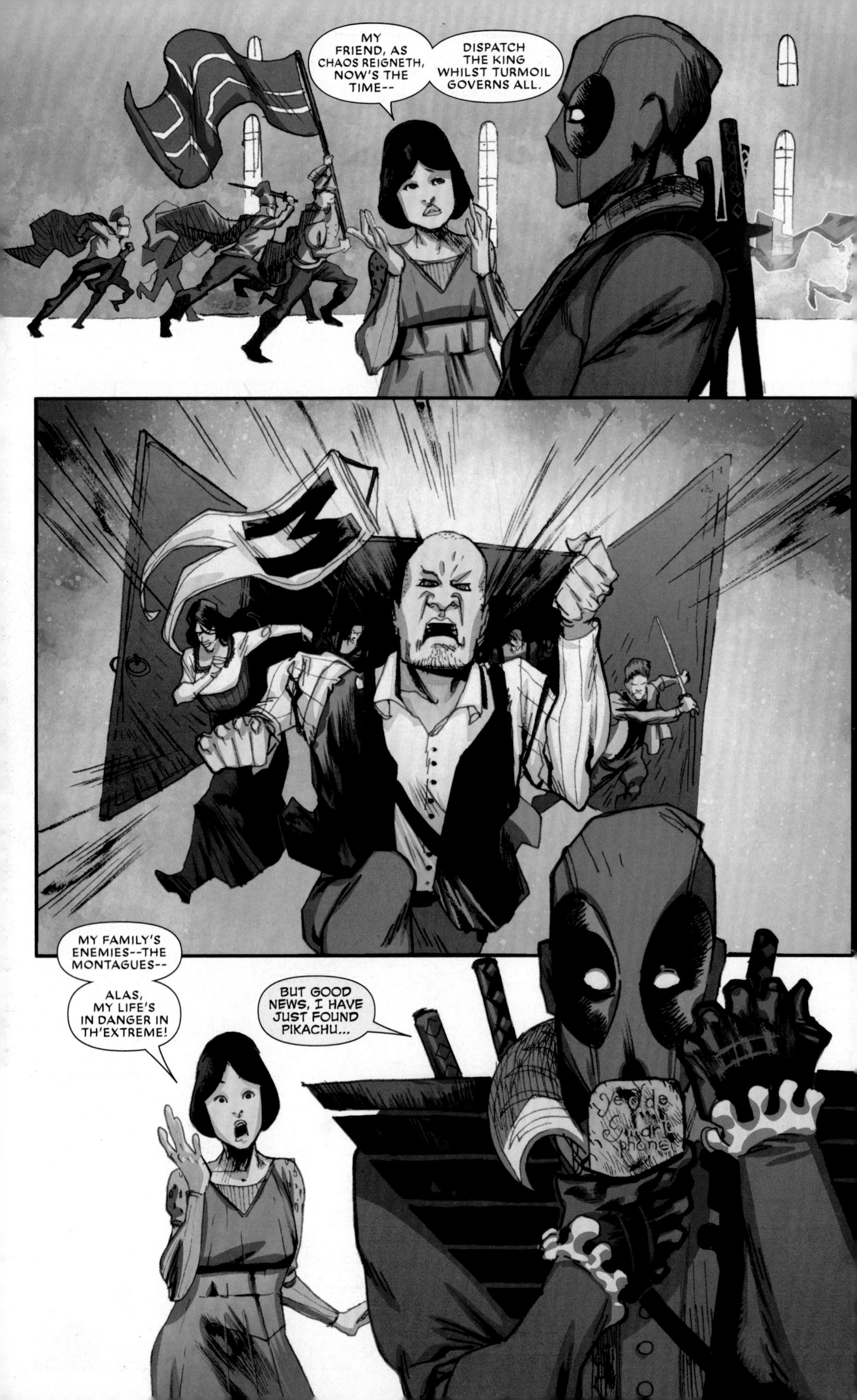
MY FRIEND, AS CHAOS REIGNETH, NOW'S THE TIME--
DISPATCH THE KING WHILST TURMOIL GOVERNS ALL.
MY FAMILY'S ENEMIES--THE MONTAGUES--
ALAS, MY LIFE'S IN DANGER IN TH'EXTREME!
BUT GOOD NEWS, I HAVE JUST FOUND PIKACHU...

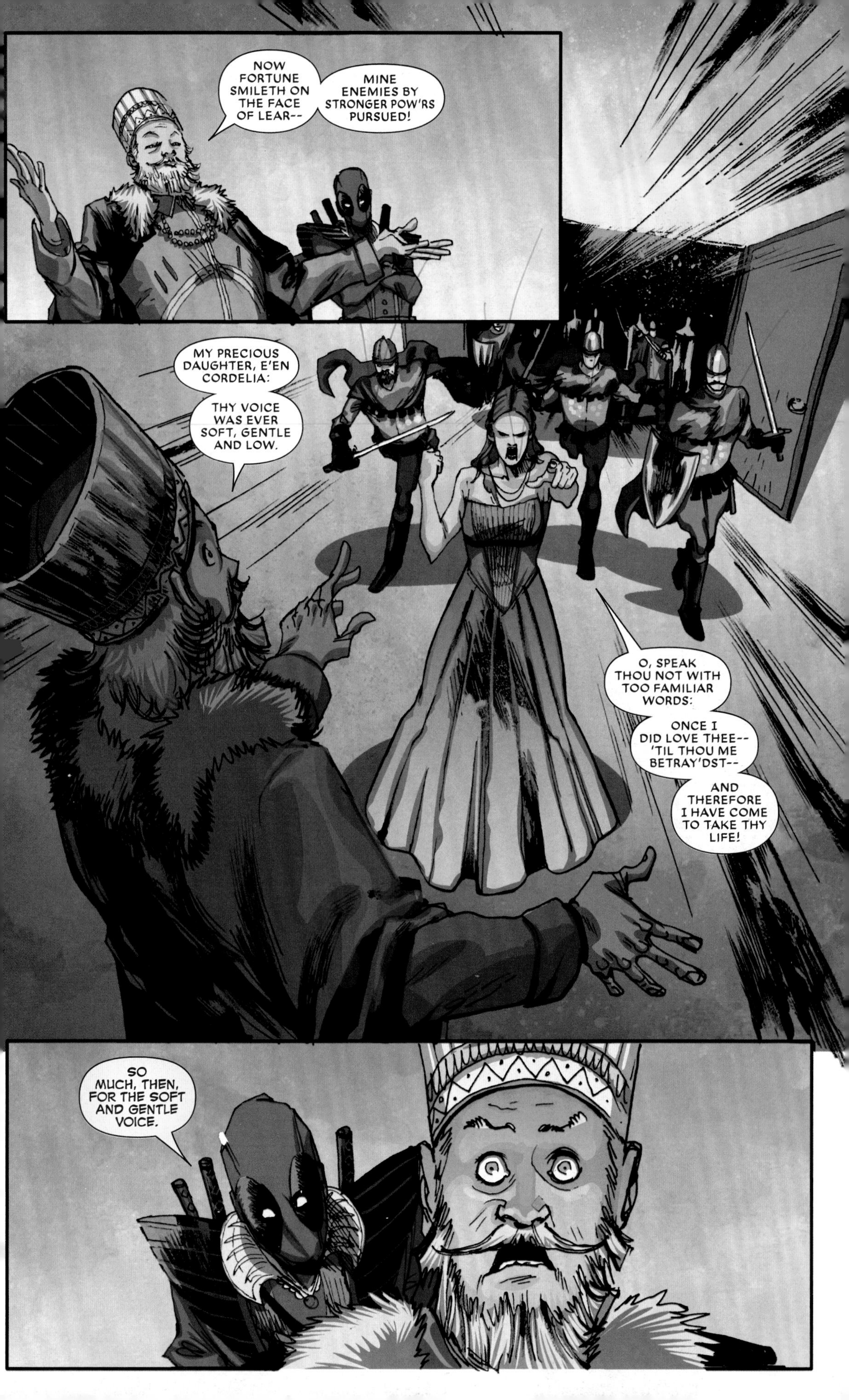
NOW FORTUNE SMILETH ON THE FACE OF LEAR--
MINE ENEMIES BY STRONGER POW'RS PURSUED!
MY PRECIOUS DAUGHTER, E'EN CORDELIA:
THY VOICE WAS EVER SOFT, GENTLE AND LOW.
O, SPEAK THOU NOT WITH TOO FAMILIAR WORDS:
ONCE I DID LOVE THEE-- 'TIL THOU ME BETRAY'DST--
AND THEREFORE I HAVE COME TO TAKE THY LIFE!
SO MUCH, THEN, FOR THE SOFT AND GENTLE VOICE.

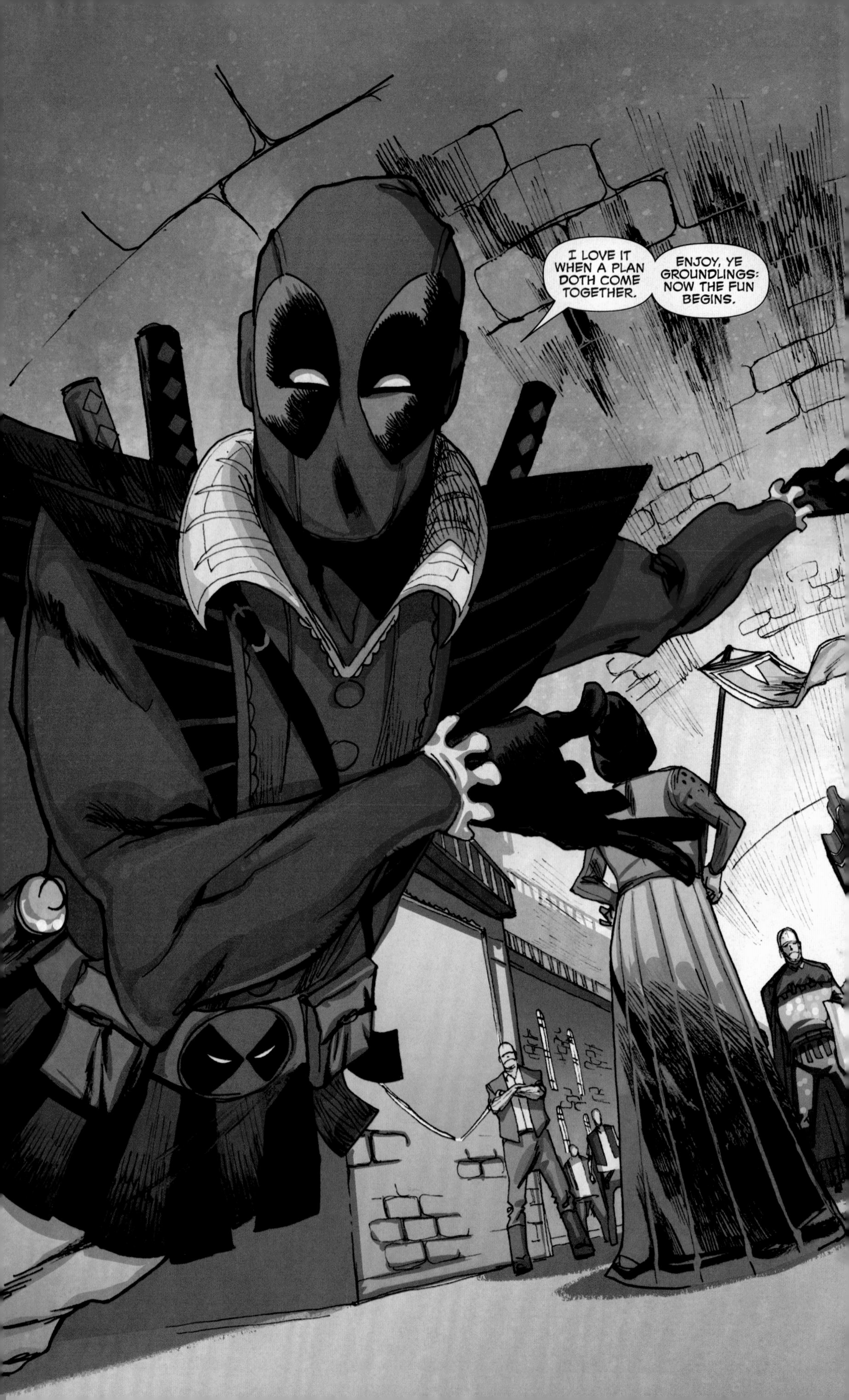
I LOVE IT WHEN A PLAN DOTH COME TOGETHER.
ENJOY, YE GROUNDLINGS: NOW THE FUN BEGINS.

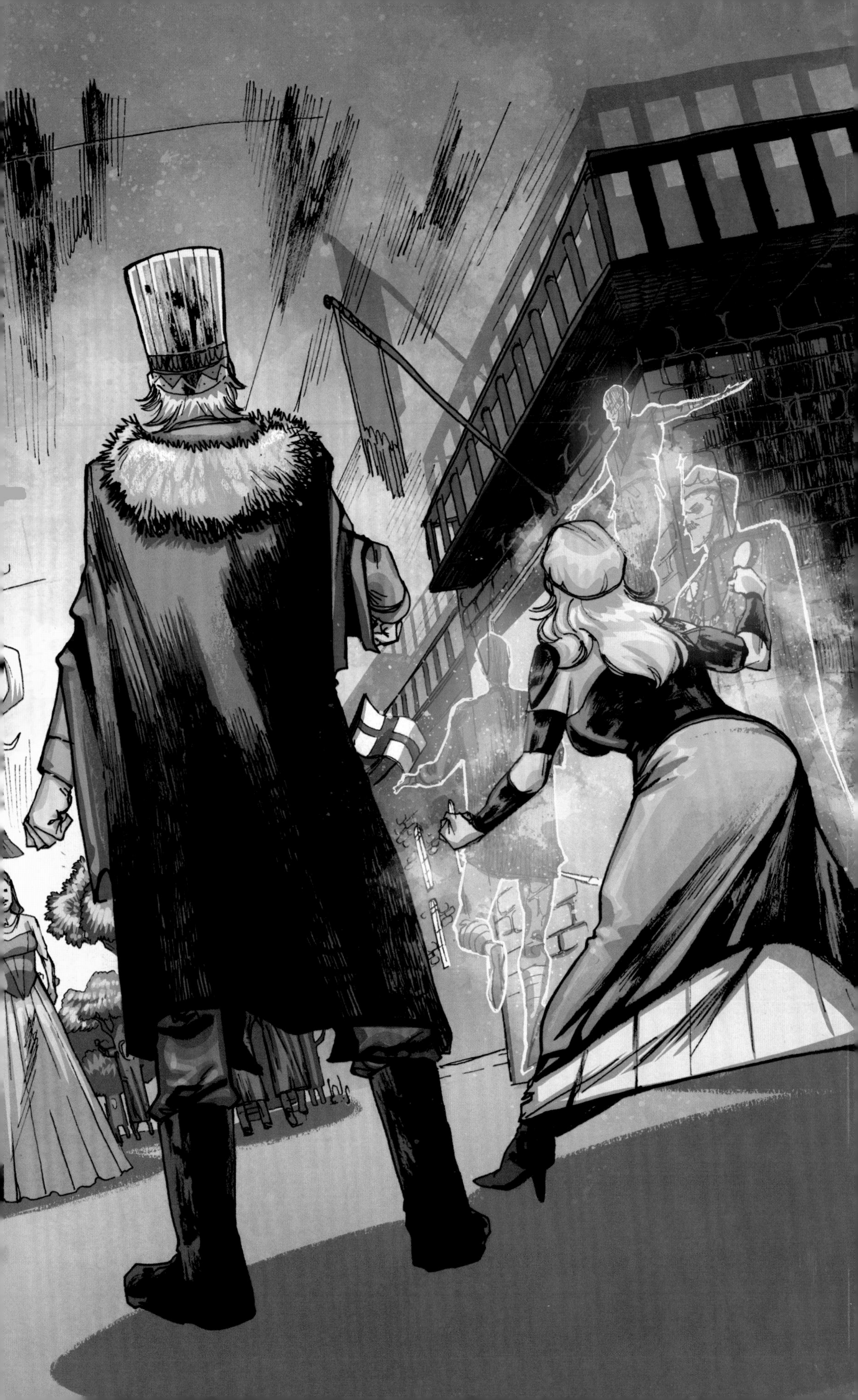

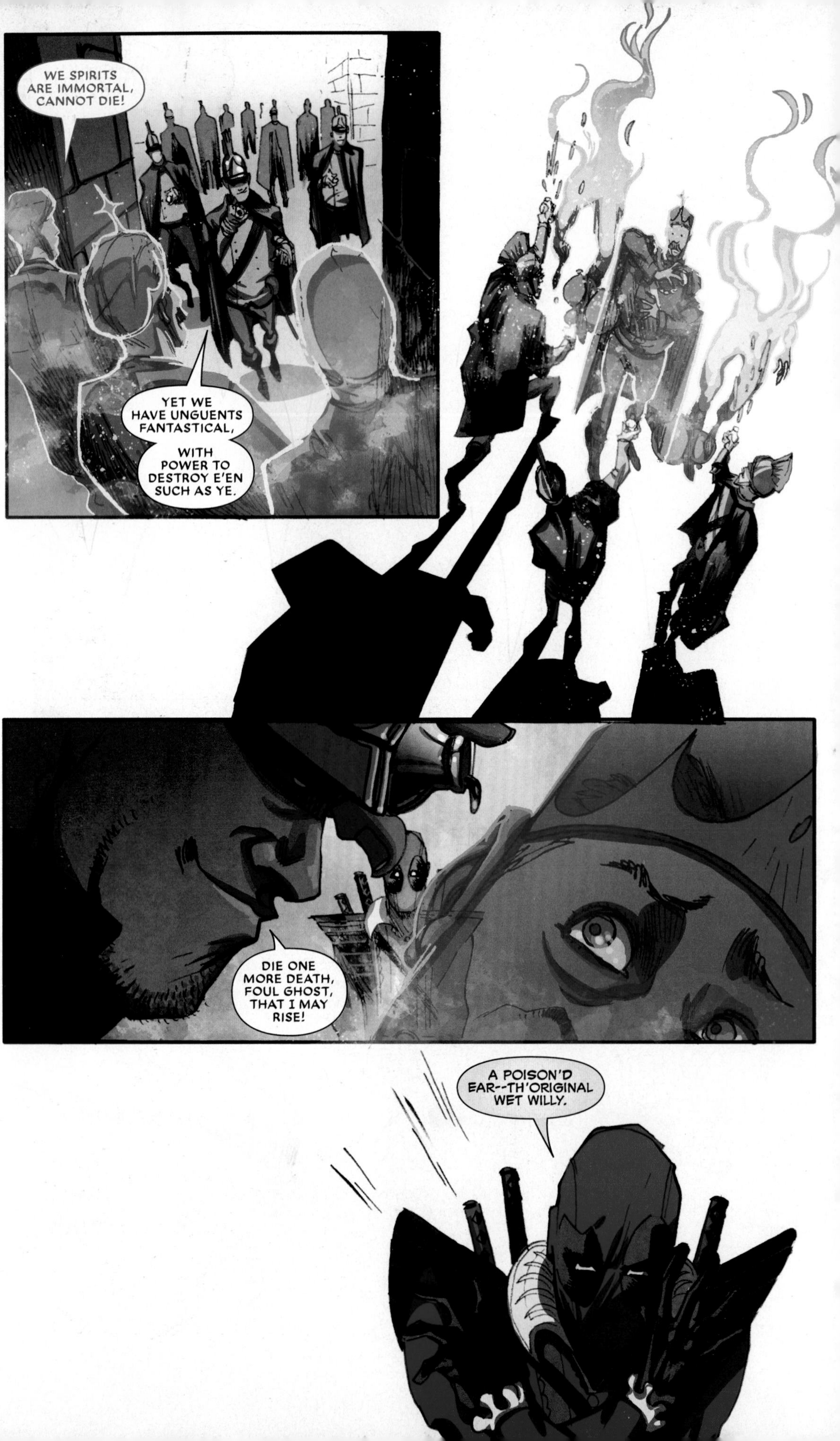
WE SPIRITS ARE IMMORTAL, CANNOT DIE!
YET WE HAVE UNGUENTS FANTASTICAL,
WITH POWER TO DESTROY E'EN SUCH AS YE.
DIE ONE MORE DEATH, FOUL GHOST, THAT I MAY RISE!
A POISON'D EAR--TH'ORIGINAL WET WILLY.

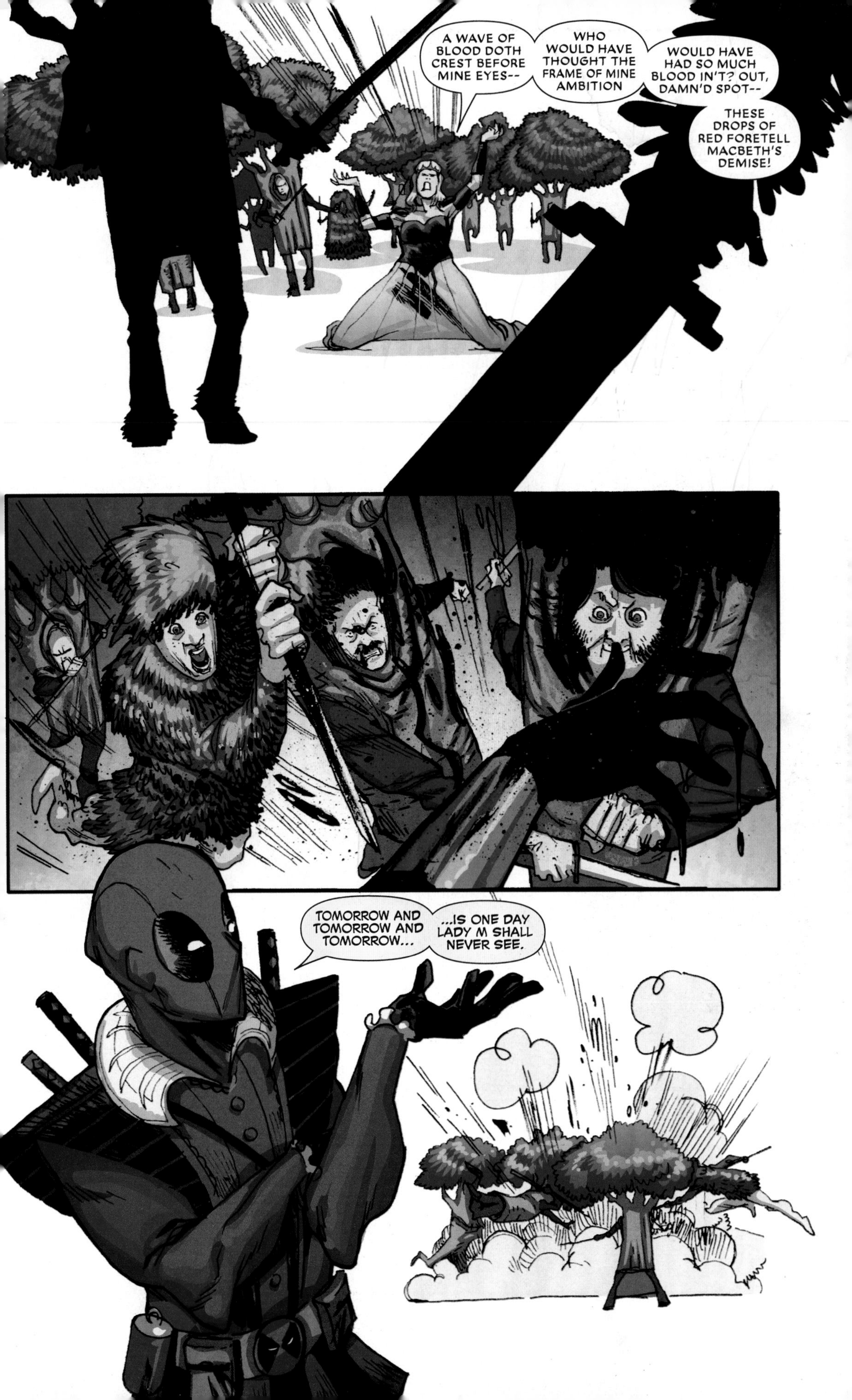
A WAVE OF BLOOD DOTH CREST BEFORE MINE EYES--
WHO WOULD HAVE THOUGHT THE FRAME OF MINE AMBITION
WOULD HAVE HAD SO MUCH BLOOD IN'T? OUT, DAMN'D SPOT--
THESE DROPS OF RED FORETELL MACBETH'S DEMISE!
TOMORROW AND TOMORROW AND TOMORROW...
...IS ONE DAY LADY M SHALL NEVER SEE.

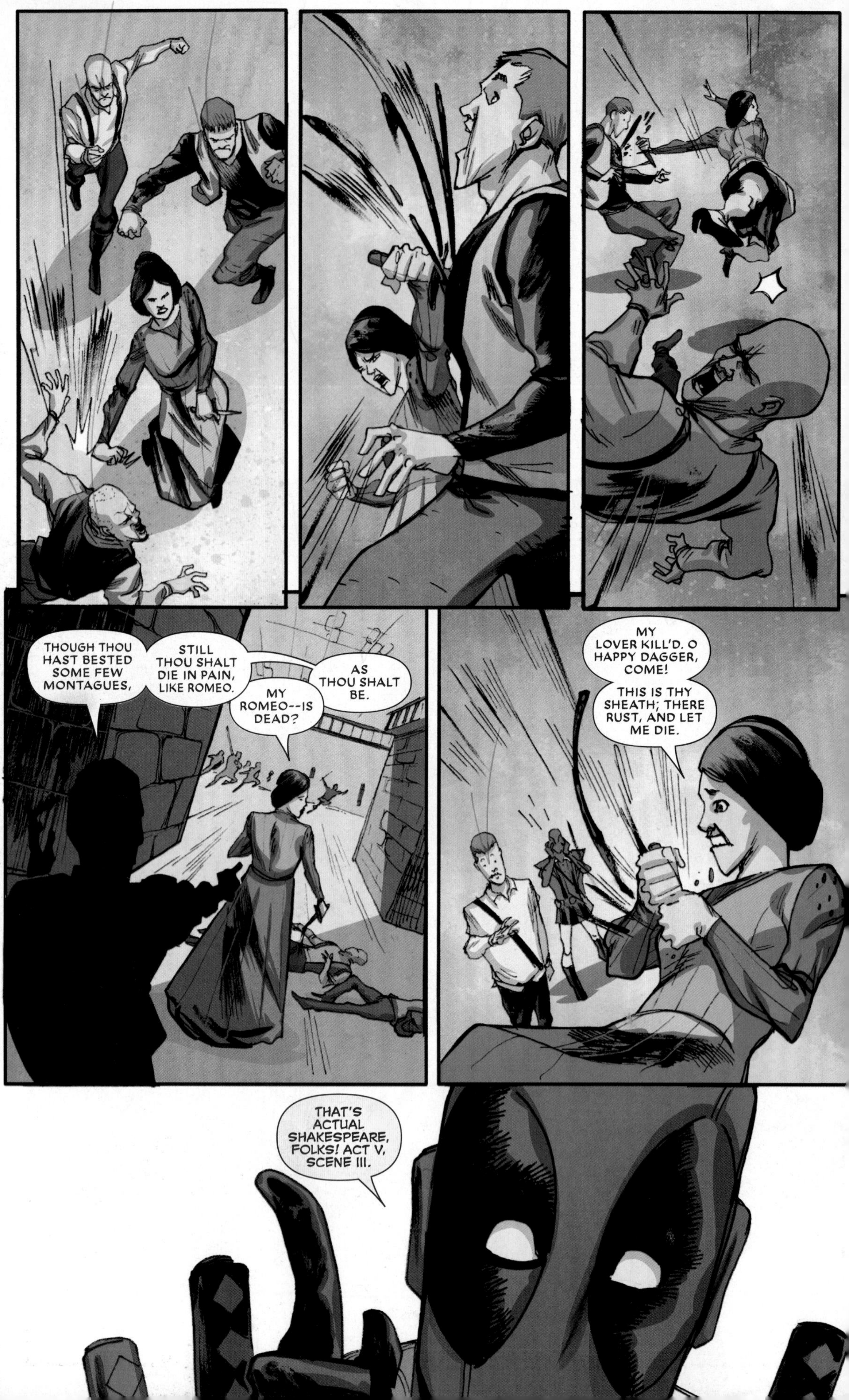

THOUGH THOU HAST BESTED SOME FEW MONTAGUES,
STILL THOU SHALT DIE IN PAIN, LIKE ROMEO.
AS THOU SHALT BE.
MY ROMEO--IS DEAD?
MY LOVER KILL'D. O HAPPY DAGGER, COME!
THIS IS THY SHEATH; THERE RUST, AND LET ME DIE.
THAT'S ACTUAL SHAKESPEARE, FOLKS! ACT V, SCENE III.

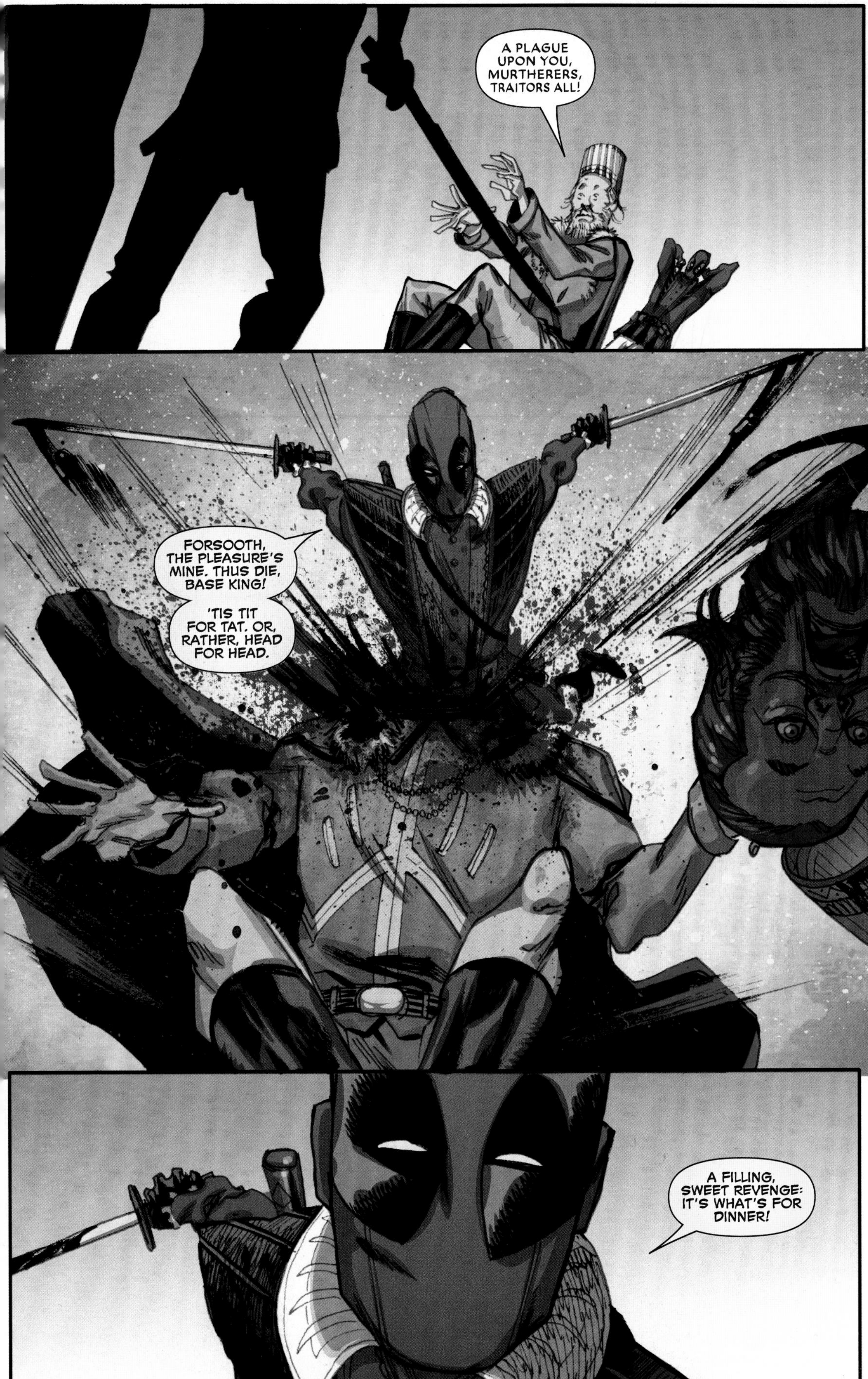
A PLAGUE UPON YOU, MURTHERERS, TRAITORS ALL!
FORSOOTH, THE PLEASURE'S MINE. THUS DIE, BASE KING!
'TIS TIT FOR TAT. OR, RATHER, HEAD FOR HEAD.
A FILLING, SWEET REVENGE: IT'S WHAT'S FOR DINNER!

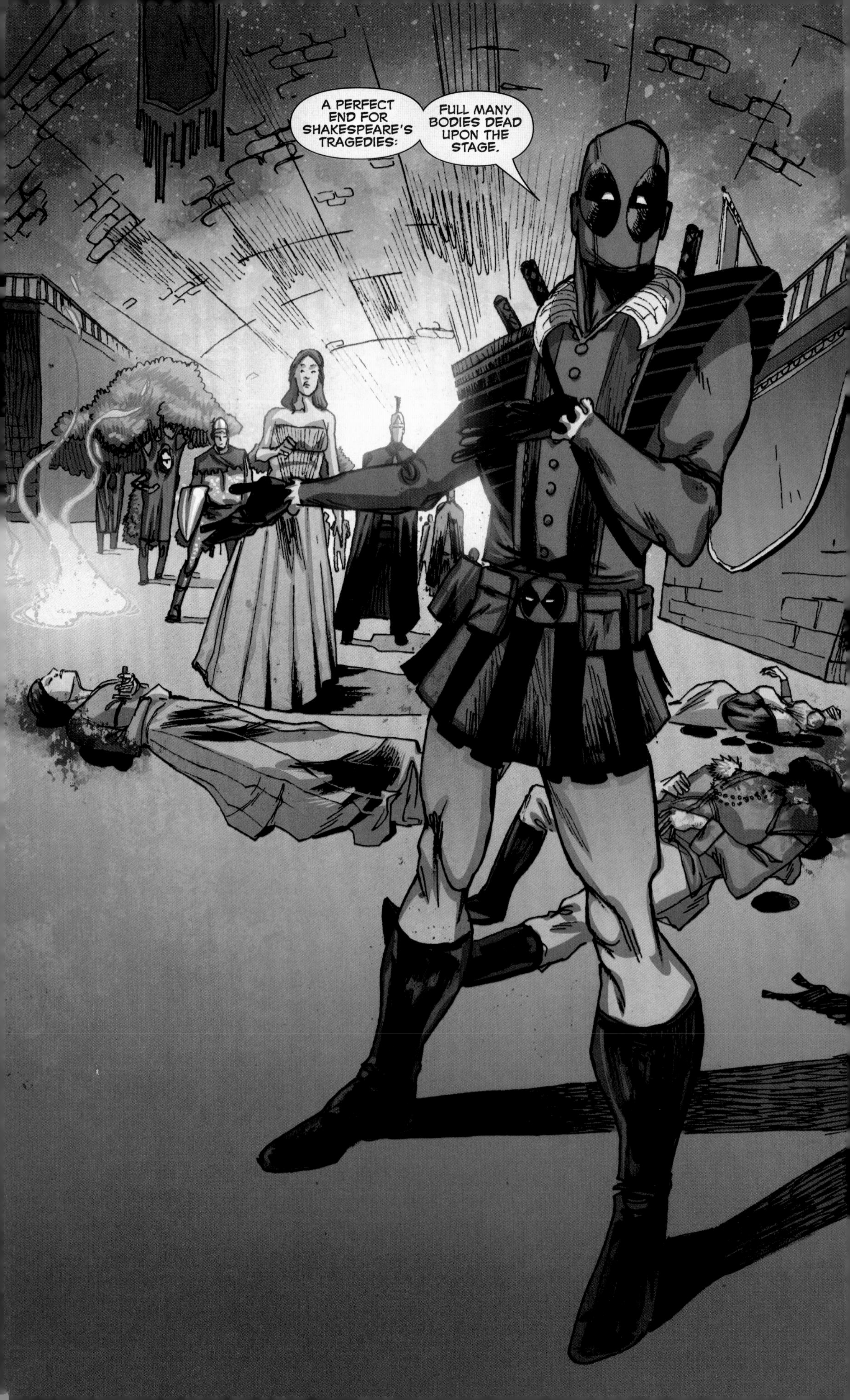
A PERFECT END FOR SHAKESPEARE'S TRAGEDIES:
FULL MANY BODIES DEAD UPON THE STAGE.

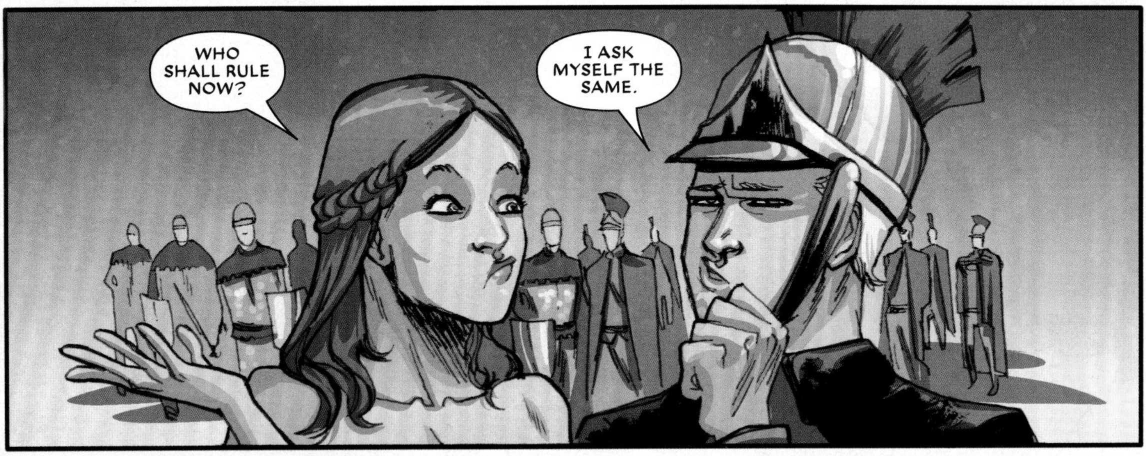
WHO SHALL RULE NOW?
I ASK MYSELF THE SAME.

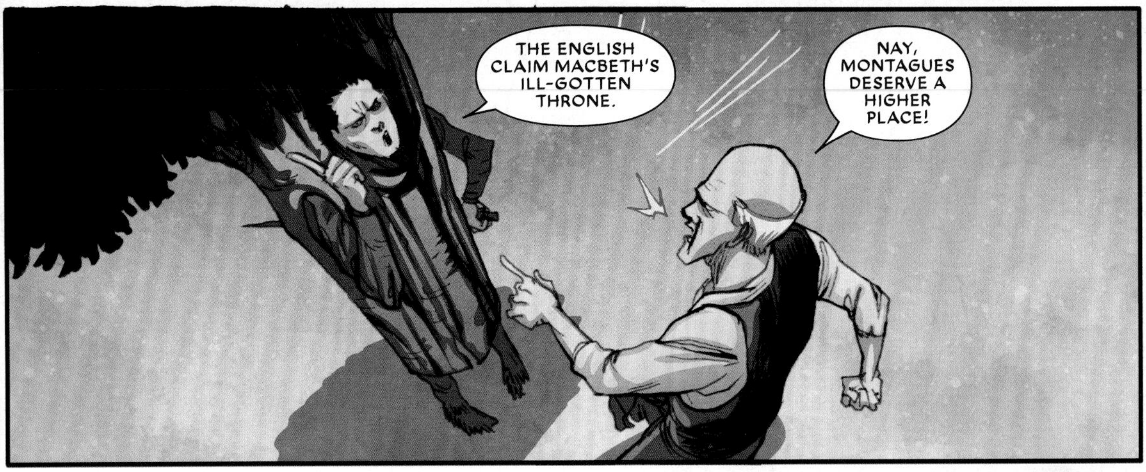
THE ENGLISH CLAIM MACBETH'S ILL-GOTTEN THRONE.
NAY, MONTAGUES DESERVE A HIGHER PLACE!

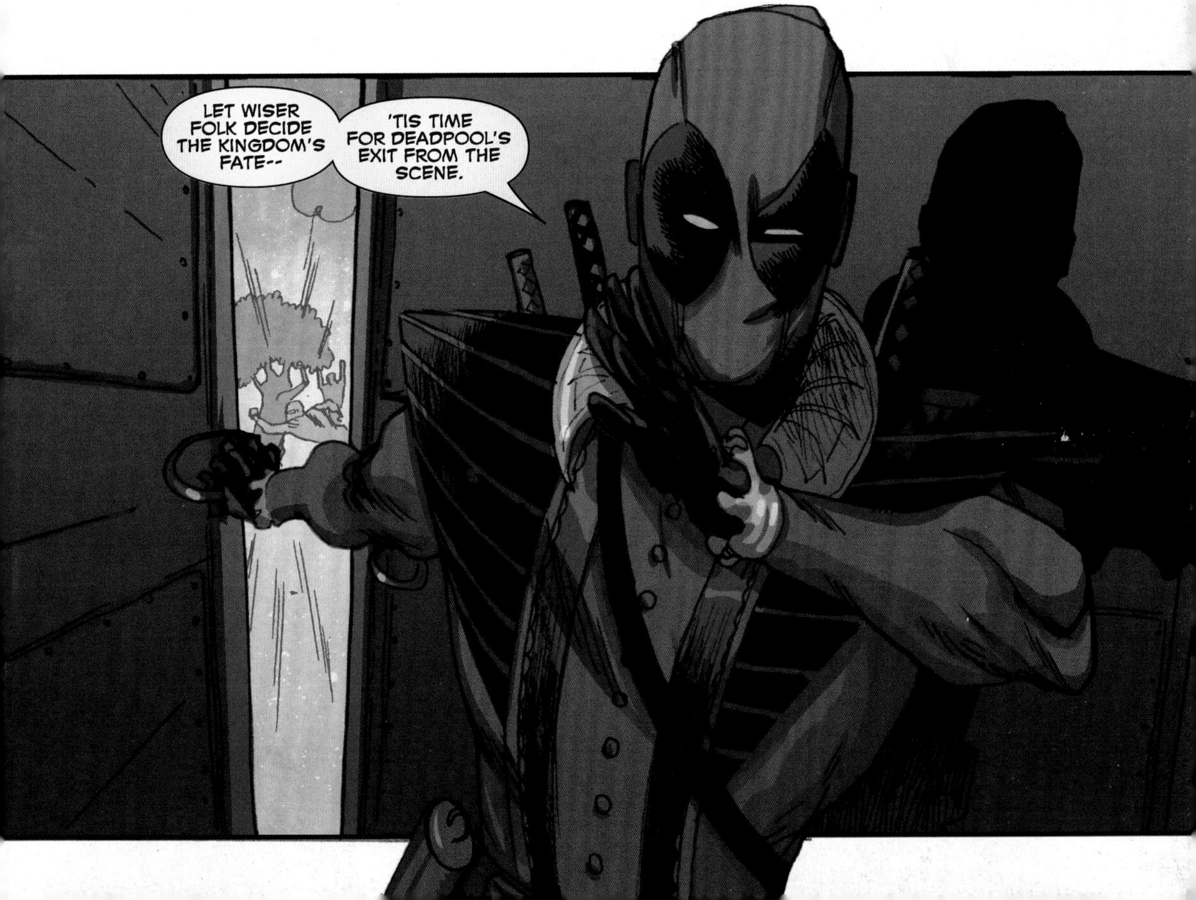
LET WISER FOLK DECIDE THE KINGDOM'S FATE--
'TIS TIME FOR DEADPOOL'S EXIT FROM THE SCENE.

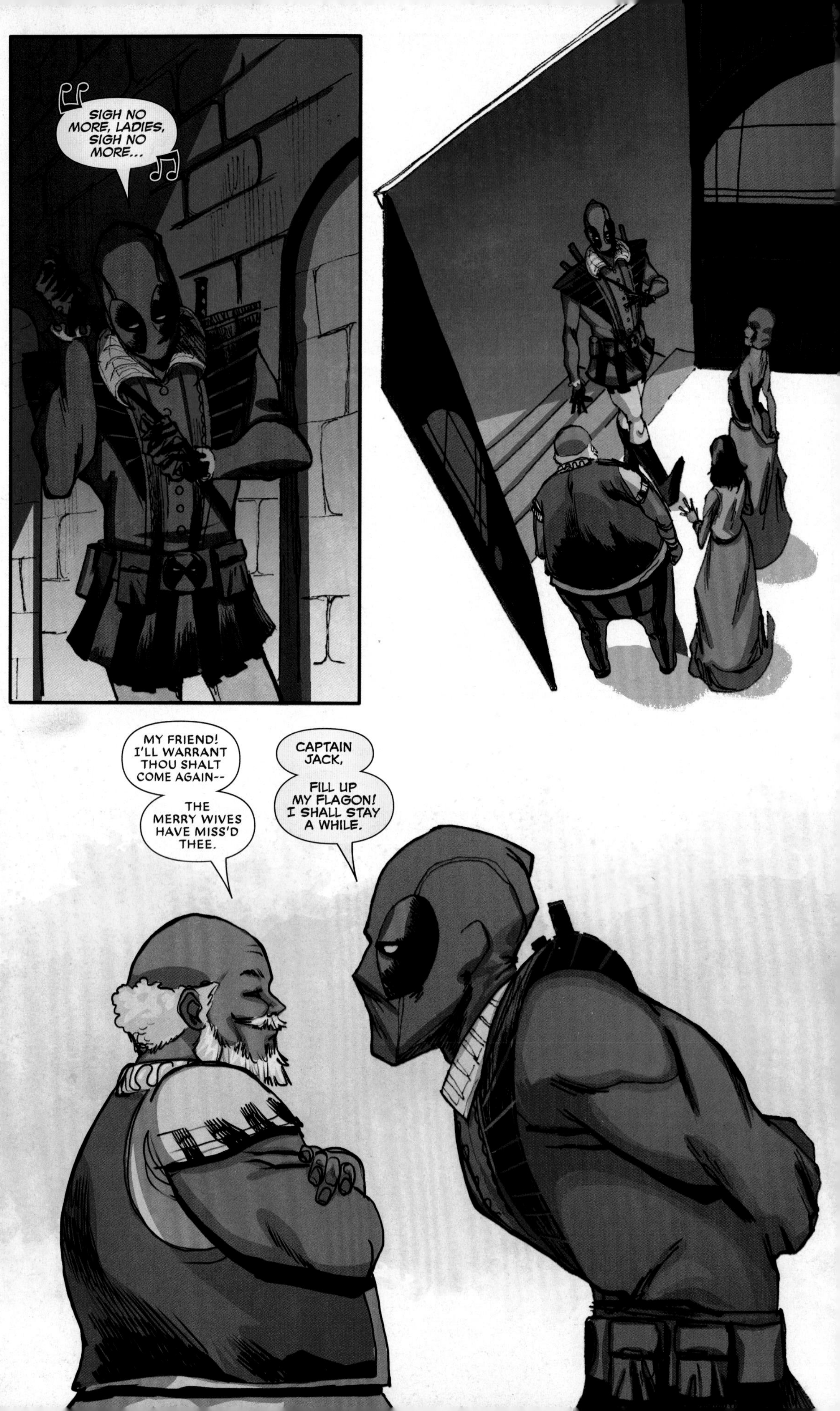
SIGH NO MORE, LADIES, SIGH NO MORE...
MY FRIEND! I'LL WARRANT THOU SHALT COME AGAIN--
THE MERRY WIVES HAVE MISS'D THEE.
CAPTAIN JACK,
FILL UP MY FLAGON! I SHALL STAY A WHILE.

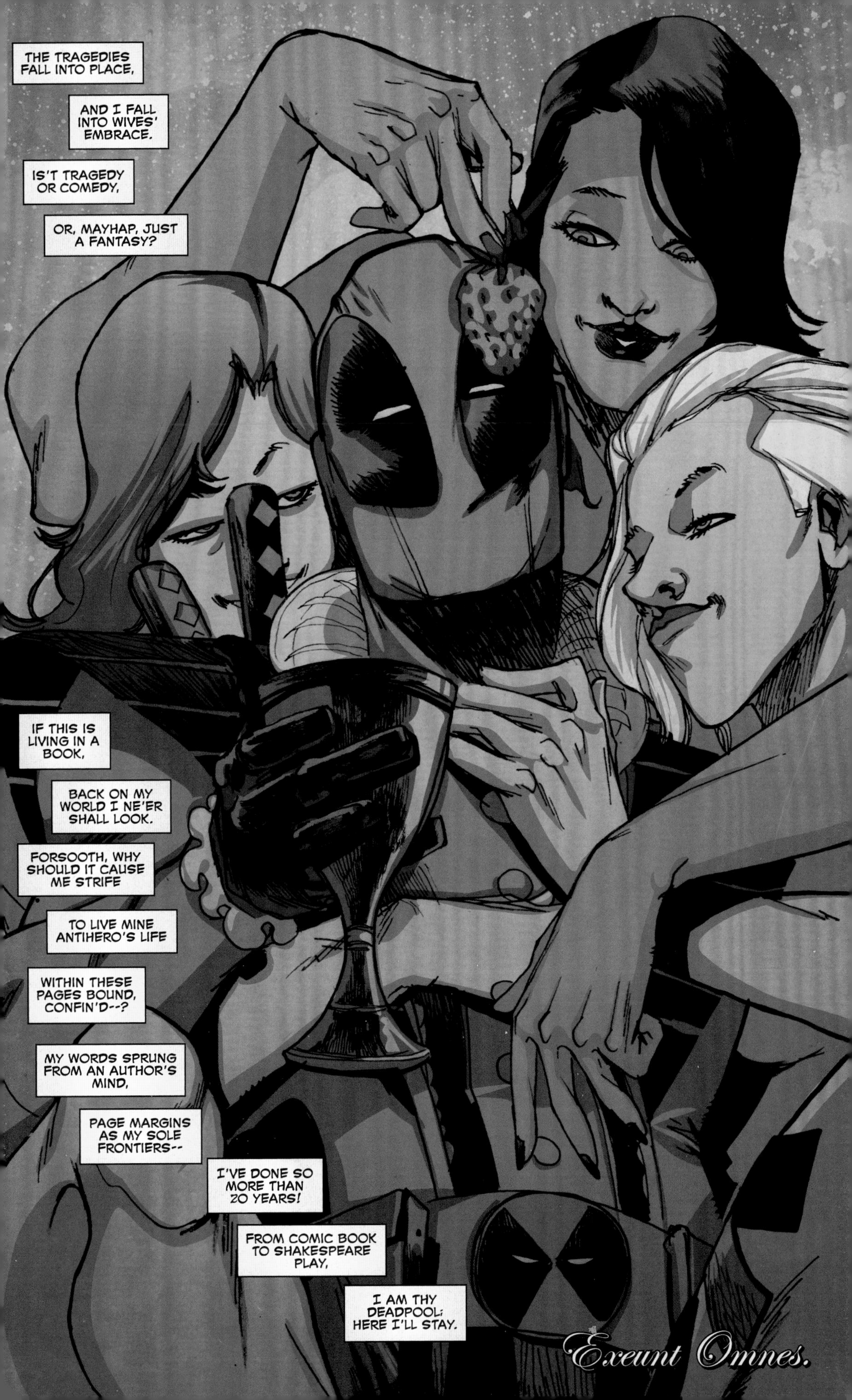
THE TRAGEDIES FALL INTO PLACE,
AND I FALL INTO WIVES' EMBRACE.
IS'T TRAGEDY OR COMEDY,
OR, MAYHAP, JUST A FANTASY?
IF THIS IS LIVING IN A BOOK,
BACK ON MY WORLD I NE'ER SHALL LOOK.
FORSOOTH, WHY SHOULD IT CAUSE ME STRIFE
TO LIVE MINE ANTIHERO'S LIFE
WITHIN THESE PAGES BOUND, CONFIN'D--?
MY WORDS SPRUNG FROM AN AUTHOR'S MIND,
PAGE MARGINS AS MY SOLE FRONTIERS--
I'VE DONE SO MORE THAN 20 YEARS!
FROM COMIC BOOK TO SHAKESPEARE PLAY,
I AM THY DEADPOOL; HERE I'LL STAY.
Exeunt Omnes.

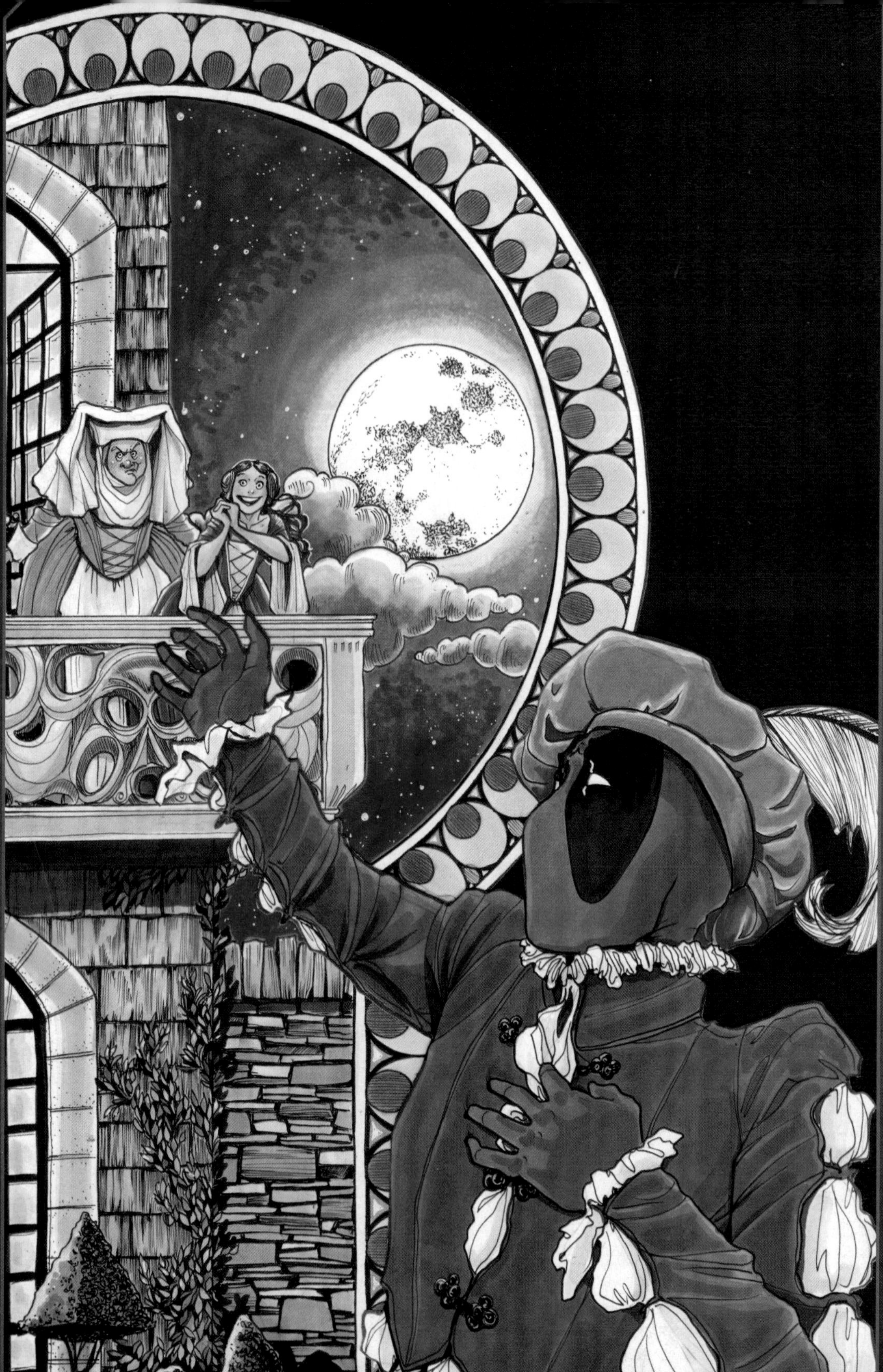

#21 variant by JANET LEE

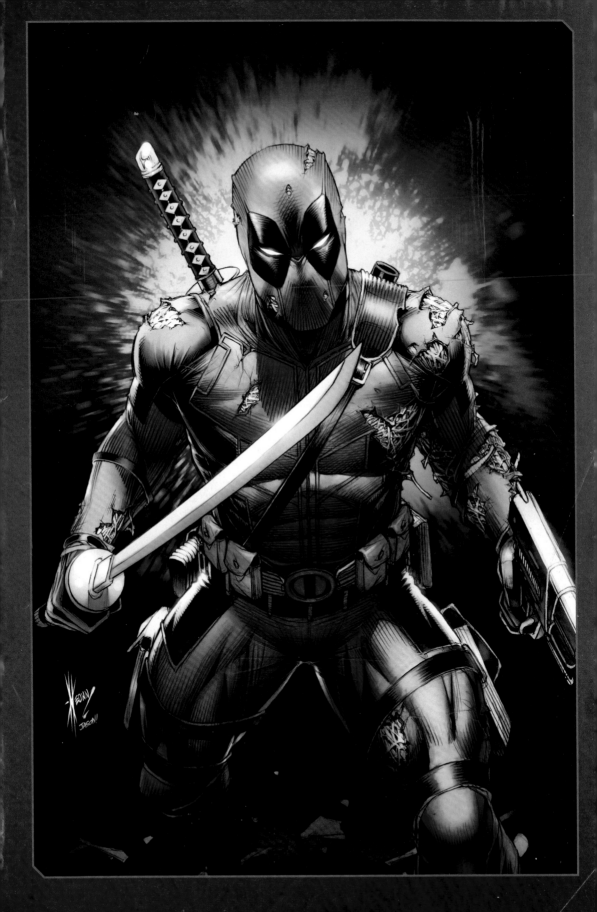

#26 variant by DALE KEOWN & JASON KEITH

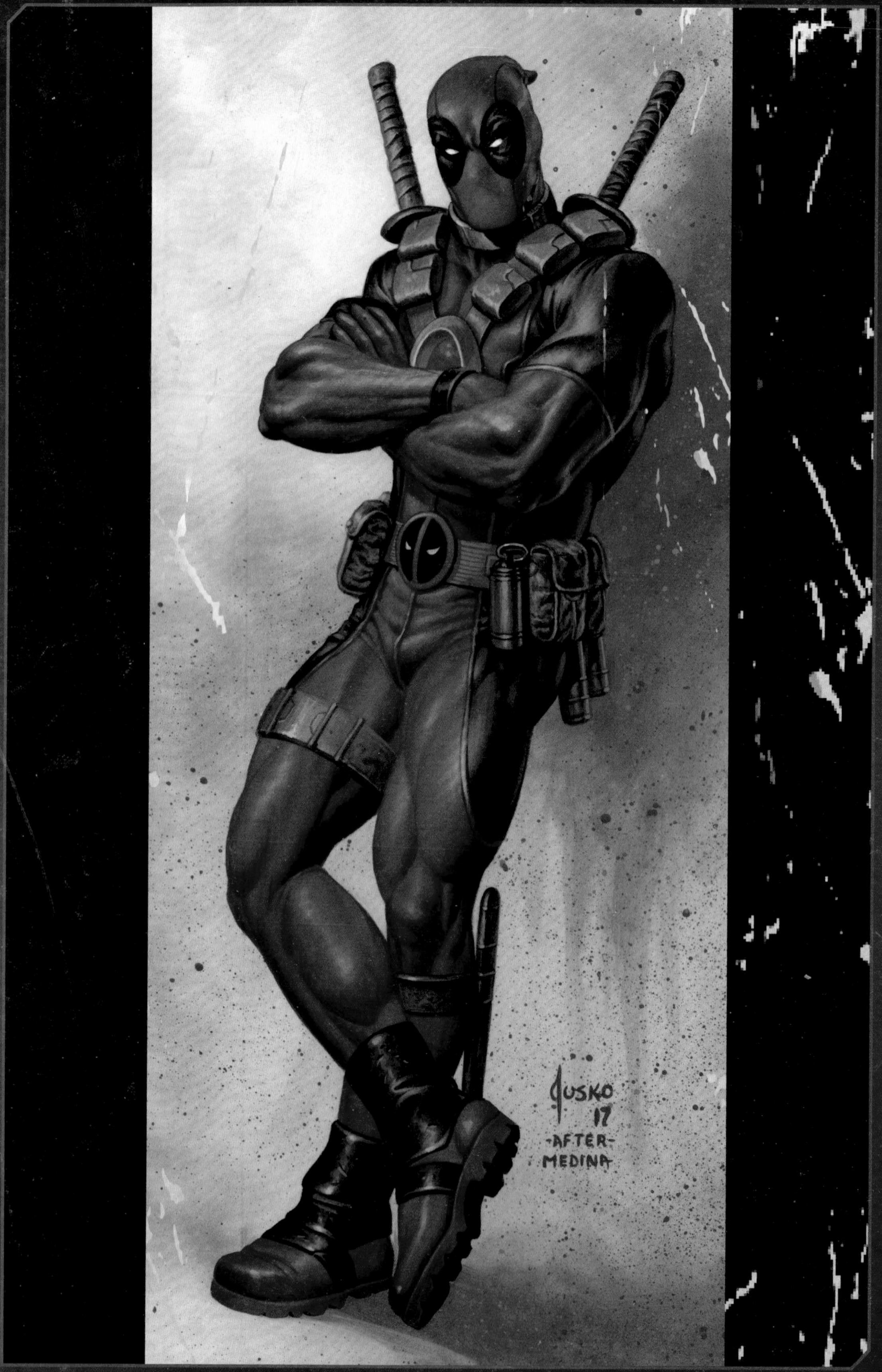
JUSKO
17
-AFTER-
MEDINA

#26 corner box variant by JOE JUSKO